COURTSHIP, MARRIAGE, AND THE FAMILY IN CANADA

Courtship, Marriage, and the Family in Canada

EDITED BY

G. N. RAMU

Macmillan of Canada

Canadian Cataloguing in Publication Data

Main entry under title:
Courtship, marriage, and the family in Canada

Bibliography: p.
Includes indexes.
ISBN 0-7705-1772-2

1. Marriage–Canada. 2. Family–Canada.
3. Courtship. I. Ramu, G.N., date.

HQ560.C68   301.42′0971   C79-094410-3

Printed in Canada for
The Macmillan Company of Canada Limited
70 Bond Street
Toronto, Ontario
M5B 1X3

Contents

COURTSHIP, MARRIAGE, AND THE FAMILY IN CANADA

Acknowledgements

I wish to thank the seven contributors to this volume for their conscientious and scholarly efforts to summarize a wide range of research materials in a coherent and readable manner and under relatively stringent editorial constraints.

I would also like to express my deep appreciation to Nicholas Tavuchis for reading many chapters and offering valuable criticisms and suggestions, many of which have been incorporated in this volume.

I am grateful to the editorial staff at Macmillan Canada, and especially Virgil Duff, for unstinting support of this project. Finally, I owe a considerable debt, which can only be partially discharged here, to Mrs. Kathy Jaworski, Mrs. Jean Anazia, and Mrs. Sally Hall for typing various versions of the manuscripts often under pressing conditions but always with care and cheer.

G. N. RAMU

Introduction

G. N. RAMU

The primary objective of this book is to provide undergraduates in Canadian universities with a systematic introduction to certain selected aspects of courtship, marriage, and the family in Canada. The 1970s represent an important phase in the development of sociology of the family in Canada. Besides innumerable articles, essays, and monographs, several edited works have appeared for the first time (for a review of these see Ramu and Tavuchis, 1977). In the essays included here, the contributors have attempted to identify and synthesize significant concepts and research findings in order to stimulate and inform students and other readers about issues that affect all of us.

Although our initial goal was to offer a comprehensive analysis of all aspects of marriage and the family in Canada, we fell short of accomplishing that goal for practical reasons. The main difficulty was a lack of pertinent research in many areas, e.g., implications of changing legal norms for marriage and the family, linkages between the family and other institutions, and sociological explanations of demographic trends. Even with respect to the specific issues dealt with in this book, the empirical materials are far from adequate because there are many conspicuous gaps in the present state of knowledge in the area of family sociology. Thus, this work serves as an overview of the field and also alerts us to what is as yet unknown in Canada about courtship, marriage, and the family.

To the extent that the themes of individual chapters permit, the organizing theme is based upon the concept of the family life-cycle. Nevertheless, other theoretical perspectives are neither ignored nor slighted for the sake of intellectual commitment to a specific conceptual framework. In an endeavour which involves several scholars with different theoretical, methodological, and personal orientations, a common theoretical approach is neither desirable nor easy to achieve. Each of the contributors has attempted to examine selected empirical materials in the context of major contemporary theoretical perspectives. This, we hope, will result in a broader understanding of Canadian marriage and family patterns from diverse points of view.

In the following pages, we propose to present an introductory perspective to each of the topics discussed in various chapters, and provide essential demographic information on marriage and the family in Canada.

SOCIETAL INTEREST IN FAMILY FORMATION

Family formation is an intricate and protracted process tempered by culture, class, ethnicity, kinship, religion, and other social determinants. Societal concern with the family stems from numerous considerations but for our purposes two are especially pertinent: reproduction and socialization. Most societies are concerned with the maintenance of their population levels in the face of mortality. A relatively stable population is critical for the survival of institutions such as economy, polity, and so on. Historically, the family has been found to be the most dependable and efficient agency for ensuring legitimate reproduction. Therefore, historically and cross-culturally, societies have evolved ways to motivate individuals to get married and form families.

It is not, however, enough that children are born in an identifiable and accountable unit: they also have to be protected, comforted, and trained for a long period of time before they become fully accredited members of society. Fundamentally, children have to be introduced to such important elements of social organization as norms, values, roles, language, and customs in order for them to become social beings. This process is known as socialization. With the exception of a few human societies, the family is fixed with the responsibility of socializing the newly-born. Consequently, reproduction and socialization are essential for an orderly continuity of the population and social organization, and in most societies the family seems to be the unit which is charged with and accomplishes both tasks. Given the importance attached to these tasks, it is not surprising that most societies exercise varying degrees of control over this matter.

Such controls are expressed in matters pertaining to social definitions of maturity, age at marriage, mate-selection, and premarital and extra-marital sexual relationships, to cite a few. For example, in most societies marriage, as a ritual, a public ceremony, or a legal contract, is required prior to the birth of a legitimate child. The event of marriage is a public demonstration of the couples' commitment to each other and also an implicit endorsement of its goals—reproduction and socialization. In order to bring adult members of the opposite sex together in matrimony, certain structural conditions have evolved. As Moon points out in Chapter 2, in traditional societies this is accomplished in a relatively simple and direct manner where parents of the marriageable adults, in consultation with the relevant kin, select appropriate partners. Here, marriage is too important to be left to the individuals who are considered to be ill-equipped to make such vital decisions; similarly marriage is viewed as the alliance of families and not individuals. In addition, the maintenance of family and kinship traditions is critical and any freedom in mate-choice may disrupt cultural continuity.

In modern industrial societies such as Canada's, marriage, with certain minor restrictions, is perceived as an essentially individual matter. Parental or kin intervention is relatively minimal, although not inconsequential. Adolescents are encouraged to come together under various conditions with the ultimate goal of selecting the most suitable person for marriage. Two questions may be raised here. First, what motivates a person to seek a marriage-partner? Second, in such an apparently random mode of mate-selection, how is the continuity of social structure ensured?

The motivation for young males and females to participate in marriage "markets" basically stems from cultural expectations and a socialization process that begins from birth. As Goode (1959) and Greenfield (1965) suggest, the mate-selection process in societies such as Canada's heavily hinges on the notion of "romantic love". A person is socialized to believe that falling in love is a normal and necessary experience and that the marriage is both the natural and desirable culmination of this state. The function of a romantic-love ideology is to encourage individuals to develop, through dating and other forms of social interaction, a sustained attachment to someone of the opposite sex.

Despite the stress on individual autonomy, the subtle intrusion of societal influences and controls is evident. As Moon outlines in Chapter

2, despite the principle of free choice in Canada there is sufficient evidence that social and cultural determinants, e.g., race, religion, class, etc., play an important role in restricting the final choice of a mate even when individuals are not aware of such constraints. In brief, there is a careful filtering of those who are eligible to engage in dating and courtship activities. This is an important fact to be kept in mind while considering aspects of mate-selection in Canada since few readers will be (or have been) immune from it.

THE COURTSHIP PROCESS

Although no definition exhausts the complexities of human relationships, the courtship process, as it is commonly understood, refers to a varied but often protracted relationship between an unmarried adult male and female both with an intention of marriage. In Canada, this relationship is governed by such subjective considerations as romantic love and companionship as well as subcultural norms regulating marriage and family systems. In most cases, casual dating signals a formal initiation of the courtship process although few would consider marriage at this state. Nevertheless, dating is important as a training ground in addition to the ways in which it satisfies such needs as recreation, experimentation with sex, ego gratification, companionship, and sharing. Further, it indirectly helps adolescents to break away from their parents socio-emotionally. Thus in most instances dating sets the stage for a series of social encounters leading to marriage.

Despite the apparent freedom available to those who date, as Moon's discussion of various theories of mate-selection suggests, the field of eligibles is determined by various demographic, cultural, and social conditions. For instance, there is considerable evidence to show that only after social determinants, such as residential propinquity, class, religion, race, ethnicity, etc., make their effects felt, do personal and psychological attributes begin to play an important part in the ultimate choice of a person's partner.

These observations further indicate that even in societies where individual autonomy in matrimonial matters is permitted, the larger societal and purely impersonal factors exert indirect controls. To illustrate this point, we shall briefly consider the patterns of intermarriage in Canada.

If we examine the Canadian data on interfaith marriages in the last five decades (Heer and Hubay, 1975) we note that, on the one hand, there is an increasing tendency to marry across the religious boundaries but, on the other, only a small proportion of Canadians actually do so. In 1927 only 5.8 per cent of all Protestant, Catholic, and Jewish brides and grooms married spouses of a different faith, and by 1972 the proportion had increased to 21.5 per cent—roughly a 400 per cent increase in fifty years. Yet when considered in the context of the ideology of free choice, there is a conspicuous tendency to marry within one's own religious group, e.g., about 80 per cent still do so.

Such a tendency is apparent in relation to ethnicity as Kalbach's (1976: 70–71) analysis of the propensity among seventeen ethnic groups to intermarry shows. He calculated the index of the propensity to intermarry by taking the ratios of actual to expected proportion of families with native-born husbands and wives of a different ethnic origin. The range in ratios of actual to expected proportions varies from close to zero to almost one (see Table 1:1).

These data clearly demonstrate that certain ethnic groups (Jewish, French, British) demonstrate a higher propensity to intermarry than others, although the general tendency is one of ethnic endogamy. In

Table 1:1 Propensity to Intermarry for a Selected Number of Ethnic Groups

Ethnic Origin of Native-born Husband	Canada	Toronto	Montreal
Scandinavian	0.905	0.946	0.941
Italian	0.815	0.706	0.759
German	0.781	0.912	0.913
Ukrainian	0.711	0.771	0.788
Asian	0.524	0.398	0.533
British	0.494	0.613	0.525
French	0.300	0.794	0.359
Jewish	0.162	0.117	0.078

Source: Ratios based on special tabulations provided by Statistics Canada, 1971 census (Kalbach, 1976:71).

short, the profile of who marries whom suggests that society exerts indirect controls over the courtship process. Freedom of choice is relevant only within the field of eligibles. As Moon points out in Chapter 2, restrictions operate even at the stage of dating whose main function is recreation and socialization.

Dating

In general, dating is closely linked to courtship in Canada. It enables adolescents and adults of the opposite sex to engage in various kinds of activities ranging from "fun-seeking" to more serious "romantic involvement". This process is essential for those who are interested in extending a casual heterosexual relationship into a more permanent bond such as marriage. The social importance of dating becomes accentuated when we consider that family and kinship groups (with some notable exceptions, e.g., Hutterites) have little direct participation in mate-selection, that individuals are encouraged to choose their own spouses, and that the social expectation stipulating romantic love is an essential ingredient in the final decision.

Dating does not occur in a social vacuum. In Chapter 2, Moon examines how religion, class, and psychological and personal attributes determine the dating patterns among Canadian adolescents and adults. It is clear from his discussion that the forces of endogamy, i.e., marriage within one's own group, and homogamy, i.e., marriage between individuals with similar social characteristics, even operate at such a preliminary phase of mate-selection as dating.

Prompted by the increasing number of divorces, and the bitterness and discord that lead to "empty-shell marriages", many sociologists and others take the position that dating, as an institutionalized means of testing mutual compatibility for a long-life partnership, is a crude and unreliable method. Dating remains mostly a recreational, ego-gratifying, and potentially exploitative relationship, which often involves little more than a game, an exercise in impression management, and a social context that encourages misperceptions which can have disasterous consequences if marriage ensues. Moon alludes to some of these points, especially in his discussion of several Canadian studies in which the respondents failed to recognize some of these pitfalls.

PREMARITAL SEX: VALUES AND BEHAVIOUR

What is the impact of changing sexual standards on the courtship process? To what extent does a sexual relationship precipitate or remain independent of the decision to marry? Although it is difficult to offer conclusive responses based on empirical materials, in Chapter 3, Hobart assesses the nature of premarital sexual attitudes and behaviour in Canada in an effort to glean some clues to such questions.

Hobart identifies a general transition in sexual standards—from a traditional morality to a new morality. At one end of the spectrum the old morality advocated abstinence—no sex before marriage—and at the other supported the double standard—premarital sex as a male prerogative denied to females with the exception of those viewed as being outside the marriage market, e.g., lower-class women, prostitutes, etc. The new morality is more permissive and sees non-marital sex as an equally legitimate alternative to sex linked with marriage. For example, the "love standard" asserts that intercourse is acceptable between *loving* partners regardless of their marital intentions or state. Mutual love and affection are sufficient justifications for a sexual relationship. A radical extension of this new morality is the "fun standard" which asserts that sex is acceptable between partners who both want to engage in a sexual relationship whatever their marital status, stage of the courtship process, or affectional commitment.

The degree of sexual permissiveness depends largely on a person's family, ethnic, religious, class, and community (rural or urban) background. In a careful, thoughtful analysis of premarital sex standards in America, Reiss (1960) outlines two basic types of sexual *behaviour*: body-centred, emphasizing the purely physical dimension of sex, and person-centred, involving an affectionate relationship between those who engage in sexual acts. This is roughly what Hobart defines as the "fun standard" and "love standard", respectively. However, Reiss further classifies North American sexual *attitudes* into four categories (1960: 83–84) and these merit brief mention because they provide a perspective for an understanding of differences in sexual permissiveness found by Hobart in his recent national study reported in Chapter 3.

1. *Abstinence: Premarital intercourse is wrong for both the man and the woman regardless of circumstances.* This is the keystone of the official

normative code for premarital sexual behaviour. Premarital sex is forbidden on religious and moral grounds. Hobart finds this pattern prevailing among such groups as Catholics and Jews in Canada.

2. *Permissiveness with affection: Premarital intercourse is acceptable for both men and women under certain conditions, e.g., when there is a commitment to a relatively permanent relationship such as engagement or when love or strong affection is present.* This attitude in many ways corresponds to what Hobart terms as the "love standard". One implication of this value is that when a couple have reached "the engagement" phase of their courtship, they can justifiably engage in sexual intercourse since the potentially disruptive social consequences, e.g., illegitimacy, are minimal or can be remedied. Another implication is that the couple need not have any marital plans but so long as they have a mutually strong affection, they can maintain a sexual relationship without any further justification. From this point of view, sex becomes a factor independent of the courtship process.

3. *Permissiveness without affection: Premarital intercourse is acceptable for both men and women regardless of the amount of affection or stability present, providing there is physical attraction.* Here, sex is body-centred and becomes an end in itself. For instance, those who engage in sex during their casual dating would subscribe to this standard.

4. *Double standard: Premarital intercourse is acceptable for men, but is wrong and unacceptable for women.* The double standard is deeply entrenched in most societies, including Canada's, reflecting the continuation of an age-old tradition of male dominance and the assumption (unfounded) about a man's superior physical and sexual prowess.

In Chapter 3, Hobart, using data from a comprehensive national survey of premarital sexual attitudes and behaviour, demonstrates that the four types of sexual standards conceptualized by Reiss are evident in different degrees in various parts of Canada. He establishes that younger Canadians are becoming increasingly more permissive although the pull is toward permissiveness with affection—a love standard. Although the double standard continues to flourish in Canada, females seem to be "catching" up with males in their premarital sexual activities.

MARRIAGE: ORGANIZATION AND INTERACTION

The definition and goals of marriage differ from culture to culture. Yet certain common features can be identified for analytical purposes. Stephens's criteria, which Nett uses in Chapter 4, are relevant for a cross-cultural understanding of marriage. In most traditional societies, the societal rather than the personal goals of marriage are stressed (see Ramu, 1977; Wolfe, 1972: Chapter 8). Marriage is seen as a means to ensure an orderly continuity of culture and society, the conferring of adult status, the ensuring of legitimacy, and the controlling of sexuality. Although these are implicit functions of marriage in Canada, Nett notes that marriage constitutes the core of family life: "it has a psychological value for adults for whom it provides a 'place' to meet their needs for security, order, and development" (Nett, Chapter 4:63).

In Canada, as in other modern industrial societies, marriage is increasingly defined as a voluntary association backed by various legal rights and obligations rather than as a sacred institution. Its basic features include (ideally) a relatively enduring commitment between two individuals based on each other's ability and desire to meet mutual needs such as love, affection, communication, companionship, finance, sex, parenthood, etc. As Nett suggests, the stress on individualism, the emergence of new definitions of sex roles, and the increasing economic independence of women in marriage have buttressed the "associational character" of contemporary Canadian marriage. At the same time, deeply entrenched customary definitions continue to exert a conservative influence that tempers the complete transformation of marriage as a total association in which both partners enjoy equality in all aspects of their lives.

The discussion in Chapter 4 implicitly highlights changes in the structure of marital relations. For example, secular values such as individuality and equality have undermined the traditionally hierarchical male-female relationship and consequently have upset, in varying degrees, the complementary relationship based on male authority and female subordination. The increasing participation of the wife in the labour force has reduced her "dependent" status and this has resulted in a need for realignment of power structures. Such an alteration has not been easy to accomplish without *conflict* and *fierce bargaining* based on the philosophy of exchange. The cumulative effect of such changes in contemporary

Canada has been that marriage is no longer a relationship that can be taken for granted, but one that requires constant attention in order to make it enduring and satisfactory.) The success and stability of this relationship depends on the constant reinforcement and re-evaluation of commitments by husband and wife.

On the one hand, as Nett infers from certain opinion surveys, there is a disillusionment about marriage and its personal utility *vis à vis* social expectations, and interpersonal problems are generated from both within and without marriage. On the other hand, as census data suggests, these increasingly problematic aspects have not seemed to deter individuals from marrying; people continued to marry in record numbers during the past decade.

The increasing popularity of marriage does not clearly establish whether there is a new resolve to correct the anomolies attributed to the traditional conception of marriage. Neither does it suggest that the associational character of marriage is gaining ground. But what it undoubtedly indicates is the continuing attraction of marriage whatever the risks and pains it entails. In the next section, we shall present certain demographic aspects of marriage in Canada.

DEMOGRAPHIC ASPECTS OF MARRIAGE

In the last decade in Canada, nine out of ten persons of marriageable age have been married at least once. The proportion of the married population is gradually increasing and this indicates that vocal disillusionment about marriage notwithstanding, most people still marry. For example, in 1965, 43.6 per cent of the Canadian population (20,000,000) were married and this figure rose in 1971 to 45.3 per cent (21,500,000). In the following paragraphs we will present a brief account of marriage rates and age at marriage in Canada.

Marriage Rates

There are several methods of ascertaining the marital state of the population in a society. One way is to count the number of marriages contracted in a given year. Thus, we can say that in Canada, in 1972, some 200,470 marriages were contracted. Although such a datum would tell us whether the number of marriages increased or decreased relative to past years, it would not provide us with an accurate statistical or demographic profile.

Consequently, demographers use two methods to calculate marriage rates. One is called the "crude rate" and this involves counting the number of marriages per 1,000 population in a given year. It is crude because the population base used includes those who are ineligible to marry, for example, infants and very old persons. To offset this bias, a more refined method called the "marriage-rate index" is used by the demographers. This measure refers to the number of married in a given year from a population which includes only those who are marriageable— single, divorced, and widowed adults. "The marriage index expresses the number of registered marriages in a year as a percentage of a weighted average of unmarried men and women" (Boyd, *et al.*, 1976: 16). Table 1:2 provides the crude marriage rate as well as the marriage-rate index for selected years.

Table 1:2

Crude Marriage Rate (Per 1,000 population)		Marriage Rate Index, Canada, 1951–72*			
1921	7.9	1951	74	1962	63
1931	6.4	1952	73	1963	62
1941	10.6	1953	74	1964	63
1951	9.2	1954	72	1965	64
1956	8.3	1955	72	1966	66
1961	7.0	1956	72	1967	68
1966	7.8	1957	70	1968	68
1971	8.9	1958	68	1969	70
		1958	68	1970	70
		1959	68	1970	70
		1960	65	1971	70
		1961	64	1972[a]	71

*Boyd, *et al.* (1976).

[a]Calculated from Statistics Canada, *Population Estimates by Marital Status, Age and Sex for Canada and Provinces* (1972), and *Vital Statistics*, Preliminary Report (1973).

Source: Unpublished Statistics Canada tabulations.

The data in Table 1:2 indicate that marriage rates and indices fluctuate from time to time. The reasons for such fluctuations, as stated by Boyd, *et al.* (1976: 16–18), Kalbach (1975: 61), and Wakil and Wakil (1976: 382–83), include major political events such as war and economic crises such as depression, recession, or inflation. For example, the major economic event of this century, the Great Depression, was accompanied by a steep decline in the marriage rate. Before and after the Second World War and during the period of economic recovery from the Depression, the rate rose to 10.9—the highest ever in Canadian history—and this resulted in not only a postwar "marriage boom" but also a "baby boom". An offshoot of this baby boom was an increase in the marriage rate during the seventies.

Age at Marriage

A consideration of age at marriage is sociologically important because it gives us clues regarding certain structural aspects of marriage in a given society. For example, where an individual (especially the male) is expected to complete his educational or occupational training and to acquire a job prior to marriage, the age at marriage tends to be relatively high. In such a situation, the age difference between the bride and bridegroom is likely to be large, e.g., ten years (see Ramu, 1977: 51–54). Such an age discrepancy cannot fail but colour interpersonal relations, such as decreasing the probability of egalitarianism and enhancing the authority of the husband.

In Canada, marriage is increasingly becoming independent of educational and occupational status and as a result there is a trend toward early marriages. As Kalbach (1976: 95) notes, the average age at marriage for all bridegrooms declined from 28.9 years in 1941 to 27.3 years in 1971. But for those who are marrying for the first time during this period, the decline was somewhat more rapid—from 27.6 years to 24.9 years. In Table 1:3, the mean and median age at first marriage for brides and grooms for selected years is given.

The over-all profile of age at marriage for the last half-century reveals two significant trends. First, there is a gradual but sustained decrease in age at marriage of both males and females. Second, there is a corresponding decrease in age differences between the bride and the bridegroom.

Table 1:3 Age at Marriage of Persons Never Previously Married, Brides and Grooms, Canada, 1941–73

| Year | Age at Marriage | | | | |
| | Mean | | | Mean | |
	Brides	Grooms		Brides	Grooms
1941[a]	24.4	27.6		23.0	26.3
1946[a]	24.1	27.1		22.5	25.4
1951	23.8	26.6		22.0	24.8
1956	23.4	26.1		21.6	24.5
1961	22.9	25.8		21.1	24.0
1966	22.6	25.2		21.2	23.7
1967	22.6	25.0		21.2	23.6
1968	22.6	25.0		21.3	23.5
1969	22.7	25.0		21.4	23.5
1970	22.7	24.9		21.4	23.5
1971	22.6	24.9		21.3	23.5
1972	22.6	24.8		22.3	24.1
1973	22.3	24.7		21.2	23.5

[a]Does not include Newfoundland, Yukon, or Northwest Territories until 1951.
Source: Statistics Canada, *Vital Statistics*, Vol. II, *Marriages and Divorces* (1973), Table 7.

For example, in 1921, the difference was 4.4 years and in 1971 it stood at 2.5 years.

What implications would such trends have on marital relations in Canada? Some of the issues raised by Nett can be understood in the context of such demographic changes. The American experience in this regard suggests that early marriages are prone to instability. Although it is difficult to establish a clear causal relationship, in general we can notice that as the age at first marriage declines, there is a corresponding increase in the divorce rate. The second consequence is that when one marries at 22 or 23 years of age, it is safe to assume that one is not well settled economically in light of Canadian educational/occupational realities. This would mean in some cases that marriage is likely to serve as a brake on personal achievement and that in student marriages, for example, initial stages of marital life are likely to show signs of stress and strain. On the other hand, not having children or one spouse working would affect this. The third consequence of early marriage is that given the longevity of those born after the Second World War, the duration of marriage will be longer than that of previous generations and this has serious implications for the nature of marital life.

To illustrate the last point, early age at marriage in conjunction with increased longevity has an effect on the life-cycle of women, especially, in relation to their child-bearing and -rearing tasks. According to current statistical indicators of fertility behaviour, a woman in Canada will complete her child-bearing and child-rearing by the time she is in her early thirties. This means she will have approximately thirty years of her life to devote to other pursuits. Given the generalized aspirations of self-fulfillment, personal accomplishment, and so on, stemming from too optimistic a belief in feminism and other ideologies, she will have enough time and energy either to get into the labour force or update her skills (assuming she has any) in order to improve her chances in a competitive labour market. Such aspirations when they cannot be materialized, especially in a tight economy, can lead to large-scale frustration and bitterness. Hence, the decline of age at marriage should be seen from the point of view of the varied social consequences it is likely to generate.

The progressive convergence of ages at marriage of males and females suggests, among other things, that age proximity can facilitate egalitarianism in male-female relations. When both husband and wife are close in age and have comparable educations, it is difficult for one to arbitrarily play a superordinate role and expect the other to be a subordinate. In Chapter 5 Nett refers to the increasing importance of the notions of equality and partnership in a marriage. We can assume that the near equal ages of the spouses contribute to the egalitarian character of marriages in Canada.

ASPECTS OF FAMILY

In 1971, approximately nine out of ten children born in Canada were born to those who were legally married. This signifies an essential and institutionalized relationship between marriage and parenthood. One of the social functions of marriage is to legitimize the birth of children. The social expectation that marriage be a prerequisite for the family has not altered despite various reform movements.[1] The societal interest in the family formation stems, as we noted earlier, from its concern for an orderly replacement of its population (reproductive function of the family) and culture (socialization function of the family). In Canada, marriage is the stepping stone to a family for a majority of the population despite the publicity given to "alternate lifestyles". In this book certain selected aspects of the family, such as the socialization, the relationship between the family and kinship networks, and ethnic patterns, will be examined in detail.

DEMOGRAPHIC CHARACTERISTICS

Family and Household

The Canadian census definition of the family stresses either affinal (marital) and consanguinal (blood) relationship or merely a consanguinal relationship. Thus, "the family consists of a husband and wife, with or without never-married children, or a (lone) parent with one or more children who have never married, living together in the same dwelling" (Census Canada, 1961, Vol. II, Part 1:14). The census family, then, includes what sociologists define as the nuclear family and the single-parent family.

A household, on the other hand, is a broader concept which includes many co-residential groups including the family. "The household is a person, a family, or a group of persons occupying one dwelling" (Census Canada, Bulletin 2.1–5, Vol. II, Part 1). As Wargon (1976: 162) informs us, "household data tell us how many Canadians live *alone*, how many live in *families* formed through conjugal or blood-ties or their equivalent (e.g., adoption), and how many live in groups created by *unrelated persons* sharing the same dwelling" (emphasis in the original).

Thus, all census families are households although all census households are not families.[2] A census family is a cultural and kinship unit whereas a household may be a residential and demographic unit. In Table 1:4 data on numbers of households and families for four decades beginning with 1941 are given.

The data in Table 1:4 clearly reflect the dramatic increase in numbers of both the families and households. It is evident that the number of Canadian families doubled during the period indicated and that this is in direct correspondence with the growth of the population in the same

Table 1:4 Households, Census Families, and Average Number of Children, Canada, All Census Years, 1931–71

| | Households | Census Families | |
	Average No. of Persons	Average No. of Persons	Average No. of Children
1931	4.4	4.2	—
1941	4.2	3.9	1.9
1951	4.0	3.7	1.7
1956	3.9	3.8	1.8
1961	3.9	3.9	1.9
1968	3.7	3.9	1.9
1971	3.5	3.7	1.7

Source: Wargon (1976:173).

period. However, the changes in the number of households are striking. Based on her detailed analysis of census materials, Wargon (1976, 1977) notes a substantial increase in the non-family households, especially single-person households. "One-person households increased more than three times over 1951–71, an addition of more than 500,000 such households to the count of 252,435, bringing the total of one-person households to 811,835 in 1971" (Wargon, 1976: 173).

How can such an increase in the non-family or single-person households be explained? Wargon (1976: 174) suggests that the increase stems from a tendency among the young and unmarried to live separate from their families of origin, and a preference on the part of those who are fifty-five years or older to live alone. While this explanation may support our common assumptions about residential patterns of youth and the aged, one should be cautious in such interpretations because the census data are a synchronistic record of the population at one point in time. For example, many young people may move in and out of their parental home depending upon social and economic circumstances and hence evade the attention of the census which does not provide us with time-series data. This may be compensated for by utilizing periodic household surveys and samples, but the problems of eliminating exact patterns remain.

Family Size

Despite the increase in the population, and the number of families and households in the last four decades (as evident from Table 1:4), the size of the average Canadian family has remained relatively stable in the last forty years, i.e., parents and two children. Although it appears that the size of the family has diminished in the last century, recent trends do not indicate that the present size will diminish. In summary, demographic and sociological data indicate that the Canadian family is nuclear in structure, neolocal in residence, and conjugal in ideology.

Fertility[3]

If, as stated at the outset, one of the major functions of the family is reproduction, how do we assess whether Canadian families are performing this function? Social demographers periodically examine this aspect of family life in two ways using measures referred to as the fertility rate and the birth rate. The fertility rate is an index of the fertility of a population, usually measured by the number of children that have been born per year per 1,000 potentially fertile females. For statistical purposes, age-specific fertility rates are calculated by sorting women into certain categories such as 15–19 years, 20–24 years, and so on, up to 45–59 years. Birth rates are calculated in two ways. The crude birth rate refers to the number of births per year per 1,000 members of the total population including children and the aged. The refined birth rate, on the other hand, refers to the number of children born per 1,000 females of 15 years or over. In Tables 1:5 and 1:6, the fertility rates and birth rates are given.

The data on the fertility rates and crude birth rates demonstrate a steady decline from 1926 with an all-time low in 1973. From an historical point of view, Table 1:5 suggests that more and more Canadians now prefer to have either one or two children. There has been a significant change in the attitudes of Canadians towards ideal family size and this, in turn, seems to be reflected in their fertility behaviour. For example, a Gallup Poll taken in 1945 indicated that only 17 per cent of Canadians claimed that two or fewer children were the ideal number whereas 60 per cent thought four or more ideal. But a poll taken in 1977 found that

Table 1:5 Fertility Rates, Canada, Selected Years, 1926–73

	Age-Specific Rate							Total Fertility Rate
	15–19	20–24	25–29	30–34	35–39	40–44	45–49	
1926–30	30.0	140.7	174.4	149.4	110.1	48.3	5.8	3,293
1931–35	27.7	121.7	159.3	136.0	96.8	40.6	5.2	2,937
1936–40	27.0	119.4	145.8	123.3	84.9	34.0	4.1	2,692
1941	30.7	138.4	159.8	122.3	80.0	31.6	3.7	2,832
1946	36.5	169.6	191.4	146.0	93.1	34.5	3.8	3,374
1951	48.1	188.7	198.8	144.5	86.5	30.9	3.1	3,503
1956	55.9	222.2	220.1	150.3	89.6	30.8	2.9	3,858
1961	58.2	233.6	219.2	144.9	81.1	28.5	2.4	3,840
1966	48.2	169.1	163.5	103.3	57.5	19.1	1.7	2,812
1971	40.1	134.4	142.0	77.3	33.6	9.4	0.6	2,187
1972	38.5	119.8	137.1	72.1	28.9	7.8	0.6	2,024
1973	37.2	117.7	131.6	67.1	25.7	6.4	0.4	1,931

Source: Statistics Canada, *Vital Statistics*, Preliminary Annual Report (1973).

Table 1:6   Crude Birth Rate, Canada, 1921–73

Year	Rate per 1,000 Population
1921	29.3
1931	23.2
1941	22.4
1946	27.2
1951	27.2
1956	28.0
1961	26.1
1966	19.4
1971	16.8
1972	15.9
1973	15.5

Source: *Canada Year Book* (1961–75) and other census reports.

15 per cent considered four or more children as the ideal number. However, the percentage of those favouring the small size (two or fewer) rose sharply to 55 per cent. The rest preferred three children.

Discussing the reasons for a declining fertility rate Wargon (1976: 163) observes, "The important demographic factors were the coming of age, during the late 1950s and 1960s, of smaller numbers of young people (since they represented the lower birth rates of the 1930s) and the decline in the childbearing of married women in the youngest reproductive ages." Most demographic accounts (see also Boyd, *et al.*, 1976: 30–32; Kalbach, 1976: 103–04; Nett, 1976: 56), offer little sociological explanation for the reduced fertility rate but it is possible to make some plausible speculations. In general, although most Canadians conform to the norm of parenthood by having one or two children, the increasing cost of child-rearing, smaller-family ideals, economic pressures, and the tendency of women to complete their child-bearing and -rearing responsibilities before they are 34 years of age appear to encourage the high incidence of small families in Canada.

Socialization

It is through the complex process of socialization that a new-born infant is made human and trained in those skills that are deemed necessary for the infant to become an accredited member of society. In virtually all societies the family is entrusted with this critical responsibility *viz.*, to facilitate an orderly inculcation of the significant social heritage among its new members.

As we have pointed out elsewhere (Ramu, 1976: 308–12), socialization entails, among other things, conferring of an initial identity in terms of gender, ethnicity, class, and religion; provision (or lack thereof) of structured opportunities for educational and occupational accomplishments; and the exposure and training of the new-born into role models which are based on gender-identity.

About a decade ago, there was little concern about the nature and purpose of socialization and it was somewhat taken for granted. As evident from Nett's presentation in Chapter 5, in contemporary societies many aspects of socialization have been subjected to severe criticism and consequently many ethical and secular concerns have become explicit points of contention and confusion. One of the major concerns has been the appropriateness or the desirability of arbitrarily socializing children into male-female roles which are differentially evaluated and rewarded. The Canadian studies discussed in Chapter 5 clearly indicate that the family directly or indirectly promotes rigid gender-based role identities. One consequence of such studies, in conjunction with the increase in public statements by various ideological reform groups, is that many arguments have been advanced concerning the desirability of socialization predicated upon rigid gender-based roles.

Kinship Networks

In our discussion of the demographic aspects of the family, we indicated that the Canadian family is basically neolocal in character, i.e., families maintain separate households, and that young people tend to move out of the family home in order to form single-person households. Such facts reflect an inherent social ideology related to the kinship system in Canada. The pattern of youth moving out even before they are married may represent the increasing commitment of individualism and self-reliance as well as a diminishing concern for residential integration with parental families. Such a pattern of neolocality also reinforces the emphasis given to the marital bond as opposed to other familial ties. In essence, the ideology, demography, and realities of family life in Canada do not support the extended-family ideals or household arrangements found in other societies.

In Chapter 6, an attempt has been made to identify the nature of kin networks in Canada. In an urban society which places heavy emphasis on achievement, self-reliance, conjugalism, and economic independence, one would expect to find an erosion of kinship networks. Nevertheless, as Goode (1963: 75) notes, "The extended kin network continues to function and include a wide range of kin who share with one another, see one another frequently, and know each other. . . ." Such networks are voluntary, selective, and relatively free from normative pressures or a sense of compelling obligation to belong to them. Despite popular notions about the shallow, impersonal, and egocentric nature of urban family bonds, empirical evidence summarized in Chapter 6 clearly shows that one turns to relatives in times of personal joy or crisis. Moreover, occasions such as marriage, civil and religious holidays, or death act as foci for kinship solidarity. In sum, urban kinship networks continue to play an important role in linking individuals and families into wider structures, providing emotional satisfactions, and providing a variety of services and mutual aid.

Family and Ethnic Patterns

If one of the major goals of socialization is the maintenance of social structure, then in Canadian society, social differentiation based on language, ethnicity, religion, and class will continue to be salient for as long as the present socialization practices prevail and are consistent with today's political ideology of pluralism. Sociological discussions have often taken the stance that the family not only encourages a pluralistic social order but also represents such an order because of its different forms. For example, Ishwaran (1971: 372–95; 1976: 23–28) identifies several ethnic and regional family patterns in an effort to demonstrate variations. Elkin (1968: 31) unequivocally states, "There is no one Canadian family. With its distinctive geography and history, Canada is much too heterogeneous to have one or twenty distinctive family types. As the geographical setting, and the social-class, religious, ethnic, occupational, and other groupings vary, so do our families."

The validity of this assertion is examined by Tavuchis in Chapter 7. Although recognizing the family's role as the first line of defense against eroding influences, he suggests that ethnicity is becoming less salient and consequential from a socio-historical point of view. On the basis of available information, he notes that the demographic distribution of ethnic groups (Quebec apart) masks the dominance of English, as a language or culture, as a homogenizing force. Ishwaran (1971, 1976) also supports this position by delineating the trends of uniformity in Canadian families. Therefore, if ethnicity is viewed from the point of view of the family, trends of uniformity rather than diversity appear to be more prominent and patent.

DIVORCE AND REMARRIAGE

As we indicated in our preceding discussion of courtship and marriage, the freedom of choice in mate-selection, and various socio-psychological expectations of marriage have contributed to a shift in marriage from its traditional character to that of an association. The sense of permanence which is endemic to any institution is weakened under such a structural arrangement. The stability of marriage is a function of the stability of mutual and exclusive commitment, love, and the ability to meet the myriad needs of the partners. Divorce often results when there is a serious erosion of such a commitment or when people have high expectations which are not fulfilled.

Marriage in our society is ideally viewed as taking precedence over all other relationships—filial, sibling, friendship, and so on. It is the only relationship where we see a convergence of needs—biological, psychological, economic, and social—and a sustained arrangement to meet these needs in a specific dyad. The burdens placed on this bond are extremely heavy and intense. Hence, there is a concerted societal effort to preserve the stability of marriage. As Peters points out in Chapter 8, the legal framework until recently has been directed toward such a conservative function. Yet, as evident from the divorce statistics he presents, a small but increasing proportion of those married seem to be unhappy mainly because the spouse has not been able to deliver what was anticipated. Thus, divorce is not only indicative of the inability or unwillingness to cope with and adapt to such enormous pressures, but also represents a societal recognition for a mechanism to deal with unhappy marriages where commitment, communication, and affection no longer exist.

For an understanding of Peters's discussion of divorce statistics and procedures, one should take into account the autonomous nature of courtship and marriage in Canada. Divorce (like other social patterns) is differentially generated and distributed among various social strata. For example, those marriages that have few institutional supports and a weak economic base are likely to entail a high risk of divorce (see Levinger, 1965; Goode, 1956).

Remarriage

A consideration of remarriage also reveals that marriage as a social institution or association is firmly rooted in Canada. For instance, Schlesinger's discussion, in Chapter 9, reiterates the understanding that divorce is an act against the marital partner, not against marriage itself since the divorced often remarry soon. Those who remarry are apt to modify their behaviour within the second marriage in order to enhance its longevity. Such an effort, by all indications, results in an improvement in the quality of marital life although there is no clear evidence about its durability.

Any discussion of divorce and remarriage tends to leave an impression on the reader that all is not well with marriage and the family in Canada. Such an impression is reinforced by sensationalized media stories about the geometric increase in divorce rates. From a sociological point of view, this aspect of marital life is unduly distorted. Although divorce rates have registered a dramatic increase in the last decade, interpreted in context they do not necessarily lead us to the conclusion that marriage and the family are in a state of crisis or disorganization. In fact, Canada has the lowest divorce rate (see Chapter 8) among all the industrialized societies including Britain and the United States.

ALTERNATIVES

The sustained durability of marriage and the family in the face of many challenges and changes raises the question of periodic efforts by individuals and groups to search for alternative arrangements which are more flexible. Historically, such efforts date back to Plato who held that marriage and family diminish a person's commitment to the State and hence, should be abolished in the pursuit of excellence and virtue. Following Engels's (1942) discourse on the monogamous family as the first expression of capitalism, Bolsheviks in Soviet Russia between 1918 and 1936 engaged in an abortive effort to reconstruct family patterns. During this century, many Jewish immigrants in areas which are now part of Israel, successfully tried to institute a communal form of family (Spiro, 1956). Numerous intentional communes were established in the United States that attempted to modify or abolish existing family patterns both on a religious and secular basis (Kanter, 1977).

In the last two decades several attempts have been made by individuals and groups to develop alternatives to contemporary marriage and family forms. In his discussion of the reasons for the emergence of such alternatives, Whitehurst in Chapter 10 suggests that the decline of shared values and the weakening of social controls, together with an emphasis on secularism, unfettered individualism, liberalized opportunities for women, easy divorce, and an increasing tolerance of sexual permissiveness, have encouraged the search for alternate marriage and family styles.

In Chapter 10, Whitehurst discusses such variant forms and alerts us to the relative lack of information concerning their incidence and dynamics. Yet, one should recognize that the potential impact of these movements or arrangements goes beyond sheer numbers or their more notorious practices. For example, the practice of "living together" before marriage, if it becomes widespread, would, in fact, alter our courtship careers and residential arrangements. Similarly, the drawing up of a contract stipulating details of obligations, rights, and routine chores, *if* it becomes popular, would change the nature of marital relations. The effect of these alternatives examined in Chapter 10 should be understood not only in terms of what they are now but also in relation to the implications for future marriage and family ties.

Notes

1. The public interest in this aspect is obvious from various newspaper reports. For example, on November 31, 1977, the *Winnipeg Free Press* on its first page had a report based on Statistics Canada's monograph with bold headlines as follows: *Family Life is Still Strong*. The Statistics Canada report reassured Canadians that "Despite increased divorce rates and lower birth rates, family life remains a strong social institution and is not disintegrating as some would believe . . . family life has undergone some major changes in ten years since the last count (1961) because of certain social trends. But it was in a state of reorganization not disorganization."
2. Adapted from Ramu (1976: 299).
3. In this introductory chapter, we deal with only two official functions of the family—reproduction and socialization. For a discussion of other functions in Canadian context, see Ramu, 1976.

The Courtship Process:

Dating and Mate-Selection

SUENG GYU MOON

Nearly all societies place a high premium on marriage and, therefore, not only expect but also encourage their members to marry. The choice of a mate(s) and eventual marriage, however, are guided by complex rules and regulations, some of which are explicit and others less obvious. In this chapter, we propose to briefly explore the social and structural conditions governing mate-selection processes in Canadian society.

PERSPECTIVES ON MATE-SELECTION

Norms or rules concerning such basic issues as who can marry whom, who has the final decision-making power in choosing a mate, and the criteria of desirability and eligibility are essential features of any marriage market or system. Sociologically, such constellations of values and actions are viewed in terms of preferential mating and patterns of mate-selection.

Preferential Mating

Rules which circumscribe the field of eligible mates in terms of preferences and prohibitions are found in every society. The criteria underlying such preferences and prohibitions differ from one society to the other. For example, in Canada the incest taboo prohibits marriage and sex between people related in certain ways and thus limits one's pool of eligibles. Thus, one may not marry one's mother's brother's daughter but in some cultures one may be encouraged, if not expected to do so. Therefore, norms related to incest indirectly result in various forms of exogamy, i.e., an exclusion of certain classes of persons from the universe of eligible mates. On the other hand, there are social pressures to choose a mate from one's own group, e.g., ethnic, religious, race, or class. This stipulation is defined as endogamy. Generally endogamy is the most preferred pattern of mate-selection and, as we shall see later, is common in Canada.

Patterns of Mate-Choice

Once the field of eligible mates has been established in terms of exogamy and endogamy, how does a person go about choosing a mate? The method, again, varies from one society to the other and is dependent upon societal concern for the preservation of social differences. In societies which place a high emphasis on the maintenance of social differentiation, the choice of a mate is likely to be made by the parents and other significant kin such as elders. In contrast, where there is a minimal interest in preserving rigid barriers or where elders do not extend authority or power, individuals are likely to choose their own mates within certain limits. The Canadian mate-selection pattern, ideal-typically, falls into the latter category. Some of the main features of such a system have been documented in the sociological literature (e.g., Zimmerman, 1947; Goode, 1959, 1963; Marsh and O'Hara, 1961; Stephens, 1963; and Larson, 1976) and include:

1. Emphasis of individualism as opposed to familism.
2. Conjugal family with neolocal residence and disappearance of uni-lineal kinship system.
3. Greater freedom and independence of the couple, financially or otherwise, from the family of orientation and no subordination of the wife to her mother-in-law or to her husband's kin members.
4. Enhanced status of children and women, and association with an increasingly egalitarian and democratic family system.
5. Increased use of person-centred criteria in mate-selection with the view that marriage is a personal matter.
6. Greater freedom from parental control in mate-selection with a minimum of parental interference.

7. Wider opportunities for increasingly frequent, intimate, and open interaction between the sexes.
8. Institutionalized dating and courtship systems.
9. Emphasis on romantic love as an institutionalized basis of selection.

Of the above, perhaps romantic love as an institutionalized basis of mate-selection may be singled out as the most important element which distinguishes the free-choice system from the arranged-marriage system. As pointed out by Goode (1959), since love attachments may occur in any society and since love is potentially disruptive of lineages and the social-stratification system, it must be controlled or channelled in some way. Thus in arranged-marriage systems, such customs as child marriage, kinship rules defining eligible mates, segregation of potential mates, and chaperonage are employed to control love relationships. By contrast, the free-choice system permits or encourages love relationships after exogamy and endogamy have extended their influence, with the source of control internalized in the person and supported by peers, parents, or others.

In Canada, where mate choice is *formally* free, love is certainly important for marriage, but it is expected to be found within the limits of the permitted social groupings. This would imply that one has to consider many other factors along with the love relationship in the process of getting to know the opposite sex and of moving the relationship toward an increasing commitment. Consequently, we turn now to various factors which explain some dimensions of the mate-selection process under the free-choice system.

FACTORS IN MATE-SELECTION

Some of the factors which will be outlined here fall into two categories: socio-psychological and structural. Though Canadian evidence on how each of these factors influences the mate-selection process is scarce, it is generally assumed that these are part and parcel of the western courtship system and, hence, of relevance for Canada.

Socio-Psychological Factors

Certain characteristics, such as perceived personality traits and the extent to which an individual's needs are gratified by another, have been considered by some sociologists as critical to the choice of a mate. For example, some investigators (Cattell and Nesselroade, 1967; Schelhenberg and Bee, 1960) found a tendency for "like to marry like". With regard to such traits as intelligence, attitudes, physical appearance, aspirations, etc., such a tendency may be conceptualized as a special case of "homogamy".[1]

On a related dimension, Winch (1958: 89) hypothesized that "in mate-selection each individual seeks within his or her field of eligibles for that person who gives the greatest promise of providing him or her with maximum need gratification." After postulating a series of twelve specific needs and three general traits, he suggested that the specific need patterns of the couple are complementary rather than similar. Accordingly, a man with a need for dominance, for example, would choose a girl with a need for deference from among several candidates within the eligible field. Although his empirical test on the basis of a small sample confirmed his theory, a number of subsequent studies undertaken by others have not lent support to the idea of complementary needs.[2] Instead, most of these studies showed that the couples either seemed attracted on the basis of "need similarity" or were characterized by a combination of similarity and complementarity.

To what extent each one of us carefully assesses these factors during the courtship process is unclear. But it is safe to assume that some evaluation of personality traits in terms of temperament, the ability to adjust, and the capacity to meet mutual needs, does occur before one decides to marry.

Structural Factors

In a context where the emphasis is on freedom of choice, romantic love may be a necessary condition for marriage but is not always a sufficient one, because various structural conditions screen individuals on certain criteria before their romantic involvement. We may consider here two of these: proximity and endogamy.

In the last four decades several studies have shown that a large proportion of people tend to select their mates from within their neighbourhood, from the place of work, or within schools or colleges that they attend. The common factor is proximity. It is also important here to recognize the manner in which prospective mates are filtered socially in terms of certain characteristics, e.g., most residential areas reflect a concentration of people in terms of race, ethnicity, or class. Therefore, segregated neighbourhoods, *per se*, encourage endogamous alliances. The Canadian data, in general, tend to support the prevalence of religious endogamy as late as the 1970s. Of all Canadians who married in 1975, 61 per cent chose their mates within their own faith.[3] If we focus our attention to the grooms of three major religious categories, i.e., Jewish, Catholic, and Protestant, the endogamous rates in that year were 84.6 per cent, 79.5 per cent, and 77.3 per cent, respectively.[4] Similarly, most ethnic groups, with the possible exception of Scandinavians, show very high to moderately high degrees of ethnic endogamy with rates ranging from 52 per cent to 92 per cent.[5] It is also generally agreed that there is a pronounced tendency for most people to marry within their own class.

The specific ways in which these factors operate in "screening" or "filtering" in the mate-selection process is not clear, but it appears that many social institutions exert direct or indirect pressures toward endogamy so that individuals gradually narrow down their own field of eligible mates and eventually reach the final choice. It should be pointed out, however, that these factors seem to operate together rather than separately. In fact, many studies in Canada and the United States have already shown the interlocking nature of religion, ethnicity, social class, and residential segregation.[6] Any combination of these factors may exist, but social class seems to be crucial relative to others, while religion and ethnicity appear to be much more closely associated with each other than other combinations. Thus, as in the case of propinquity, each of these variables appears to reinforce the other in the persistence of endogamy.

DATING AND COURTSHIP IN CANADA

Functions and Stages of Dating

In Canada, one usually chooses a mate through the socially approved method of dating. Thus, most young Canadians start dating during their fourteenth or fifteenth year and carry on this heterosexual interaction until marriage which takes place, on the average, at the age of 22.6 for women and 24.7 for men.[7] Somewhere along the line (which spans no less than a period of eight to ten years) every groom and bride must at some point have engaged in courtship in the sense that they seriously considered their dating partners as potential spouses.

The distinction between courtship and dating may be made analytically by viewing the former as an activity directed toward a member of the opposite sex with a serious intent of marriage and the latter a playful or less-committed activity. However, given the essential ambiguity of intentions and actions it is more useful to view dating and courtship on a continuum with various identifiable stages such as casual dating, casual going-steady, serious going-steady or "going with", and engagement, as suggested by Adams (1975).

Sociologists have distinguished a number of purposes and consequences of dating: recreation, socialization, personality development, satisfaction of ego needs, status placement, sexual gratification, and selection of a mate.[8] They further agree that these functions are "not *all* performed at *all* stages of *all* dating relationships" (Adams, 1975: 190), but rather, that certain combinations may occur depending upon the intensity and duration of interaction between the dating couples. Thus, the functions of recreation and socialization are more likely to be salient in casual dating whereas personality development and ego needs would be more important for those going-steady. Moreover, each stage seems to reflect a different level of intimacy in terms of sexual behaviour ranging from holding hands to petting and sexual union.

Most Canadian empirical studies have relied on responses from university students and this clearly limits our ability to generalize.[9] On the other hand, if we interpret the data with caution they do provide us with some suggestive findings and implications.

Some Basic Trends and Sex Differences

One of the earliest empirical studies was conducted by Mann (1968a) in Ontario in mid-1960s and found that regular dating starts at the age of fourteen for girls and fifteen for boys at school parties and dances, and house parties. After a few years of multiple dating most girls started going-steady for varying lengths of time at sixteen. The experiences of these adolescents conformed closely to the stages outlined previously and the various forms of sexual intimacy associated with these stages. Thus, at the time of the survey, roughly 15 per cent of the boys in the sample[10] had had sexual intercourse while 74.3 per cent of the girls and 53.1 per cent of the boys had already engaged in necking and petting. In the same sample, Mann also found that 78 per cent of the girls and 66 per cent of the boys had gone-steady at least once. In general, the girls tended to have had dates more frequently and with more different partners than the boys.

Most of the patterns Mann found, especially the sexual differences in dating patterns, were substantiated by Wakil's study (1973a) of dating practices on a prairie campus.[11] Even with such variables as age, class, religion, marital status, and community of origin (rural/urban) controlled, Wakil found that females in general started dating slightly earlier, dated more frequently, and had gone-steady earlier than males. When different ages were taken into account, females again dated more individuals than the males, with the exception of rural females over twenty years of age. With respect to rural-urban differences, Wakil's data show that, as a whole, both males and females of urban origin started dating slightly earlier than their rural counterparts, and urban males more frequently than their rural counterparts, although both differences were only slight.

Perhaps the most significant and provocative finding of Wakil's study is the absence of *homodating*[12] (in-group dating in terms of structural variables such as economic background, religion, ethnicity, and nationality) except for rural males and females. All other individuals—whatever their status characteristics, dated across category boundaries. Although Wakil's other findings are fairly consistent with most of the American studies, the lack of "homodating" is radically different from most of the previous findings. In the absence of subsequent comparable studies, no generalization could be made, but because of its challenging nature, we will come back to this point very shortly.

ORIENTATIONS TO DATING AND MATE-SELECTION

Since Waller's pioneering study (1937) on dating, much attention has been directed toward the problematic aspect of such relationships as perceived by dating partners. One of the areas explored in this connection has been the attitudes and values of young people regarding various aspects of dating and mate-selection.

With respect to attitudes and evaluations of dating relationships, Whitehurst and Frisch (1974) have studied dating practices among 679 students (47 per cent of whom were males) through interviews on a southwestern Ontario campus. The data show that dating was "essentially a sociable (but not socially or status) oriented pleasurable activity", but "not especially marriage oriented". The dating experiences of the respondents were described as warm (82 per cent), very pleasant (80 per cent), real human involvement (71 per cent), and educational (69 per cent). Moreover, it was growth oriented (61 per cent) rather than antagonistic, and non-status oriented (60 per cent). However, there were some sex differences in the subjects' perceived and actual dating experiences. In the area of perception, for instance, males were seen as less cooperative (*vs.* antagonistic), more oriented to having fun rather than interested in courtship, and more sexually oriented, while females were perceived as less growth (*vs.* exploitation) oriented. Except for these four dimensions, the remaining nine dimensions, which were intended to measure the respondents' perceptions, did not show any sex differences, and this basic similarity of perception between the sexes is interpreted by Whitehurst and Frisch as a reflection of our "homogenizing" socialization system which tends to minimize differences.

This "homogenizing" effect is also well reflected in mate-selection preferences. According to Wakil (1973a), the six traits (out of 32) indicated as most desirable by both sexes, regardless of their community of origin were: dependability and honesty, faithfulness and loyalty in marriage, consideration and understanding, pleasant personality and disposition, emotional maturity, and good sense of humour. The only minor exception was that urban males rated being "sexually responsive" high enough to replace "dependability and honesty" in the list of the top six. With the lack of similar data from other parts of the country, Wakil does not make a generalization of his findings for most university students in Canada, but his findings correspond very closely to those in the United States.

It might be of interest to compare Wakil's sample with the young people living in an ethno-religiously oriented community in Ontario. According to Ishwaran's study (1977) of a relatively closed Dutch community, religious compatibility was given the first rank by the boys and the sixth by the girls. By contrast, for Wakil's sample "similar religious background" was given much lower standing, at 20th to 22.5th places, depending upon sex and community of origin.

Role consensus or perceived role consensus appears to play a part in mate-selection. Indeed, role congruence between the couple would certainly contribute to stability in the marriage. In this connection, Hobart (1972) reports a study dealing with attitudes towards various marital-role issues as perceived by a sample of 700 English- and 404 French-speaking university and trade-school students. With regard to the concept of "egalitarianism", Hobart found the English-speaking sample distinctly more egalitarian, but not in all dimensions. The English-speaking students were more egalitarian in such matters as "personal characteristics of marriage partners, social life, and education expectations", but not in the area of a wife's employment. French-speaking women students were highly egalitarian in their views concerning a wife's employment, while French-speaking men students were still characterized by "traditionalism" in most areas. Although the females in both samples were more egalitarian than the males, this difference was much more pronounced in the French-speaking women. The analysis suggests that "there are more powerfully entrenched definitions of marital roles in the French-Canadian culture than in the Anglo-Canadian culture."

SOME SIGNS OF CHANGE AND UNCERTAINTY IN ATTITUDES

The absence of "homodating" in Wakil's study (1973a) may be explained in light of Whitehurst–Frisch's concepts of "no-marriage and fun-oriented" and "education-growth-oriented" attitudes of college students. Nevertheless, and despite the limitations of the sample, this negative finding may give us some insight into the practice of dating as a phase in the courtship process. Apart from the increased incidence of inter-religious and inter-ethnic marriages shown by Canadian census data, we have several other empirical studies indicating that young people are disenchanted with marriage and the family as we know it. Compared with their counterparts in the United States, for example, Whitehurst and Plant (1971) found that Canadian students were more conventional but more alienated and were more inclined to consider alternatives to the standard marriage forms.[1] They appear to be more aware of prob-

lems in marriage, especially marital roles, and this is reflected in the more
negative comments toward marriage and the legal aspects of the family.)
Although Canadian youth place an extremely high value on open and
honest communications with their mates (Whitehurst, 1973), they "tend
to dismiss the difficulties faced by others with a naive faith that they
will somehow do better—never fully understanding the means to the end
as either unattainable or extremely difficult to achieve" (Whitehurst,
1975: 5).

CONCLUSIONS

The implications of the previous discussion of courtship in Canada are
clear.

First, more factual data on the process of courtship in Canada are
sorely needed before any theoretical statements can be validated concerning who marries whom and in which contexts.

Second, such studies should make it a point to try and sort out the
relative weights of such sociological considerations as class, religion, etc.,
both independently and in combination, insofar as they are pertinent to
dating and courtship systems.

Third, Canadian patterns must be viewed in larger contexts which
calls for comparative research within and between nations and cultures.

Notes

1. Following Kephart's suggestion
   (1972), we are using the term
   "homogamy" in a narrower sense in
   this chapter. Thus, it is used to refer
   to only a similarity of physical or
   psychological traits, while endogamy
   is used to refer to group similarities
   such as race, religion, nationality,
   and social class.
2. Bowerman and Day (1956), Schelhenberg and Bee (1960), Levinger,
   Senn, and Jogensen (1970), and
   Murstein (1970).
3. Kalbach and McVey (1976: 98).
4. Heer and Hubay (1975: 88, Table
   6:2).
5. Kalbach and McVey (1976: 97).
6. Kephart (1972: 310–12), Kalbach

(1975: 69–72).
7. This figure is based on Wakil
   (1973a) and Mann (1968).
8. In fact, these figures are mean ages
   for those who married for the first
   time in 1973. See, Kalbach, (1975:
   63–66).
9. Kephart (1961: 296–300), Adams
   (1975: 189–93).
10. Most of the studies are included in
    the selected bibliography at the end
    of this chapter.
11. The main sample, consisting of
    eighty boys and forty girls, is a two
    per cent randomized sample of 6,000
    students at a mid-Ontario college.
    In addition to this, Mann also
    studied two more samples. For

more details, see Mann (1968).

12. Wakil's sample consisted of 166 males and 134 females.

13. The term "homodating", coined by Wakil, refers to the dating between pairs of similar background characteristics. For more detail, see footnote 1 of Wakil (1973a), p. 286.

14. For this study, a sample of 276 midwest American university students was compared with 222 Ontario university students from similar-sized cities and similar-sized university settings. For more detail, see Whitehurst and Plant (1971: 76–77).

SELECTED BIBLIOGRAPHY

ECKLAND, BRUCE. "Theories of Mate Selection", *Eugenics Quarterly*, Vol. 15, pp.
1968   71–84.

FREEMAN, LINTON C. "Marriage Without Love: Mate-Selection in Non-Western
1974   Societies", pp. 354–66 in Robert F. Winch and Graham B. Spanier, eds.,
Selected Readings in Marriage and the Family, New York.

GOODE, WILLIAM J. "The Theoretical Importance of Love", *American Sociological*
1959   *Review*, Vol. 24, pp. 38–47.

———. *World Revolution and Family Patterns*, New York.
1963

HOBART, CHARLES W. "Orientations to Marriage Among Young Canadians", *Journal*
1972   *of Comparative Family Studies*, Vol. 3, pp. 171–93.

LARSON, LYLE E., ed. *The Canadian Family in Comparative Perspective*, Scarbor-
1976   ough. See especially, Kalbach and McVey's article, "The Canadian
Family: A Demographic Profile", pp. 94–108, and Larson's article,
"Courtship and Mate Choice", pp. 111–19.

MANN, W. E. "Sex Behaviour on the Campus", pp. 115–26 in W. E. Mann, ed.,
1968   *Canada: A Sociological Profile*, Toronto. First appeared in W. E. Mann,
"Canadian Trends in Premarital Behaviour", *Bulletin of the Council for
Social Service of the Anglican Church of Canada* (Toronto, 1967).

WAKIL, S. PARVEZ, ed., *Marriage, Family, and Society: Canadian Perspectives*, To-
1975   ronto. See especially, chapters 1 and 2 (by Wakil), 6 (by Heer and
Hubay), and 7 (by Carisse).

WHITEHURST, ROBERT N. and BARBARA PLANT. "A Comparison of Canadian and
1971   American University Students' Reference Groups, Alienation and Attitudes Toward Marriage", *International Journal of Sociology of the
Family*, Vol. 1, pp. 75–82.

——— and G. R. FRISCH. "Sex Differences in Dating Orientations: Some Compari-
1974   sons and Recent Observations", *International Journal of Sociology of
the Family*, Vol. 4, pp. 213–19.

The Courtship Process:

3

Premarital Sexual Attitudes and Behaviour

CHARLES W. HOBART

The past two decades has been a period of revolutionary change in the sexual mores in North America. In the media, sophisticated "skin magazines" such as *Playboy* and *Viva* and movies featuring nudity and the depiction of sexual acts have gained widespread acceptance and even respectability. The sexual-responsiveness research of Masters and Johnson (1966, 1970) has given rise to sexual therapy in which opposite sex therapists engage in sexual foreplay and intercourse with "clients". The line between old-fashioned pornography and art, advertising, education, and science has become increasingly blurred, as has the line between therapy and prostitution.

There are numerous indications that many people in North America are responding to this new freedom, and perhaps to the basic malaise of the family in "post-industrial" society, in an unprecedented variety of ways, including sex before marriage, living together without marriage, and "swinging" though married.

Most of these patterns have originated in Europe or the United States, but their effects on Canada are apparent to even the casual observer. "New morality" standards are now reflected in this country's mass media. There are in fact two new moralities in addition to the two "old moralities"—the "abstinence" or no sex before marriage standard, and the "double" or premarital sex for men but not for women standard. The moderate new morality, essentially an extension of the abstinence, sex only after marriage standard, is the "love standard". This asserts that coitus is acceptable between *loving* partners, before or after marriage, but that sex without mutual love is immoral even after marriage. The more radical new morality, essentially an extension of the double standard, is the "fun standard". This asserts that intercourse is acceptable between partners who both *want* to participate, whether married or not, but that it is not acceptable, even between married partners, where one does not want to.

In this chapter we shall review the evidence of the impact of such recent developments on courtship and sexual relationships among young Canadians. Following a section dealing with recent theoretical writings, we shall review major Canadian research relating to changes in sexual attitudes and sexual experience. The chapter concludes with a more detailed consideration of findings from a recent reiterative study which surveyed student attitudes and behaviours across Canada in 1968 and 1977.

THEORETICAL ORIENTATIONS

Theories explaining variations in sexual attitudes and sexual behaviour range from psychological theories of sexual drives and motivations, to explanations of sexual norms in terms of the functions of these norms for other structures in the society. In between there are a number of other psychological, social-psychological, and sociological theories which have some explanatory value. However, none explains much of the variation in observed sexual attitudes and behaviours within the same society, much less between societies. We will briefly review several influential social-psychological and sociological theories.

There are three categories of social-psychological theories which have been applied to this area: the interaction, reference-group, and exchange theories.

Interaction theories run a gamut with some inductively based theories, such as the oft-demonstrated propositions that sexually permissive attitudes and behaviour vary inversely with age at first date (Bell and Chaskes, 1970; Freeman and Freeman, 1966) and at steady dating (Hobart 1972b), and directly with love relationships) (Eastman, 1972; Christensen and Gregg, 1970), number of persons dated (Hobart, 1972b), and steady dated and engagement experience (Hobart, 1972b). Kirkendall and Libby (1966: 48) have emphasized that "a sexual relationship is an interpersonal relationship and as such is subject to the same principles of interaction as are other relationships". Kirkendall (1961: 7) has essentially explored the approach that sexual relations, like other interpersonal relations, may increase cooperative attitudes, self-respect, faith and confidence in people, and fulfillment of individual potentialities, and may dissolve the barriers separating people and create greater integrity in relationships. He further argues that relationships having these consequences are right, and by implication are reinforcing. On the other hand, it is apparent that sexual relationships, like other relationships, may also be destructive of people and may have quite contrary consequences to those Kirkendall discusses.

The reference-group theorists have typically tested the hypothesis that the sexual attitudes/behaviour of an individual will tend to be a function of his perceptions of the norms or expectations of his normative and comparison reference groups, irrespective of the direction of influence. These researchers have often conceptualized parents as a conservative reference group which loses its influence during adolescence, and the adolescent peer group as a liberal reference group gaining influence, thus explaining the often-observed tendency for adolescents to become more permissive during this period. However, this same formulation, of course, explains the continued non-permissiveness of young people with strong conservative, church-based reference groups (Mirande, 1968; Clayton, 1972; Teevan, 1972; and Davidson and Leslie, 1977).

Exchange theorists conceptualize all continuing social relationships as essentially exchange processes in which each party seeks to maximize his/her benefits and minimize his/her costs. This approach was implicit in Waller's discussions of "rating and dating", and of "dalliance" relationships years ago (1938): the "biggest men on campus" attempt to date the most popular "campus queen" and such interest is reciprocated because each benefits from the high rating of the other. In dating, women will seek to exchange a minimum in sexual favours for a maximum of entertainment provided, or of affection. The support for propositions derived from exchange theory is provided by Davidson and Leslie (1977).

Structural functional theory explores the functions or consequences which some structures or practices of a society have for other aspects of the system, either the large, societal system, or a component subsystem, such as the family. For example, structural functionalism emphasizes the importance of norms prescribing premarital chastity for perpetuating unambiguous kinship definitions, or for maintaining control of property inheritance in the hands of a kinship group. It may be applied for an analysis of contemporary changes in sexual mores. Reiss (1967) is the most recent proponent of this perspective and based on his research findings he concludes that:

The degree of acceptable premarital sexual permissiveness in a courtship group varies directly with the degree of autonomy of the courtship group (in respect to family influences) and with the degree of acceptable premarital sexual permissiveness in the social and cultural setting outside the group (p. 167).

Reiss's research on premarital sex has precipitated further investigations directed at confirmation or negation of his major findings. Essentially, subsequent findings by Heltsley and Broderick (1969), Middendorp, et al. (1970), Maranell, et al. (1970), and Bayer (1977) have not totally confirmed some of Reiss's assumptions. Reiss, of course, questions their conclusions on the grounds of validity.

More recently, working with Miller (1974), Reiss has proposed an essentially eclectic theory postulating that sexual permissiveness is a function of personal liberality, traditional level of perceived sexual permissiveness (PSP) of one's membership groups, affection in dating relationships, orientation to marriage and family roles, individual egalitarianism, potential for PSP in one's basic parentally derived values, perceived PSP of parents, importance of parental reference groups, perceived PSP of peers, responsibility for other family members, physical attractiveness, courtship participation, and individual courtship autonomy (1974).

Less ambitiously, Clayton's "contingent consistency model" in many ways anticipates Reiss's more recent approach. Clayton's model seeks to account for sexual behaviour in terms of attitudes and "contingent factors" mediating between attitudes and behaviour (1972). These factors include group properties such as relevant group norms, personal properties such as personal attractiveness, perceived group properties such as perceptions of the sexual experience of comparison groups, and behavioural opportunity factors such as whether housing arrangements are shared or not. This theory is an attempt to combine reference-group theory with findings concerning the relevance of some attitudinal influences and aspects of the physical setting to explain variations in coital experience. Clayton found some support for hypotheses derived from this theory.

In 1969 Christensen proposed his "theory of relative consequences" which states:

Both the behaviour itself and the resulting effects of premarital sexual intimacy are in part dependent upon differing cultural norms, plus the conversion of these norms into individual values; and the negative consequences are greatest in restrictive societies, where behaviour is most deviant from existing standards (both cultural and personal) (p. 220).

This theory accounts for behaviour cross-culturally among societies where cultural norms may differ widely, and predicts, in a way suggestive of structural-functional approaches, that the more stringent the standards the more punitive the response to deviation.[1]

Some imaginative attempts have been made to combine these components into more comprehensive theories, particularly by Clayton (1972), Burr (1973), and Reiss and Miller (1974), but none has yet appeared which explains the criterion attitudes and behaviours definitively. Nevertheless the preceding review does provide a basis for predicting increased premarital coitus in Canada. The conditions associated with or facilitating premarital sex specified by Reiss and Miller, and Clayton are generally relevant in Canada. Let us see to what extent this expectation is supported by the findings of relevant Canadian studies.

PREMARITAL SEX RESEARCH IN CANADA

Most Canadian studies have used small convenience samples of students. We shall review the findings from Canadian research in this area by examining attitude studies first and studies of reported premarital sexual behaviour thereafter.

Attitudes Towards Premarital Sexual Experience

The earlier Canadian studies which collected attitudes include: Mann's studies of students at four eastern Canadian universities, Perlman's, *et al.*'s studies of students at a Prairie university, and Hobart's research involving studies at several technical schools and universities in eastern and western Canada which will be reported in the next section.

The Mann Research. W. E. Mann conducted four studies of premarital sexual behaviour in different universities in Canada between 1965 and 1969.[2] The two based on samples having the highest response rate will be reviewed here: one at the University of Western Ontario in 1965 based on a random sample of 120 students, representing 96 per cent of those contacted (Mann, 1967) and one at York University in 1969 based on 153 responses from 85 per cent of those contacted (Mann, 1970). Essentially the same questionnaire was given to both samples.

Mann's data appear to suggest that changes occurred in permissive attitudes between 1965 and 1969, though the differences may reflect in part differences between Toronto and Western Ontario. Thus, he found that 39 per cent of men in the later York sample, as compared with only 5 per cent of men in the earlier Western sample, believed sexual intercourse was justified when pinned or ringed.

Cross-tabulated analysis showed that for both the Western and York samples,[3] age was directly associated with sexual permissiveness. Protestant students at Western were more frequently accepting of genital petting and of intercourse than were Catholics. The less religiously devout students accepted a much more permissive standard of sexual behaviour for engaged couples than the more devout, the percentages accepting intercourse being 46 per cent and 9 per cent, respectively, for students at Western. Also, Western sample members approving of intercourse following engagement increased steadily with the size of the home community from 22 per cent for rural residents, to 45 per cent for metropolitan residents. Among the York students, the trends were similar. At both schools those from middle-class backgrounds were more accepting of sexual intimacy for engaged couples than those from working-class backgrounds.

The Perlman Research. Perlman (1973) reports on findings from several small surveys of students enrolled at the University of Manitoba. In respect to permissiveness attitudes he presents the responses from a random sample of 156 students surveyed in 1970–71, to the items of the Reiss sexual-permissiveness scale. Unfortunately he does not report separately on the acceptability of various degrees of intimacy for male and for female participants. Sixty-seven per cent of the male and sixty per cent of the female respondents were accepting of coitus when the participants were engaged. Those accepting coitus when the participants were in love included 65 per cent of the men and 53 per cent of the women. Sexual intercourse between affectionate participants was acceptable to 55 and 42 per cent of the male and female respondents, and coitus between "not particularly affectionate" participants was acceptable to 20 and 13 per cent respectively.

Correlations showed that religiosity was highly correlated with permissiveness with those highly devout, and Catholics most conservative, and Jews, and those without religious preferences, most permissive. Devoutness was more strongly predictive of conservatism than was religious affiliation. Neither the size of the respondents' homes nor the level of their parents' incomes were consistently related to permissiveness.

Premarital Sexual Experience

The Mann Research. Mann reports on the "lifetime sexual experience" of his sample members, that is, the maximum degree of sexual intimacy ever experienced with a partner of the opposite sex. For the male samples (including 93 men at York and 80 at Western), 50 per cent of those at York (35 per cent at Western) had experienced intercourse, 23 (27)[4] per cent had experienced no more than genital petting, 3 (10) per cent had experienced no more than petting the girl's breast under clothing, and 12 (15) per cent had experienced no more than necking, kissing, or holding hands. For the female samples (including 60 women at York and 40 at Western) 37 (15) per cent had experienced intercourse, 40 (31) per cent had experienced no more than genital petting, 7 (23) per cent no more than breast petting beneath clothing, and 7 (23) per cent no more than necking, kissing, or holding hands.

Mann reports on the relationship between sexual behaviour and ten personal and social characteristics for his two samples: sexual permissiveness is significantly and directly associated with age, infrequent church attendance or prayer, size of community, living in impersonal settings while at university rather than with family or friends, lenient home discipline, unhappy home life, lower income (at Western) and upper-middle-class family standing (at York), and with dissatisfaction with the kind of sex instruction provided by parents.

The Perlman Research. Perlman (1973) provides data on the reported premarital sexual experience of students enrolled in a personality course in 1969 and again in 1970. Among the former 56 per cent of the men and 43 per cent of the women reported intercourse experience, while for the 1970 class these proportions were 54 and 30 per cent, respectively.

In another, related study Perlman (1973) reports on correlations between personality traits and sexual experience among 209 introductory psychology students at the University of Manitoba. Men reporting "a greater number of coital partners" were found to be typically dominant, nurturant, understanding, and low in social recognition, that is, they had little need to be held in high esteem. By contrast, girls reporting a greater number of coital partners tended to be low in dominance, exhibitionism, nurturance, sentience, and the pursuit of leisure-time activities.

A RECENT REITERATIVE STUDY OF CANADIAN TRENDS

Hobart collected data from students enrolled in a number of universities and technical schools across Canada in 1968 (Hobart, 1972b) and again in 1977 using essentially the same questionnaires. The 1968 student samples were drawn from universities in Alberta, Ontario, and Quebec (one school in each province), and from technical schools in Alberta and Quebec. The 1977 data were collected again from the same schools as were contacted in 1968, and from one university and one technical school in Nova Scotia and of British Columbia, and one technical school in Ontario.

The sexually relevant components of the questionnaire include items dealing with sexual-permissiveness attitudes, including the "Reiss Premarital Sexual Permissiveness Scale", reported details of sexual experience, reported reactions to sexual experience, as well as numerous questions on family background.

In the 1968 study, a total of 1,104 responses were obtained from randomly drawn samples at the five schools where the data were collected (Hobart, 1972b). The later data were collected during the winter of 1976–77 from university and technical students in the Maritime provinces, Quebec, Ontario, the Prairie provinces, and British Columbia. The

Table 3:1 Attitudes of Anglophone Sample Members Towards Various Forms of Sexual Permissiveness For Males in 1968 and 1977 By Sex: Percentages

	1968 Sample			1977 Sample		
	Total	M	F	Total	M	F
Kissing not acceptable if not affectionate toward partner	16	9	22	18	14	23
Premarital petting never acceptable	8	6	10	7	7	7
Petting acceptable if engaged	92	94	90	93	93	93
Petting if feel strong affection	80	86	74	90	92	88
Petting though not particularly affectionate toward partner	45	63[a]	29	48	63[a]	36
Intercourse if engaged	59	67[b]	52	82	87[b]	77
Intercourse acceptable if in love	57	64[b]	50	81	85	77
Intercourse if feel strong affection toward partner	44	52[b]	37	70	78[b]	63
Intercourse though not particularly affectionate toward partner	25	38[a]	13	32	46[a]	18
No premarital intercourse	41	33[b]	48	18	13[b]	23
Number of respondents	681	329	352	1628	796	832

[a] Signifies differences between males and females are significant at 0.01 level.
[b] Signifies differences between males and females are significant at 0.05 level.

sampling design of this later study called for the random selection of 100 each of male and female students, aged between 18 and 25, who were not of Oriental or African extraction and were not members of religious orders. The final sample consists of 2,062 students, including 413 Francophones and 1,649 Anglophones. Over 75 per cent of the students contacted filled out questionnaires in eight of the ten schools surveyed in 1976–77.

In the following pages we shall first consider data on the attitudes of students with respect to premarital intercourse, and then on their reported intercourse experience and their reactions to that experience. Differences between such samples, significant at the five-per-cent-confidence levels or beyond, are identified as statistically significant.

Table 3:1 lists some attitudes of Anglophone sample members toward various forms of permissive behaviour for males and Table 3:2 presents data on attitudes towards these same behaviours for females. Tables 3:3 and 3:4 contain similar data for Francophone students. The Anglophone data show that there has been a decided increase in permissiveness. In terms of permissiveness for men (Table 3:1), the data show, in particular, a significant increase in acceptability of intercourse if engaged or in love (from about 59 per cent acceptance in 1968 to 82 per cent in 1977), as compared with a slight increase (from 25 to 32 per cent) in acceptance of intercourse without affection. There is a slightly greater increase in acceptance of intercourse for engaged men among women than among men (from 52 to 77 per cent as compared to 67 to 87 per cent). Note, however, that there is no reduction in the proportion of staunch conservatives: those disapproving of kissing by a non-affectionate couple remains at about 18 per cent.

The data in Table 3:2, showing permissiveness with respect to females, generally reflect a similar pattern. Among the *four* conditions we examine here, attitudes of males and females toward intercourse when engaged by males and females—the greatest increase was registered in female acceptance of female intercourse when engaged (29 per cent). The least increase was registered by males in acceptance of male or female intercourse when engaged (20 percentage points). In the case of intercourse without affection (the "fun standard") there was a greater increased acceptance of such behaviour among women than among men.

The data in Tables 3:1 and 3:2 show a greater increase in acceptance

Table 3:2 Attitudes of Anglophone Sample Members Towards Various Forms of Sexual Permissiveness For Females in 1968 and 1977 By Sex: Percentages

	1968 Sample			1977 Sample		
	Total	M	F	Total	M	F
Kissing not acceptable if not affectionate toward partner	23	17	29	19	16	22
Premarital petting never acceptable	11	9	12	7	6	7
Petting acceptable if engaged	89	91	83	93	94	93
Petting if feel strong affection	76	82[b]	69	88	90	86
Petting though not particularly affectionate toward partner	30	45[a]	17	43	57[a]	30
Intercourse if engaged	56	66[b]	47	81	86[b]	76
Intercourse acceptable if in love	51	61[b]	42	80	83	76
Intercourse if feel strong affection toward partner	37	49[a]	26	68	60[b]	75
Intercourse though not particularly affectionate toward partner	13	24[a]	4	27	39[a]	16
No premarital intercourse	44	36[b]	53	19	14[b]	24
Number of respondents	681	329	352	1627	795	832

[a]Signifies differences between males and females are significant at 0.01 level.
[b]Signifies differences between males and females are significant at 0.05 level.

Table 3:3 Attitudes of Francophone Sample Members Towards Various Forms of Sexual Permissiveness For Males in 1968 and 1977 By Sex: Percentages

	1968 Sample			1977 Sample		
	Total	M	F	Total	M	F
Kissing not acceptable if not affectionate toward partner	67	60[b]	78	28	24	32
Premarital petting never acceptable	26	20	31	10	7	12
Petting acceptable if engaged	74	80	69	90	93	88
Petting if feel strong affection	58	70[a]	45	74	79[b]	67
Petting though not particularly affectionate toward partner	15	23[b]	8	38	48[a]	29
Intercourse if engaged	54	60	47	91	91	91
Intercourse acceptable if in love	50	56	42	84	84	84
Intercourse if feel strong affection toward partner	37	49[a]	24	65	70	61
Intercourse though not particularly affectionate toward partner	14	22[b]	6	32	39	27
No premarital intercourse	46	40	53	9	9	9
Number of respondents	377	190	187	411	189	222

[a]Signifies differences between males and females are significant at 0.01 level.
[b]Signifies differences between males and females are significant at 0.05 level.

of male and female intercourse with affection (the "love standard") than in acceptance of male and female intercourse without affection (the "fun standard") among both men and women. This suggests that there has been a more rapid increase in acceptance of sex with affection than in sex without affection. In terms of the total sample we find a 25 per cent increase in acceptance of the love standard for men, and a 27 per cent increase in the love standard for women, as compared with a 7 per cent increase in acceptance of the fun standard for men, and a 14 per cent increase in this standard for women. The data further show that the greatest increase in permissiveness was registered in the case of women's attitudes toward sex with affection for women, a 33 per cent increase in acceptance, as compared with a 21 per cent increase in male acceptance of sex with affection for men.

Turning to the Francophone data, those in Table 3:3 on the acceptability of male sexual behaviour show a general significant increase in acceptance of various kinds of sexual behaviour. Thus, opposition to kissing without affection reduced by more than one-half. Acceptance of intercourse under various conditions roughly doubled for the total sample but was typically much greater on the part of women than men. Thus, female acceptance of male intercourse without affection increased almost five-fold, as compared with almost a two-fold increase among men. Those rejecting all premarital intercourse for men were only one-fifth as numerous in the latter as compared with the earlier sample.

The patterns in Table 3:4, relating to acceptability of female sexual behaviour, are very similar but somewhat stronger. Again, there was vastly increased acceptance of non-affectional kissing. In the case of acceptance of female intercourse without affection, there was a 22-fold increase in acceptance by women, and almost a 3-fold increase by men.

The data in Tables 3:3 and 3:4 also show a decline in the differential acceptance of various practices of women as compared with men, with the former tending to surpass the men in terms of increasing permissiveness. This is particularly apparent in the reduction of the differential from 25 percentage points to 12 percentage points in acceptance of male petting with a non-affectionate partner and a reduction from 30 to 15 percentage points in acceptance of such female petting. It is seen in reduction of this differential in acceptance of intercourse for engaged

Table 3:4 Attitudes of Francophone Sample Members Towards Various Forms of Sexual Permissiveness For Females in 1968 and 1977 By Sex: Percentages

	1968 Sample			1977 Sample		
	Total	M	F	Total	M	F
Kissing not acceptable if not affectionate toward partner	73	65[b]	81	34	30	38
Premarital petting never acceptable	30	24	37	6	3	5
Petting acceptable if engaged	70	76[b]	63	95	97	94
Petting if feel strong affection	51	66[a]	36	71	79[b]	64
Petting though not particularly affectionate toward partner	9	14	4	32	39[b]	26
Intercourse if engaged	51	60[b]	42	91	92	91
Intercourse acceptable if in love	46	52	40	84	86	83
Intercourse if feel strong affection toward partner	33	45[a]	20	63	68	59
Intercourse though not particularly affectionate toward partner	7	13	1	27	34	22
No premarital intercourse	49	40[b]	58	9	8	9
Number of respondents	399	203	196	411	189	22

[a]Signifies differences between males and females are significant at 0.01 level.
[b]Signifies differences between males and females are significant at 0.05 level.

men and women, and in respect to acceptance of non-affectionate kissing as well.

There are some interesting differentials between the Francophone and the Anglophone samples. The 1968 data show that generally both male and female Francophone respondents were more conservative than were the Anglophones. This was particularly true of intimacy without affection, as in non-affectionate kissing, where the differential for each sex was about 50 percentage points, and reduced to insignificant differences, but yet in the same direction in favour of the Anglophone sample in the case of affectionate intimacies.

The 1977 data show a very great change in this pattern. It is generally true that these data show few statistically significant differences between the male and female sub-samples of the two language samples, in responses to these sexual permissiveness questions. Francophone women were still more conservative than Anglophone women in respect to petting or intercourse with affection. But they had "overtaken" Anglophone women, and were significantly more permissive than the latter in respect to intercourse for engaged couples. Francophone men were more conservative in respect to non-affectionate petting involving women, but they were more permissive in respect to male petting with affection, than Anglophone men. Thus, we must conclude that in respect to *profession* at least, the Francophone's samples changed dramatically in the interval between 1968 and 1977, and that the latter sample was no less permissive than Anglophone students surveyed the same year.

PREMARITAL SEXUAL EXPERIENCE

Data on premarital sexual experience of the 1968 and the 1977 Anglophone samples are found in Table 3:5 and those for the two Francophone samples are found in Table 3:6. It is perhaps to be expected in situations were strong motivations are at work, that there are sizable discrepancies between profession and practice, and these discrepancies are reflected in our data.

The data in Table 3:5 reflect rather sizable increases in intercourse experience, amounting to 20 and 15 per cent respectively in the case of Anglophone women and men. The data for the Francophone samples (Table 3:5) show great increases in the experience of women. Thus,

Table 3:5 Incidence of Various Sexual Experiences Among 1968 and 1977 Anglophone Sample Members, With Information on Relationship with Partners By Sex: Percentages

	1968 Sample			1977 Sample		
	Total	M	F	Total	M	F
Has never petted	8	9	8	10	10	11
Has ever petted	92	91	92	90	90	89
Respondent in love with all petting partners	25	10[a]	38	21	17	25
Has petted, but not below waist	12	10	14	8	6	9
Has petted below waist	80	82	78	82	84	80
Respondent was in love with all below-waist petting partners	42	27[a]	59	44	34[a]	52
Has experienced intercourse	50	56[b]	44	68	73	63
Respondent engaged to all intercourse partners	20	14[b]	29	11	9	13
Respondent in love with all intercourse partners	50	34[a]	70	53	45[b]	60
Number of cases	699	336	363	1585	773	812

[a]Signifies differences between males and females are significant at 0.01 level.
[b]Signifies differences between males and females are significant at 0.05 level.

Table 3:6 Incidence of Various Sexual Experiences Among 1968 and 1977 Francophone Sample Members, With Information on Relationship with Partners, By Sex: Percentages

	1968 Sample			1977 Sample		
	Total	M	F	Total	M	F
Has never petted	33	20	47	14	17	12
Has ever petted	67	88ᵃ	53	86	83	88
Respondent in love with all petting partners[1]	Not Available[1]			40	35	44
Has petted, but not below waist	20	17ᵃ	23	7	7	6
Has petted below waist	47	71ᵃ	30	79	76	82
Respondent was in love with all below-waist petting partners[1]	Not Available[1]			58	50	63
Has experienced intercourse	47	63ᵃ	30	62	59	65
Respondent engaged to all intercourse partners[1]	Not Available[1]			5	6	5
Respondent in love with all intercourse partners	46	38ᵃ	56	64	62	66
Number of cases	369	194	177	407	186	221

[1]Unauthorized changes were made in the French version of the questionnaire by a research assistant in Quebec in 1968.
ᵃSignifies differences between males and females are significant at 0.01 level.
ᵇSignifies differences between males and females are significant at 0.05 level.

those with petting experience increased from 53 to 88 per cent, those with below-belt-petting experience increased from 30 to 82 per cent, and those with intercourse experience more than doubled, from 30 to 65 per cent. The surprising consequences of these increases is that slightly more Francophone women than men reported intercourse experience.

Our data permit us to make some inferences concerning the relative degree of practice of the love standard. The data in Table 3:5 show that in terms of the total sample, there was no significant increase in adherence to the love standard, either with respect to petting or with respect to intercourse. In both samples adherence to the love standard was much more general among the women than among the men (by 32 percentage points and 18 percentage points in 1968 and 1977 in the case of petting, and by 36 and 15 percentage points respectively in the case of intercourse). These data thus do reflect erosion in adherence to the love standard during this period on the part of women, which is statistically significant in the case of the proportion in love with all intercourse partners. They also reflect a slight but consistent increase in adherence to this love standard on the part of men, which is statistically significant in the case of the proportion in love with all intercourse partners. Thus, the recent data reflect a statistically significant convergence in the degree of adherence to the love standard on the part of men and women in 1977 as compared with 1968, in respect both to petting and to intercourse.

The 1968 data show that significantly more Anglophone women than men said they were engaged to all their intercourse partners. This proportion declined among both men and women between 1968 and 1977, but only the decline among women was statistically significant. However, this decrease generally suggests the decline of commitment to marriage, as contrasted with love without commitment, as justifying intimacy. This suggests the strengthening of the love standard at the expense of even the attenuated abstinence standard that intercourse after engagement implies.

The Francophone data show that the result of changes between 1965 and 1977 is a distinct erosion of male behavioural adherence to the fun standard, such that Francophone men and women report that they adhere to the love standard to an equally large extent. This is substantiated by the large proportions of Francophone respondents reporting they were in love with all their "heavy petting" partners.

Comparison of the Anglophone and the Francophone data shows that for the 1968 sample significantly more Anglophone than Francophone women said they were in love with the relationship partners. In the later samples this difference was reversed, though not statistically so, and a significantly higher proportion of Francophone than Anglophone men said they were in love with their intercourse partners. In the later samples this difference was reversed, though not statistically significantly so, and a notably higher proportion of Francophone than Anglophone men said they were in love with their intercourse partners. The same pattern is found in terms of relationship with petting partners where the differences between the two language samples are significant for both men and women. On the other hand, the Francophones reported intercourse only with fiancés, only about half as frequently as did the Anglophones. These relationships seem clearly to imply a stronger commitment to the love standard among the Francophone than among the Anglophone respondents.

SUMMARY AND CONCLUSIONS

In this chapter we have reviewed briefly the major theoretical discussions which have sought to explain premarital sexual permissiveness among young people, and some of the Canadian studies of sexual permissiveness among post-secondary-school students. We have also presented a more extensive discussion of the findings of two reiterative studies made by Hobart at a number of post-secondary schools across Canada in 1968 and 1977.

On the basis of the theoretical material reviewed in this chapter it is clear that while there are eclectic collections of empirically supported propositions, there is no single comprehensive theory that can explain variations in sexual permissiveness. Perhaps the problem lies in the heterogeneity of the behaviour to be explained. Recall that Perlman found that sexual experience was associated with dominance in men but with submissiveness in women. Perhaps the conditions of permissiveness are different in yet other ways for men and women. Since the reasons for sexual compliance among women may be quite varied in differing circumstances, perhaps there is a need to identify sub-categories of pre-marital sexual behaviour.

At the strictly empirical level the material we have reviewed reflects four sets of convergences. In the first place, while data from the late 1960s suggest that the American students studied were typically more permissive and more sexually experienced than Canadian students, the more recent studies show not only parallel trends between these two categories, but suggest that the patterns are indeed convergent. Second, while the earlier Canadian studies showed sizable discrepancies between male and female respondents in terms of permissiveness and sexual experience, the later studies suggest that women are indeed "catching up" with men. Third, Hobart's earlier study showed that Francophone Canadian students were generally less permissive and less sexually experienced than the Anglophone students. However his 1977 study shows that the intercourse experience rate for Francophones is convergent with that of the Anglophones (although surprisingly the rate for Francophone men shows a decline) and that Francophones now express more permissive attitudes than do the Anglophone respondents. Finally, there is convergence among Anglophone and Francophone respondents of both sexes on the strength of support for the dominant love standard, which gained during the past nine years at the expense of the standard permitting sex only when engaged or married.

More detailed consideration of the data from Hobart's studies show some surprising discontinuities between the results of the two surveys. Most of the surprising discontinuities are found in the Francophone data, particularly in respect to the sharply increased acceptance of sexual intercourse for women, acceptance of sexual intercourse by women, and experience of sexual intercourse by women. There is also convergent acceptance of the love standard by Francophone men and women, the result of greatly increased male acceptance and slightly increased female acceptance of this standard. As a result of these changes, the data show that the erosion of the double standard appears to be much more complete among Francophones than among Anglophones. Thus there are no significant differences between male and female Francophone respondents, in the proportions sexually experienced, or in reported painful reactions following first intercourse experience.

What can be the explanation for these dramatic changes in attitude and experience among the Francophone women? No answer is apparent from the preliminary analysis of the currently completed data. However, a hint is found in some of the 1968 data, in a section dealing not with sexual permissiveness, but rather with egalitarianism in respect to marital role expectations (Hobart, 1972a). These data showed that in respect to a number of marital role areas, including the wife's authority, gainful employment, and sharing of housework, Francophone women were in fact more egalitarian than their English-speaking counterparts. Perhaps these attitudes of Francophone women have spread from morally neutral marital-role issues to the area of sexual relations, as the hold of church authority eroded. Perhaps, the greater involvement of Francophone married women in family support, apparent in the role expectations of women in 1968, has given them the power and the inclination to claim equal rights with men in sexual activity, as they have similar responsibilities in respect to family support.

Notes

1. Burr has reformulated and integrated the work of Reiss and Christensen into a precisely stated integrated system of propositions. His formulation is unfortunately too detailed and too complex to be presented here (Burr, 1973: Chapter 8).
2. The four campuses are the University of Western Ontario, in 1965, the Glendon College campus of York University in 1966, the University of Calgary in 1967, and the total student body of the main campus of York University in 1969. The rate of return from the Glendon College sample was quite adequate— 90 per cent—but the sample is small, only 74 subjects, and the population from which it was drawn is somewhat similar to that from which the York University sample was drawn in 1969. Accordingly, no further mention will be made of the findings of that study here. The University of Calgary study is based on a 100 per cent sampling of 72 students enrolled in an introductory sociology class in summer school. Thus its representativeness of the student body as a whole is so doubtful that no further mention will be made of those data. Information concerning two studies which are omitted here may be found in W. E. Mann, "Non-Conformist Sexual Behaviour on the Canadian Campus" (Mann, 1968).
3. Data for the York sample was obtained in personal correspondence with W. E. Mann. The author wishes to express his gratitude to Professor Mann for his generosity in supplying these unpublished data.
4. The figures in parentheses refer to the Western sample, and the other figures refer to the York sample.
5. Difficulties were experienced with a Quebec research assistant which resulted in these data not being available, and in his making unauthorized changes in the questionnaire, as well.

SELECTED BIBLIOGRAPHY

BELL, ROBERT R. *Premarital Sex in a Changing Society*, Englewood Cliffs, New
1966   Jersey.

BURR, WESLEY R. *Theory, Construction and the Sociology of the Family*, New York.
1976

HOBART, CHARLES W. "Orientations to Marriage Among Young Canadians", *Journal*
1972a   *of Comparative Family Studies*, Vol. 3 (Autumn), pp. 171–93.

———. "Sexual Permissiveness in Young English and French Canadians", *Journal of*
1972b   *Marriage and the Family*, Vol. 34, No. 2, pp. 292–303.

———. "The Social Context of Morality Standards Among Anglophone Canadian
1974   Students", *Journal of Comparative Family Studies*, Vol. 5, No. 1, pp.
26–40.

KINSEY, ALFRED C., WARDELL POMEROY, and CLYDE E. MARTIN. *Sexual Behaviour in*
1948   *the Human Male*, Philadelphia.

MANN, W. E. "Canadian Trends in Premarital Behaviour", *Bulletin*, The Council for
1967   Social Service, No. 198.

———. "Non-Conformist Sexual Behaviour on the Canadian Campus", in W. E.
1968   Mann, ed., *Deviant Behaviour in Canada*, Toronto.

———. "Sex at York University", W. E. Mann, ed., *The Underside of Toronto*,
1970   Toronto.

REISS, IRA L. "The Sexual Renaissance in America: A Summary and Analysis",
1966   *The Journal of Social Issues*, No. 22, pp. 123–37.

———. *The Social Context of Premarital Sexual Experience*, New York.
1967

Marriage and the Family:

4

Organization and Interaction

EMILY M. NETT

It is hard to escape the sensation of permutations in the import of marriage during this century, particularly since the 1950s. In Canada there is much popular interest in the subject of marriage, as indicated by the number of articles appearing in magazines and newspapers. Furthermore, the federal divorce law has been changed and proposals have been made for further reform (Law Reform Commission of Canada, 1975a; also, Wuester, 1975). Property laws have been modified in some provinces and reform commissions have reported to the legislatures in others (Law Reform Commission of Canada, 1975b). Federal policies affecting the relations between spouses or their rights as individuals have been instituted or changed, many in accordance with the recommendations made in the 1970 Report of the Royal Commission on the Status of Women (Advisory Council on the Status of Women, *Annual Reports*, 1974–75). In communities throughout the country, organizations are working to improve the quality of family life by offering preparation for marriage, and courses in communicating in marriage, sex education, marriage counselling, and parent effectiveness. Medical schools recently have begun to provide training for hospital personnel in problems of human sexuality. University offerings and enrolments have increased in marriage courses. Several films have been produced dealing with marriage, family planning, and human sexuality.[1] Marriage and remarriage rates continue to increase.

These indicators, and others to be discussed, point to the fact that the topic of marriage is important to Canadians; that there are numerous concerns about both the public and private aspects of marriage which have fomented considerable action; and that the marital state continues to attract most Canadian adults and even appears to have taken on greater significance in their lives despite its well-known hazards.

The objectives of this chapter are to describe the roles played by wives and husbands, to locate sources of consensus and conflict in marriage, to indicate the effect of marital negotiations on the family and the persons in marriage, and to discuss marital adjustment.

DEFINITION

A sociological perspective calls for approaching marriage both as a concept involving two persons responding to each other in a meaningful context, and as a set of societally developed and shared rules centering around basic societal prerequisites. In this chapter marriage is conceptualized simultaneously as a socio-cultural manifestation, and as a social-psychological phenomenon.[2] The definition of marriage best suited is Stephens's (1963: 5):

Marriage is a socially legitimate sexual union, begun with a public announcement and undertaken with some idea of permanence; it is assumed with a more or less explicit marriage contract, which spells out reciprocal rights and obligations between spouses, and between spouses and their future children.

Stephens's definition shares with that of Burgess, *et al.* (1971: 5) the central idea that marriage is based on the societal need to regulate sex, and ultimately, to legitimate and provide for children. Also, both agree that relative stability ("permanence") and harmony ("contract") are societal concerns. Furthermore, both spell out that security (permanence) and mutual expectations (contract) are the hoped-for outcome for the persons (woman, man, and potential offspring).

The meanings of marriage and sexuality are cultural. In some cultures marriage is valued primarily for its pragmatic virtues, whereas in others (ours appears to be such a one) the psycho-erotic aspect of the relationship is ranked high. The sociological perspective helps to distance the viewer sufficiently from the values and beliefs of the culture and to see marriage in Canadian society in the wider context of persons involved in institutional change.

THEORIES OF MARITAL ORGANIZATION

The most well-known formulation of changes in the family over time is that which describes the "transition from a traditional family system, based on family members playing a traditional role, to a companionship family system, based on mutual affection, intimate communication, and mutual acceptance of a division of labour and procedures of decision-making" (Burgess, *et al.*, 1971: 7). Burgess connected the emergence of the companionship marriage with the weakening of external factors making for family stability, such as social control by custom and community opinion. The companionship marriage is not a unity of obligations, tasks, rules, and regulations, but rather a "unity of personalities".

In developing the concept of *universal, permanent availability*, Farber (1964) delineated another feature of the emerging family: the centrality of the marriage unit in the family system. The development of a pattern of behaviour which involves the freeing of adult individuals to choose as a mate any individual of the opposite sex with whom they come into contact, involves a type of family system which Farber contrasts with one which emphasizes *orderly replacement*, or the passing along of family culture from one generation to the next with as little change as possible. Formerly it was children, as the bearers of culture, who stood as the bridge between the generations and thus as the basis of stability. For Farber, the unity in the contemporary family appears to be in the marriage linkages between spouses.

Scanzoni (1972) views the most significant and profound phenomenon touching upon marriage as the fact that female and male roles are being altered and becoming more interchangeable over time. He diagrams changes in the structure of spousal relations in terms of a continuum of married female statuses in relation to husbands, namely wife as property, wife as complement, wife as junior partner, and wife as equal partner. He attributes the change in female statuses in marriage, from wives as "property" to wives as "complements" of their husbands, to conflicts between males and females as interest groups at the macro level of society. More specifically, the factors involved have been first, the extension of the ideology of individualism and second, the striking down in modern (industrial, urban) society of the "ancient irreversibilities of ascribed roles" and the opening of "the possibility of achieved roles". He finds conflict the source of potential role modification, where it is successfully "negotiated" by the marital pair (see Safilios-Rothschild, 1977).

Another approach to the marriage process is that of Berger and Kellner (1970). They inquire into the character of marriage as a *nomos*-building instrumentality. For them marriage is a social arrangement in which persons can experience their lives as making sense in our society. It is "a *dramatic* act in which two strangers come together and redefine themselves". However, let there be no illusions; the script is already written and the two individuals are guided in their performance by social legitimations and internal applications. The stage is the nuclear family and the background music is a "pervasive ideology", the themes of which are romantic love, sexual fulfillment, self-discovery, and self-realization through love and sexuality.

Another theory of marriage as an aspect of the emergence of a sphere of "personal life" is that of Zaretsky (1977). Starting with a reformulation of the Marxian analysis of the "split" between the socialized labour of the capitalist enterprise and the private labour of women in the home, he posits another "split"—between our personal lives and our place within the "social division of labour". Proletarization having separated families from the ownership of property, an ethic of personal fulfillment has become the property of the masses of people. He views much of the search for personal meaning as taking place in the family and even posits this as the reason for its persistence.

Modelling the family after a capitalist enterprise, Becker (1965: 310), of the so-called "new school of home economists", views each marriage as "a two-person firm with either member being the 'entrepreneur' who 'hires' the other at . . . [a] salary . . . and receives residual 'profits'." Men hire women to bear children (because men cannot) and do housework (which their time is too valuable for men to undertake); women hire men to be the breadwinners and earn the wages they cannot command. The theory is based on the relative differences in the earnings of the two partners, among other gains (or costs). The theory predicts that only if the salary differentials between the sexes are eliminated will people marry and form a household for non-economic reasons.[3] The approach is essentially a theory of marital household arrangements, which are presumed to be tied to the economic institutions.

From the various ideas presented of contemporary marriage as an ideal type in mass society, emerges the following characterization: it is the relationship at the core of family life; it has psychological value for adults for whom it provides a "place" to meet their needs for security, order, and development; it supports flexibility in wife-husband roles; it is grounded in an economic system which supports a household arrangement dependent on a division of task by sex, and it creates a unity out of the various conflicts inherent in its very nature.

We shall examine each of the characteristics, with the exception of the first, in the light of Canadian research on marriage. Actually, there is little evidence to substantiate the claim that the marital bond takes precedence over the child-parent tie in Canadian families. The matter of what constitutes the focus of the family—the couple or the children— cannot be divorced from the other characteristics of marriage in mass society, however, and some "hard" facts will be presented in their discussion.

MARITAL INTERACTION IN THE CONTEXT OF MASS SOCIETY

Individualism and the New Model of Marriage

Individualism is a way of conceptualizing the world which places the person at the centre of the social world rather than the collectivity. As an ideology, it includes a set of assumptions, one of which is that the human person, not the human group, family, or state, has priority in decisions which are made when conflicts of interest occur. Individualistic norms may be part of either a religious or a secular world-view, and in fact the ideology has appeared in various forms throughout the history of western society.[4]

Is marriage in Canada tied up with an ideology of extreme individualism as some would have it, or does it rest upon the notion that the family as a unit constitutes a reality which should be supported and preserved? What are the facts as found in polls, questionnaires, and other attitudinal measures?

Comparing a sample of Ontario university students with a corresponding sample of mid-western American university students, Whitehurst and Plant (1971) found that Canadian students showed a stronger tendency to criticize legal structures and the amount of control which these exercise over the individual. Canadian students felt that change to a more liberal stance was needed in the areas of divorce, common-law, trial marriages, and adultery. Going further than the restrictions imposed by law, Canadians, similarly to Americans, criticized the structure of marriage for a loss of freedom when one marries. Juxtaposed to this idea of loss of individuality, Canadians, to a greater extent than Americans, thought of marriage as causing selfishness. It is interesting that only the Canadian youth mentioned specific categories of persons who interfered with people's marriages and who caused some type of problem. They blamed "would-be marriage counsellors", "the mass media", "Hollywood", and "sociological research", all of which, parenthetically, might be considered American imports.

Whether or not the generally negative attitudes of these youth toward marriage are shared by other university students, by young people of the same age not in university, or by those already married is a moot question. Furthermore, it is not easy to associate such reported disaffection with marriage to actual behaviour. Some (Carisse, 1975; Wakil, 1976) claim to document a decline in conjugality; others (Kalbach, 1976; Krishnan, 1977) say that marriage rates can only continue to increase. Undoubtedly some of the recent increase in marriage rates is the result of remarriage, which some (Schlesinger, 1971) take as an affirmation of faith in the institution of marriage. Furthermore, there is an indication that, for whatever reasons, younger persons are not entering into marriage as eagerly as earlier cohorts did (cf. Laing and Krishnan, 1976).

Individualism is more than a psychological perspective, or the difference between perceived restrictions and freedom. It is more than the lack of discomfort as one moves in and out of relationships with other persons, or the willingness to do so; it is also an experience, or a series of experiences.

By now it is well known that increased numbers of young persons of both sexes are living outside the family residence prior to marriage and after divorce (cf. Wargon, 1977; Chapter 3; and Chapter 10). Significantly they reside alone rather than with other non-related persons or families as they formerly did when leaving home for reasons other than marriage. Furthermore, even married persons, as the result of the diversity of work, school, and other schedules, more frequently experience social life as separate individuals rather than as the unity of wife and husband. Interestingly, the notion that separate contacts for wives employed outside the home might be a threat to spousal cohesion has not been verified (*cf.* Edwards and Booth, 1976, on extramarital affairs).

Images associated with marriage are somewhat difficult to discern in Canadian society. If individualism has truly permeated the societal construction of marriage, then we would expect the "pillars of the temple" or "oak tree and cypress" metaphor to prevail rather than the "yoked" image.[5] Income tax provisions, Canadian marriage law reform with regard to property and support, as well as pressures for material benefits for the person who contributes to the marriage by way of child care and housework so that she or he can be financially independent—all of these are premised on the idea that the marriage represents a union of two persons who remain separate and distinct for most purposes even though they have agreed to share *some* aspects of their lives. Despite these assumptions and the fact that in Canada married women do have the right to use the surname they were born with instead of that of their husband, there may be significant proportions of the population who, because of religious grounds or other traditional values, subscribe to the idea that upon marriage the woman and man do become one, that one being the husband, or the "head" of the family.

The Attack on Ascribed Roles and Role Flexibility in the Marriage[6]

Reflected in marriage, the attack on ascribed roles refers to how Canadian husbands and wives deviate from the gender assignment of childcaring functions, housekeeping tasks, and financial-provider tasks. On the basis of demographic analyses made by Nett (1976) and Boyd, *et al.* (1976), it is possible to make a strong case for a greater interchangeability of roles, with wives and husbands sharing more and more of the responsibility for providing income for the family, with some help from the husband for child care (accompanied by clear-cut declines in the number of children ever born to married women).

Balancing the picture, however, are strong sentiments for the traditional roles in some sectors of society. In a collection of *Monthly Letters* published by the Royal Bank of Canada (1972) appears the following description of "the woman's part":

A wife cannot devote herself wholly to husband and children, but they are still her first and most important responsibility. She is still the hub of the family. She is still the centre of education. She must be patient, loving and understanding. She must be strong enough to bear the weight of family troubles, while retaining her glamour and attractiveness.[7]

Participation in family life for the "man in the house" is considered important because he provides training for his sons and is "of a link between the oneness of the family and the gregariousness of the wide world" (p. 28).

Generally, though, the strength of the more traditional attitudes to sex-differentiated roles in the family has been weakened. Canadian youth have been found to be typically more concerned about inequalities in marital roles than Americans (Whitehurst and Plant, 1971). More recently, Whitehurst (1973a) discovered over half the Canadian students expected to have a different lifestyle than their parents. On the other hand Hobart's (1972) study of orientations to marriage among young Canadians in two universities and a trade school did not reveal a very high proportion with egalitarian orientations, either in the English or French sub-samples; nevertheless, fewer than a third of males and only a negligible proportion of females in either sample thought the wife's role should be that of housewife and mother only. Overall only one person in six chose the limited role of the wife as housewife and mother only.

The findings of several attitudinal studies of the youth toward marital roles must be taken as only suggestive because of methodological problems. Canadian public opinion polls, however, based on more representative samples, show strong adherence on the part of Canadian adults to the idea that the married woman's role is to care for the children in the home. Cook (1976: 6) reports as recently as a 1973 poll, 62 per cent of male and 57 per cent of female respondents felt that women's participation in the working world had a harmful effect on family life. In 1975, 75 per cent of all Canadians indicated that married women should not take a job outside the home if they have young children (cf. Women in Canada, 1977: 49–54). Age, education, and occupation, rather than sex, appear to be the determinants of these attitudes. More conservative attitudes were held by those over thirty-five, by persons with public school education or less, and by those whose occupations were skilled labourer, housewife, or who were retired.

It is perhaps significant that the published research deals mainly with the attitudes toward the wife's roles. None recognizes the fact that male participation in the labour force has actually been declining over the years, or that there exist alternatives to the provider role for males in the family, such as the three models Eichler (1975) proposes as possibilities. The extent to which men actually assume other family roles is unknown.[8]

Closely associated with who does what in the marriage is the question of who is the real boss—the husband or the wife? In one of the first examinations of Canadian marriage studies, Elkin (1964) came to the conclusion that the traditional family, with the man as "the authority and incontestable head of the household had probably given way to . . . a 'democratic' or 'partnership' type of relationship". Tremblay (1977), in a discussion of the democratization of French-Canadian family relations with the home, concludes that there are joint decisions made in strategic areas concerned with the well-being of the whole family group. He added that the idea remains of a special domain of competence for each spouse and an area over which he or she has authority. In view of their generality, the statements of Elkin and Tremblay seem sound enough; however, they lack precision. There are clues (Hobart, 1972) that younger persons of both language groups are closer together in attitudes than Tremblay's statements imply, and exhibit greater sex differences than Elkin assumes. More of Hobart's males than females, French and English, were authoritarian, with over half of the French males scoring high on this aspect of marital roles.

Nationally these is no indication of a general pattern of authoritarian marital standards. Questions about who actually makes decisions in various areas of domestic life, and who should make the decisions about these matters (*cf. Women in Canada*, 1977: 81–90), show male and female respondents both indicating that there *should be* more sharing between wife and husband. The greatest disparity between what is and what should be in the minds of the couples comes in the area of looking after the family budget. In 45 per cent of the households it is now a joint responsibility and 73 per cent believe it should be. If three out of four Canadians subscribe to sharing the power in so important an area as money, how does it happen that in only half of all marriages the goal is achieved?

There is no easy answer. Obviously marital power is a complex matter, which a simple scale including questions about either or both hypothetical power and actual influence, does not reveal much about the process of decision-making in marriage. The tendency is for each spouse to under-report his or her own power in the marriage and to attribute more power to the partner. Observations of marital interaction (Turk and Bell, 1972) show little difference between the influence of Canadian wives and husbands on the decision-making process. Furthermore, power exercised in the routine and recurring decisions in the domestic lives of the couples may be quite different from that employed in decisions which are often salient to the personal identities of the spouses, for example, sexually or culturally. A review of studies in decision-making where identity is involved (sterilization of the husband, by Grindstaff and Ebanks, 1971; mate swapping, by Henshel, 1973; moving, by Matthews, 1977; and bilingualism in marriage between French and English, by Carisse, 1976) leads to the conclusion that there is no consistent pattern with regard to the joint or shared aspect of the final decision or behavioural outcome. Some decisions are truly joint ones; others have high proportions of one spouse (husband) reportedly making the decisions.

Yet another complication in power relations in marriage is introduced by the multiformity in traditions of different segments of Canadian society, besides the English-French variations already alluded to. This is especially the case in those sub-cultures where religious beliefs support a patriarchal arrangement, as among the Hutterites (Peters, 1971), Calvinist Dutch (Ishwaran, 1971), Lebanese Muslims (Barclay, 1971), Jews (Latowsky, 1971), and Roman Catholic-Italians (Boissevain, 1976). Ishwaran, for example, indicates that the partiarchal position of the father stems from the belief that the father, as the mediator between the family and church, is the pastor of the family and the Lord (like Jesus) in the home, and of course the disciplinarian. In two-thirds of the Holland Marsh Dutch families, however, both husband and wife meted out punishment to the children. Furthermore, he admits that egalitarian ideals are "pervasive". Which ideology, the official church one or the pervasive one, influences couples playing the roles of the wife (mother) and husband (father)?

A final factor in assessing marital power is the role change in the wider society, which affects marriage relationships in all segments of Canadian society. To this we shall now turn our attention.

The Societal Split in Work and Family, and Task Substitution

Life in contemporary, large-scale, bureaucratically organized society is, to a significantly greater extent than ever before in the organizational history of the human species, characterized by the individuals' ability to segment their roles. The split between work and family has become so fundamental that until very recently women's work, housework, has not even been considered by social scientists as a form of *work*.

The far-flung suburbs of large cities have represented the ultimate in the impermeability of home and work in the twentieth-century mind. There is significance in the conclusion of the reviewer of the first full report on the suburb, who observed the following:

> . . . only the women live in Crestwood Heights, along with the young people and the professionals servicing both, while the men are, so to speak, visiting husbands from the bush—from the 'real world' of Canada's booming economy (Seeley, *et al.*, 1956; Introduction by David Riesman, p. xiii).

Clearly the picture is one of two subcultures, one for females and one for males. In the upper-middle-class families in Crestwood Heights the earning sphere is dominated by the male who shares the area of spending with other members of the family. As for duties, the investigators discovered that the general administration of the household and the feeding and clothing of the children are regarded as the wife's responsibilities. They saw no reduction in homemaking time or efforts for her since the Crestwood home is an exhibition of status and thus an aid to the male career. The Crestwood man is only "ritually responsible" for those tasks requiring physical strength—gardening, window-cleaning, putting on storm windows, etc., since in practice commercial outfits are hired to take care of them. Although the home is defined as the woman's world, the man does "help", but on a voluntary and flexible basis.

In a very different kind of community, consisting of family farm enterprises in southern Saskatchewan, where contrary to the suburban family the husbad's workplace is quite close to home, Kohl (1976) also describes a situation where household tasks are taken for granted as being women's responsibilities and not to be shared by husband and wife. However, women participate in the entire range of farm activities, including roundups, baling hay, keeping the books, fencing, feeding animals, etc., as well as being involved in community affairs. Although there is considerable variation seasonally in their "help" with the farm work, their own tasks remain routine including child care, cooking, gardening, feeding farm hands, etc. Parenthetically, Abell (1975: 371) reports 95 per cent of farm homemakers across the nation reported doing one or more farm tasks, such as operating farm machinery, driving a truck or tractor, keeping farm accounts, handling eggs and feeding livestock, as well as some field and garden work.

Kohl qualifies the rigidity in the division of labour within the house between husband and wife with the proviso that there is interaction and companionship between the spouses. She reiterates, however, that it is women who are involved in the work world of men, not vice versa.

Bennett (1976) notes that in contrast to Jasper, Hutterite women are excluded from the enterprise, while husbands have informal access to the domestic establishment. Curiously, the Crestwood Heights pattern is more like that of the Hutterite colonies than of Jasper, even though agriculture is the subsistence base for the latter two.

If Crestwood Heights and Jasper represent the extremes with regard to the way entire communities in Canada pattern relationships between the work and family roles of wives and husbands, what about the current over-all configuration for the country as a whole? In general, the survey data and time-budget studies indicate high behavioural conformity to a division of labour in which most of the household labour is performed by wives, whether or not they are in the labour force and for whatever number of hours.

Half or more of the respondents to the 1975 national poll replied that both spouses are responsible for four of fourteen areas of household work, the wife alone in six areas, and the husband alone in two (the pattern for two household activities was not clearly sexual). Areas of responsibility assigned to the sexes are traditional ones, with women involved in meals, interior home decorating, shopping, and washing the dishes, and men having responsibility for buying liquor or beer and painting the woodwork outside the house. Looking after the family budget and helping children with homework appear to be less sex linked, although in both instances fewer than half the respondents reported sharing in these activities with spouses. Deciding where to go on vacations or weekends and reprimanding the children are the only activities clearly shared by wife and husband.

Time budgets show how much of the wife's and husband's time is actually spent in the activities required to maintain a household. The two largest items, in proportion as well as average time spent on them, are daily cooking and house-cleaning (*cf.* Meissner, *et al.*, 1975: 430–31), which for the most part is the task of wives. The husbands' contribution to domestic work is insensitive to the increasing demands on time shared by couples when wives are employed outside the home. Furthermore, when the wives' job hours increase, their total workload (at home and at the place of employment) increases a great deal while their husbands' declines slightly, and the hours available for housework decline without being made up for by their husbands (Meissner, *et al.*, 1976).

The conclusion that most married Canadian women do the regular, necessary, and most time-consuming work in the household every day, is no different from findings in the United States, Sweden, the Soviet Union, and many other parts of the modern world.

Interest Groups and Conflict in Marriage

The consequences for the social order of pluralism in mass society have given rise to considerable concern. With much of the society which was once bound in traditionally assigned roles now "unbound" or "free", people are more *differentiated* with regard to how they see the world and what they want from it. Division in marriage has resulted from pluralism of the society along religious, ethnic, and language lines, and more recently, by polarization of sex interests as well.

When a woman and man marry, each brings into the marriage a lifetime of learned values, philosophies, attitudes, beliefs, and styles of coping. With the greater degree of differentiation provided by mass society each person has almost a unique background and unique experience. Although there is some attempt on the part of couples to sort out these differences in the dating period, and for marriages to be homogamous, like-marrying-like is not as certain as it was in any earlier time. (In

Canada, rates of religious and ethnic intermarriage have been declining.) Furthermore it is inevitable that even where some similarities are sought many differences will remain and some clashing will occur.

Marital adjustment is the process whereby the couple develop a working arrangement with both their own and the other's expectations and with societal realities. Problems frequently encountered in adjustment are those arising out of sexual matters, finances and employment, in-laws, and leisure time. In these areas of marital life, conflict is exacerbated by the necessity for the couple to merge two family traditions and also by the ideological positions taken by groups with political overtones which influence the wife and husband. The problems vary over the life-cycle of the couple. We shall examine each of the areas in the light of information available on marital interaction, to which Canadian investigators have addressed themselves only recently (*cf.* Nett, 1977).

Sex adjustment is frequently mentioned as a marital problem by couples seeking help with troubled marriages or on the verge of divorce. The few Canadian studies on marital sex tentatively confirm some of our common-sense notions or beliefs: that modest levels of marital discord reduce the frequency of sexual discourse between couples (*cf.* Edwards and Booth, 1976), that *severe* marital strain is associated with extramarital relationships (Edwards and Booth), and that extramarital affairs are one kind of ego-threat that can antagonize conflicting spouses, even to the point of homocide (Chimbos, 1976). Furthermore, in sexual matters wives appear to comply with husbands' suggestions, often contrary to their own wishes (Henshel, 1973). Employment of wives outside the home affects sex in the marriage: it reduces the likelihood of the wife's involvement in extramarital affairs (Edwards and Booth, 1976) and increases the probability of the spouses communicating their feelings about sex with each other (Burke, *et al.*, 1976).

These few observations suggest that sexual behaviour in marriage is related not only to attitudes learned while growing up, but also to the experiences one has in marriage and in other areas of social life. Couples who discuss their sexual feelings are generally more communicative (Burke, *et al.*, 1976).

Another area of couple adjustment is the *economic* one. Somewhat more is known about the effects of employment than about financial problems. Class differences undoubtedly are important in both connections. Conflict in working-class couples appears to revolve around the employment of both spouses. Palmer's (1972) working-class husbands took it for granted that their wives would contribute to household finances by taking employment outside the home. That did not give their wives a sense of freedom or independence; on the contrary, they felt devalued by what they considered to be inadequate support by their husbands. Moreover, the disappointment was mutual, since husbands felt a lack of support from wives for their jobs, and wives were not entirely happy with their husbands' work efforts. Employed wives being dissatisfied with their unskilled husbands as providers seemed to be a factor contributing to the higher divorce rates among these families (Palmer, 1976).

Employment of wives in the middle class has quite different effects on adjustment than it does in the working class. Instead of discrepant expectations, it results in more communication between spouses, more mutual give-and-take, or negotiation in resolving conflicts, and more agreement with spouses in numerous areas (Burke, *et al.*, 1976). However, there is some evidence of stress for the husbands of wives thus employed.[9] Wife employment appears to have different meanings at two levels of the stratification system. The identity of the middle-class wife appears to be enhanced by her job, whereas the self image of the working-class wife suffers. The effects on the husband are just the reverse; the middle-class husband loses part of his "support system" when his wife is employed outside the home, whereas the working-class husband gets financial assistance, and subsequently a status boost, from his wife when she is gainfully employed. The middle-class wife's employment does nothing directly for her husband; the working-class wife's employment does nothing directly for herself.

In-laws are a potential source of conflict for married couples. Among Canadian married couples and their parents-in-law there seems to be little conflict. For Protestant Anglo-Saxon Canadians the difficulty centres around two situational themes: husbands and wives feeling their spouses were taking sides with their own parents, and husbands feeling left out because their wives went to their mothers first about important matters to be discussed (*cf.* Irving, 1971). Disagreements between spouses and their parents-in-law occur in four areas, in the following order of frequency: child-rearing, the husband's job, how often to visit, and money.

Irving concluded that the nuclear family is quite successful in maintaining the psychological boundaries between related families, and in keeping the level of conflict over "internal matters" low.

An important aspect of marital adjustment, because the so-called recreational function assumes greater proportions in the family in mass society, is *leisure time*. Husbands have more leisure time to spend than wives (Meissner, 1977), but whether this causes marital conflict or how it might be resolved has not been asked or documented. Further, the question of how often to visit in-laws causes considerable discord between couples (Irving, 1971); on the other hand, there is a remarkable amount of spousal sharing in making decisions about weekends and vacations (*Women in Canada*, 1977).

The level of conflict and ways of coping with conflict varies considerably from the formulation of the marriage to its termination either by divorce or death. Beyer and Whitehurst (1976: 119) conclude that "over the life cycle, men and women experience such different modes of adaptation that there is an essential reversal of positive and negative meanings . . . for the sexes." With reference to values, alienation, and self-concept, men seem to experience negative effects early in their marital careers, while women respond more negatively with length of marriage. Their finding is that instrumental values, or those less deeply rooted, tend to become more consonant over the years, which they take as an indication that there are subtleties in marital dynamics that are not well understood.

Crises, either internal or external to the marriage, also enter into marital adjustment. Since many Canadian families have been uprooted from quite alien cultural surroundings due to migration, or have experienced changes introduced into their environment, marital stress is frequently occasioned by acculturation and assimilation. Incongruity between traditional roles and emerging modern Canadian roles may be experienced generationally, as among Ukrainian Canadians (Hobart, 1975a); or due to migration from cultures as different as India (Ames, 1976), or Lebanon (Barclay, 1971); or as the result of urbanization as in the case of the Japanese in Japan and to a lesser extent in Canada (Maykovich, 1971); or due to the cultural disruption that occurs when the economic bases of an entire geographical region are changed, as in the Yukon (Cruikshank, 1971). Although the conflict and its consequences for family life have been described, little explanation has been offered as to how marital balances, upset by such events, are resolved by wives and husbands who have undergone the crises.

CONCLUSIONS

The review of recent Canadian marriage research substantiates the claim that marriage is tinged with elements of individualism, that it includes attitudes favourable to flexibility in marital roles (but that household tasks remain sex-differentiated), and that Canadian marriages handle a considerable amount of conflict out of which is created a degree of marital cohesion. Offsetting these tendencies are feelings of family loyalty, responsibility for familial child-care, traditional views of husband-wife relations held in many segments of the society, and considerable value and role consensus in many areas of marriage. There appears, however, to be not much variation in the pattern of sex-associated domestic work, despite all the other changes in marriage and society.

With regard to the traditional sociological concerns, such as power, decision-making, and marital adjustment, the scant research findings are similar to those for the United States. Wives and husbands verbalize egalitarian ideals and they do influence each other reciprocally. Joint decision-making appears to be rarer than the sex-differentiated allocation of decision areas along traditional lines. Gender enters into marital adjustment with husband and wife frequently "out of phase" with each other. Canadian marriages encounter many dilemmas stemming from these issues, not the least of which is how to be a couple yet have both persons equally gratified by what goes on, as they try to construct something of meaning and value between them. They undertake such an effort in a social environment which while not exactly hostile to their endeavours is not conducive either, since both the law and custom, as well as the economy, are based on other premises. The motivation to try it, however, is culturally induced, since sex (and marriage) is perceived at least as the one "stage" on which social actors can still extemporize. However, much societal concern has been expressed to the effect that the goals of self identity, equality, and personal growth in marriage are too limited whereas the traditional goals of children, complementarity, and loyalty are more worthy.

Notes

1. See the Vanier Institute of the Family, *Catalogue* (1972) and its supplement (1974), as well as the Federation of Canada, *Family Planning Resource Catalogue* (1975).

2. Two examples of writers who have come to recognize the necessity for doing this are Safilios-Rothschild (1977) and Birdsell (1976). The latter illustrates with fertility factors, which as a socio-economic variable is conceptualized as "female labour force participation rate", and as a social-psychological variable as "wife's role extensiveness".

3. The theory has its critics, including Sawhill (1977), who argues that the reason for the labour force differentials by sex is that since women bear and rear children they fail to develop the resources for employment that men have (human capital theory).

4. Early Christianity was quite individualistic or anti-family in the sense that followers of Jesus were expected to give up domestic life and the movement was directed against two other strong collectivities, symbolized by the crown and the temple. Later, Martin Luther, on the wave of a new individualism, tried to divest marriage of the control the Church of Rome had gained over it throughout the centuries. He took the position that marriage was not a sacrament, but a civil contract between two persons, blessed by God.

5. Cole (1955: 157) quotes from an early pope, Clement, as follows: "For if the God of both is one, the master of both is also one; one church, one temperance, one modesty, their food is common, marriage an equal yoke . . . ." Quite in contrast is the often-quoted passage from the popular writer Gibran (1929) on marriage, as follows: "Love one another, but make not a bond of love. . . . And stand together yet not too near together; for the pillars of the temple stand apart, and the oak tree and the cypress grow not in each other's shadow" (15–16).

6. Interchangeability or flexibility of roles should not be confused either with equality or equity in mariage. Equality refers to similarity of condition and opportunity regardless of sex; equity, to fairness, or the distribution of justice between the spouses. If both have opportunity to pursue careers or to choose homemaking, that is equality; if they consider "fair" the exchange of one's income for the other's homemaking services, that is equity. Equality entails equity, but equity does not necessarily involve equality. Flexibility merely refers to societal approval or tolerance of tasks being assigned irrespective of sex. Boyd, *et al.*'s (1976: 44) conclusion that marriage is not yet a union of economic equals does not negate role flexibility in marriage.

7. The quotation is interesting because it is followed by a statement allegedly made by a character in a Canadian humourist's writings: "I let him think he is master in his own house, for when ladies wear the breeches, their petticoats ought to be long enough to hide them." This is precisely the situation described by Moreux (1973: 178) in a study of French-Canadian wives. It also illustrates the point that a discussion of marital roles often emerges as a description of parental roles.

8. The three are where (1) the mother and father have equal responsibility for child care; (2) the father has main responsibility, although he is part-time employed; and (3) the husband has main responsibility and is not employed outside the home.

9. Other effects of wives' labour force employment have been reported by Burke and Weir (1974), Butler (1976), and Hobart (1975b). Effects of social class are reported in Hobart (1975b) and *Women in Canada* (1977).

SELECTED BIBLIOGRAPHY

EICHLER, MARGRIT, "The Egalitarian Family in Canada", in S. Parvez Wakil, ed.,
1977   *Marriage, Family and Society: Canadian Perspectives*, Scarborough.
ELKIN, F. *The Family in Canada*, Ottawa.
1964
KOHL, S. B. "Working Together", *Women and Family in Southeastern Saskatchewan*,
1976   Toronto.
NETT, E. M. "The Changing Forms and Functions of the Canadian Family: A
1976   Demographic View", in K. Ishwaran, ed., *The Canadian Family*, revised
        ed., Toronto.
RAMU, G. N. "The Family and Marriage in Canada", in G. N. Ramu and Stuart D.
1976   Johnson, eds., *Introduction to Canadian Society: Sociological Analyses*,
        Toronto.
SEELEY, I. R., R. A. SIM, and E. W. LOOSLEY. *Crestwood Heights: A Study of the*
1967   *Culture of Suburban Life*, New York.

EMILY M. NETT

Two kinds of adult behaviour which the family plays an important part in establishing from the time of birth are gender behaviour and occupational behaviour. Since a child is either a female or a male depending on the appearance of the genitalia at birth, sex status is *ascribed*.[1] On the other hand, occupational status in Canada ideally is *achieved*, although there is considerable indication that in reality opportunities are in large part determined by family position.

Learning associated with both the gender and occupational positions (statuses) is very much affected by the function of the family which has been called "placement". In all societies the family serves to locate new members in the social structure; subsequently the family also teaches new members who they are (identity), what behaviour is expected of them (norms), and what future positions are open to them (opportunities), to some extent preparing them to fill these positions (training). This latter function is usually referred to as "primary socialization". The social class into which the child is born, as well as the child's sex category, have the most profound implications for the kind of adult the child will become, as well as for all ensuing experiences.

The process by which the individual incorporates the attitudes and behaviour considered appropriate by society is also called socialization. Thus defined, socialization is in effect role learning, since theoretically individuals come to acquire proper attitudes and behaviour as they learn the roles associated with positions they are currently assigned to, or statuses they anticipate filling. In Canadian society, gender and occupation being closely related, children incorporate ideas of what it means to be feminine and masculine as they learn to associate gender with what women and men do, or with occupational status deemed appropriate for men and women in their family and society. Thus, as Bem and Bem (1970) noted, although parents may speculate at the birth of a boy as to what his future might be, "if the newborn child is a girl, we can usually predict with confidence" what her occupation will be 25 years later since the role of homemaker is allocated solely on the basis of sex. In part the extent to which additional work roles are visualized for baby girls is determined by the level in the stratification system occupied by the family as well as by other subcultural factors such as ethnicity and residence.

In this chapter I will examine the literature on gender socialization in the Canadian family.[2] I will describe the way children are taught the *family roles* associated with their biological sex and, to some extent, their occupational roles. Furthermore, I will discuss *sex-difference stereotypes* (perceptions of typical traits, interests, and behaviours of females and males, or ideals of what females and males "are like" in Canadian families). In addition, I will include materials on *sex-role orientations* (attitudes about what is "right" and "wrong" for females and males to do). The emphasis will be on the role of the family in transmitting the culture or teaching the norms of the society or a particular sub-group in society. Only to a limited extent shall I deal with the development of *sex-role adaptations* and *sex-role identities* in the family. The former refers to evaluations of role definitions for the sexes, and the latter to the Self—and Other—evaluations of adequacy as male or female.

The procedure will be to describe in the second section the process of socialization for sex roles within the family, both theoretically and substantively for Canada; in the third section, to discuss changing sex roles; in the fourth section, to treat the impact of changing sex roles on the family; and finally, to summarize and assess the materials reviewed.

GENDER-ROLE SOCIALIZATION

Perspectives

Much of what families actually do involves teaching children the societal attitudes to their having been assigned to the female or male sex. As Hartley (1966) says,

From the young subject's point of view, sex role, child role, and self definition are blended in an unselfconscious complex of unobstructed behaviours. "Unselfconscious" because as well as the lack of awareness on the part of the child, the parents too for the most part are little aware of what they are doing.

The sexes are indeed treated differently by their parents and knowledge of gender-role definitions or stereotypes is evident in children of kindergarten age (cf. Williams, et al., 1975). Furthermore, the child's understanding of biological sex and sex-role identity develops prior to, faster than, and more completely than the child's understanding of gender-role identity (cf. Slaby, 1975; Thompson, 1975). Money (1975), in discussing the acquisition of language as the counterpart to imprinting in animals, states, "the critical period in establishing psychosexual identity appears to be approximately simultaneous with the establishment of native language."

The psychological term for how persons come to internalize societal expectations is "identification". It refers to the process whereby the individual incorporates that complex of behaviours, attitudes, and beliefs appropriate for his/her own sex as well as an image of the complex appropriate for members of the other sex (Pyke, 1976: 51).

The identification process seems to subsume at least three more specific types of processes. It is the result of differential *reinforcement*, selection and *imitation of models* acting as "significant others" (family members who, because of proximity, primacy of interaction, nurturant functions, and perceived powerfulness, are regarded by children as very important), and *interaction* with salient (cathected) same-sex and opposite-sex adults. These processes lie at the core of the various theories of childhood socialization into sex roles and identity.

Sex-role learning is only partially accounted for by differential reinforcement. Typically, *learning theory* refers to explanations of sex-role behaviour that is the direct result of training by adults. Through the four processes of socialization discussed by Hartley (1966)—manipulation, canalization, verbal appelation, and activity exposure—parents implant correct responses and weed out incorrect ones. Thus, they "manipulate" by cuddling little girls more and verbalizing more to them; they "channel" by approving the random acts of boys to protect little girls and treat them chivalrously; they "name" behaviour as feminine or masculine (and the child too) when they specify that the little girl is sweet and the little boy brave; and they "expose" children to selective activities when they provide girls with ballet lessons and boys with hockey sticks. This direct training, reacted upon by significant others, facilitates the learning of sex-appropriate traits (Bandura, 1969; Kagan, 1964).

Secondly, learning gender can be further explained by means of role theory. Role theory refers to learning sex-appropriate behaviour as the result of observation and imitation of available models, or significant others (Elkin, 1972; Lambert, 1971; Lynn, 1962).

Children play at the roles they see these adults acting out. In the statistically normal nuclear household they are exposed daily to the parental roles of mother-father, the marital roles of husband-wife, and the occupational roles of homemaker-provider.

Finally, *psychoanalytic theory* presents a third mechanism by which sex-role identification takes place. Underlying tensions resulting from the libidinal attractions between children and both their same-sex (pre-oedipal) and opposite-sex (oedipal) parents, everywhere regulated by cultural prohibitions in the intimate family (incest taboos), lead to differential infantile perceptions and evaluations of genital anatomy. In the context of complementary parental roles and their meanings, assigned on the basis of sex, such reactions result in a variety of behavioural, trait, and attitudinal differences being strongly associated with sex (*cf.* Parsons, 1955; Winch, 1962; Chodorow, 1974).

As a result of these three subprocesses of internalizing, all relevant to the total socialization of children into their many gender roles, people develop a sense of their own sexual identity, a sex-role orientation according to cultural or sub-cultural standards or images, and a set of behaviours anticipatory to adult role-taking. To the extent that families rear their children in such a way as to either reinforce sex stereotypes or teach undifferentiated behavioural adaptations for girls and boys, children learn what is expected of them as males and females. Moreover, parents provide an emotional climate in which, from birth, the libidinal energies of children must be redirected from forbidden expressions into socially acceptable ones, and the children themselves, actively involved in their own maturing, interpreting the biological and cultural facts of their parents' interaction with each other and with their children, perceive the imposition of those taboos in a most self-defining manner. Identification, like learning, is a psychological problem, but it is important to sex-role-appropriate behaviours being learned by children in the family, since in the nuclear family there is a parent of each sex and they are the representatives of the sexes that the children relate to as daily models of sex behaviour, including occupational aspiration and choice.

CANADIAN SOCIALIZATION PATTERNS

The official document on child-rearing, published by the government, *The Canadian Mother and Child* (1967), prescribes the care of the very young child in a manner which is remarkably indistinguishable for girls and boys. Except for the fact that linguistically the baby is invariably male in sex, and that the book is addressed to mothers only and assumes a more vital interest on their part (*cf.* p. 123), the publication appears relatively free of sex stereotypes.

In actual families, however, such is not likely to be the case to any great extent. Ambert (1976) gives a concise summary, as follows:

little boys and girls are dressed differently or in sex-typed colours. . . . Girls are provided with toys that are miniatures of the instruments their mothers use in the homemaker and nursing roles, and boys are given toys that are replicas of objects that serve the counterpart function among men—the latter toys also happen to encourage rougher play, activity, creativity, mastery, and curiosity, girl toys, on the other hand, encourage passivity, observation, simple behaviour, and solitary play. . . .

Little girls are encouraged to socialize more, to verbalize more, a prelude to their future "expressive" role in our society. . . . Girls will cook and feed toddlers as well as change them and put them to bed. Boys, in contrast, may simply be asked to play with them or keep an eye on them. . . . mothers tend to be more particular about girls' appearances and mind less when boys are dirty. . . . Little girls learn to thrive on the "she is so cute" exclamation—a prelude to their subsequent function of ornament and bodily companions for men in our society.

When children ask what they will do when they grow up, the little girl is frequently told she will be a mother and wife, whereas . . . boys are first made aware of all the appropriate jobs that a parent can meaningfully describe to a three- or four-year-old.

There is a considerable variation in the degree to which families impress upon their children the traditional expectations for girls and boys, but the picture seems an accurate one for most Canadian families. Survey data which depict young Canadians expecting a clear differentiation of parental roles (Hobart, 1973) corroborate the learning of differentiated roles in the family.

An important aspect of sex-role learning not to be entirely separated from reinforcement, as Bandura (1969) notes, is *the model provided by significant others* and the societal representations of parents. With regard to the latter, Pyke (1975) surveyed books, designed for pre-school children and published by Canadian firms, to determine the existence and strength of sex-role stereotyping to which very young children are subjected. The conclusion is that sex-role stereotyping is prevalent in very recent books, despite efforts of feminist organizations to lessen it. Few women are shown in salaried roles, and those occupations in which they are shown are teachers, dancers, nurses, maids, nuns, etc.; male figures have a larger number of occupations. Females are shown in homemaking and child-caring roles; the father's occupational role is "hazy". At home, according to Pyke (1976, p. 69):

The typical family scene shows daddy reading the newspaper while mommy sews. It is even more unusual to find a woman behind the wheel of a car. . . . Women are never depicted engaged in volunteer services. . . . in non-occupational activities males are involved in a greater variety of enterprises than are females. . . . girls play primarily with dolls and associated paraphernalia, flowers, and skipping ropes, while boys prefer balls, bikes, boats, games, guns, toy vehicles, and wagons. Unisex toys appear to be hoops, paints and clay, stuffed toys, and blocks.

As Pyke proves with the following facts, these stereotyped conceptions of sex roles have little basis in reality; almost half of all married women are in the labour force; women are employed in a great variety of occupations, suburban mothers devote much of their time to chauffeuring children, and the female volunteer force is almost equivalent in size to the female labour force. One aspect of the sex-differentiated images appears to be realistic, i.e., that the child-care and cooking tasks in the home are still predominantly part of the "female sphere".

Not only do children perceive their parents performing in the household and outside of it as representatives of the categories "women" and "men", they also see their parents as personalities, i.e., as "feminine" or "masculine" beings. To a large extent this may be "felt" rather than comprehended intellectually in the child's earliest experiences with the parents. With the cognitive development of the child, however, parental equation of various combined aspects of their sex as a complex modality occurs. Thus the work-body-trait set is associated with the cultural prescriptions for dress, hair styles, and other aspects of sexual appearance. In Pitcher's (1975: 89) account,

One mother reports her husband's pleasure when she put their six-month daughter in a dress for the first time. "That's much nicer than those old pajamas," said the father. But he was much concerned, since they were visiting, and since the infant kept kicking up her dress, and he constantly rearranged her skirt in proper fashion. . . . One mother reports that her husband blanched when he found she had cut his [sic] daughter's hair.

Lacking in such accounts is whether the "outward" signs of sexual personality type are simultaneously presented to children by parents themselves as the living standards of "masculinity" or "feminity". That is, does the father in the example berate the mother as unfeminine when she wears clothing other than dresses? Does he evaluate her modesty traits as feminine or unfeminine? It would be unrealistic to expect parents to be perfectly consistent in these matters, and indeed there is evidence in the research for both traditional views of what constitutes femininity and masculinity as well as considerable uncertainty and ambivalence. In the public opinion polls examined by Boyd (1976) adult Canadian women and men view "being a boss" or "running a business" as unfeminine. The belief, surprisingly more prevalent among younger, better-educated males but also held by a significantly large proportion of women, contrasts with the relatively positive attitude of respondents of both sexes to the theoretical acceptance of women doctors, lawyers, and politicians.[3]

It is probable that Canadian children observing their parents in the roles of mother and father perceive both parents as behaving more flexibly than the traditionally prescribed roles warrant. Schludermann and

Schludermann (1973), expecting to find fathers perceived by Hutterite children as exercising firmer control and mothers perceived as showing more acceptance and psychological control, found neither sex perceiving their fathers as being firmer. Girls, but not boys, perceived mothers as being more accepting and psychologically controlling. Schludermann and Schludermann explain the deviance from their expectation of father perception in terms of the somewhat deviant family structure and work apprenticeship of the Hutterites, but similar findings have been reported in other community studies (*cf.* Ishwaran, 1971) of families with more "typical" male heads.

On the other hand, there is surely adequate opportunity for young persons to observe the subtle ways in which mothers exhibit "typically" feminine personalities and fathers behave in a "typically" masculine way.[4] It is known, for example, that girls and boys are more likely to have opportunities to see their mothers as more active than fathers in the "helping" relationship in marriage. Burke and Weir (1976) found wives were significantly more likely than their husbands to go to their spouse for help with their problems, were more willing to disclose feelings of tensions and reasons for their tension to their spouse, and were more involved in specific activities directed at helping their partners cope with tension. We would be more than naive if we thought this escaped the youngsters' attention. An earlier report by the youthful French-Canadian respondents in Garigue's (1968) study suggests that the youth view the mother as the emotional or "expressive" parent, and that she is the one with whom one talks things over, takes one's problems to, and reveals one's feelings to. Other studies (Irving, 1971; Piddington, 1971; Kohl, 1977; etc.) substantiate that wives and mothers are the emotional facilitators and adaptors in the family.

The same studies referred to above show that parents represent differential power to their children. The findings of Garigue and others, that there is greater fear and respect for the father, is not entirely generalizable since as later investigators of the French-Canadian family, like Tremblay (1973), have found, the authoritarian role of the father has been considerably modified in recent years. Furthermore, even Garigue had to qualify his picture of the image that children in the family hold of the father as strong and powerful by describing different patterns by age and sex as well as personality of father and child. On the whole, however, the myth of the patriarch persists, probably in the eyes of the child as well as the constructs of society.[5]

Recent American research provides a clearer picture of the complexities involved in differential patterns of parental interaction associated with the sex of the children and their self-concept and identity. In general, differential parental behaviour by sex of child, whether reported by parent or child, or as observed by the researcher, does occur. Margolin and Patterson (1975), making home observations of parent-child interaction and examining the consequences of the child's "prosocial" and "deviant" behaviour, noted that boys received more positive responses from parents than did girls. Fathers gave twice as many positive responses to sons as to daughters; mothers gave the same amount of positive responses to both sexes. No significant differences were obtained in the amount of negative consequences elicited. In Canada, Schludermann and Schludermann (1973) discovered Hutterite girls, compared with boys, described both parents as being more accepting; boys described both parents as less restrictive. In general, they conclude that Hutterite adolescents perceive their parents' behaviour along the same basic dimensions as did American, Belgian, and other Canadian teenagers with whom they were comparing them. Propper (1972) found sex differences for feeling close to parents and asking for help; adolescents tend to ask help of the same-sex parent.

A related area where differential treatment by parents occurs is with regard to encouragement given for the development of achievement orientations in children. George and Kim (1971) found, as did Breton and McDonald (1971), that Canadian high-school girls had lower educational aspirations than boys, although they frequently had better grades. More significantly as far as the family is concerned, more than one out of three fathers were highly interested in their sons' education, whereas only one out of four were equally interested in their daughters' education. This finding is of particular interest since parental aspirations were found to be similar in the various social classes represented. It is also interesting because mother's interest has been left out entirely.[6]

In sum, parents treat their girls and boys differently and children of different sexes perceive their mothers and fathers differently. Related to this, numerous studies of American children have found that parents encourage sex-appropriate activities more for boys than for girls, and conversely, will discourage cross-sex activities more in boys than in girls (*cf.* Ambert, 1976: 72, footnote 9).

CHANGING SEX ROLES

By now it is a truism that relations between women and men in mass society have been revolutionized (for demographic materials *cf.* Nett, 1976a; and Boyd, *et al.*, 1976). There is little doubt that greater opportunities have opened up for both men and women to deviate from traditional gender roles. On the other hand, as is indicated in Chapter 4, within the household husbands and wives generally adhere closely to the traditional division of labour. Further, favourable attitudes to greater equality of opportunity socially and occupationally for women, even where wives are increasingly employed outside the home, are considerably moderated by the traditional emphasis on the mother role (*cf.* Boyd, 1976; *Women in Canada*, 1976). It is, therefore, unrealistic to expect drastic alterations in social patterns as the result of the relatively small increase over the last fifteen years in the proportions of women entering secondary education or receiving advanced degrees. There have yet to be significant increases in the proportion of women in high-prestige or better-paying jobs, or in those occupations traditionally reserved for males (*cf.* Women's Bureau, 1974). Although the home and work spheres are less "impermeable" in some ways because of the increased number of women assisting male heads of households with their provider task, Boyd's (1976) conclusion summarizes the situation well: "There are many attitudinal roadblocks that yet have to be removed for gender equality to be congruent with reality." One would like to add, institutional and ideological roadblocks too, insofar as roles involve patterned expectations as well as behaviours; however, there are signs of change.

Public opinion polls starting in 1953 (Boyd, 1974; *Women in Canada*, 1976) show a secular trend toward more egalitarian attitudes. In both studies, as well as in other surveys of attitudes, women are more aware of the problems than men, and younger women more than older ones. Furthermore, women believe that the attitudes of men have changed very much during the 1970s.

Media representations of women and men too have altered some. Pyke (1976) presents a positive side to her generally pessimistic view of changes in children's books. She noted that stereotypically female activities, while still predominantly female, are more equally represented for each sex than in the children's literature of an earlier date.

Two studies have attempted to isolate factors involved in the persistence of sex-role attitudes, and in change. Loo and Logan (1977) suggest that male chivalry, as a factor in the attitudes of both male and female undergraduates in Calgary, accounts for conservatism with respect to women's roles. They found a sex difference in attitudes in that women include a "pro-feminist" factor which was lacking in males. The national survey (*Women in Canada*, 1976: 148) reports similar facts. Men, not women, perceive responsibility for children as part of general household management and also perceive a potentially threatening imposition on some traditional male roles; women, not men, perceive a factor of physical fitness and stamina as characteristic of the female, and also a pervasive factor in homemaking described as "effectiveness of management"

It is not to be concluded, however, that all men and women in Canada are like their own sex in their constellations of attitudes toward sex roles, or that there is a high degree of uniformity in the country as a whole. As a result of the *Women in Canada* study (1976: 145), six segments of the population were uncovered by the correlation analysis of forty questionnaire items, as follows: Female Chauvinist (women as superior), 6 per cent; Egalitarian, 18 per cent; Feminist/Traditional, 7 per cent; Traditional Female ("appropriate" work roles), 28 per cent; Traditional Male (women have limited ability and roles), 26 per cent; and Male Chauvinist (male dominance), 15 per cent. Combining the Feminist/ Traditional and Traditional Female categories, it can be seen that one out of three Canadian adults subscribe to more or less traditionally feminine roles for women.

There are indications of generational differences in sex-role orientations. In the national poll cited here there is a definite age factor, with the Female Chauvinist segment tending to be middle-aged, and the Egalitarian segment tending to be younger on the average. The segment with the oldest average age is the Feminist/Traditional one. Beyer and Whitehurst (1978: 114) found older males less favourable than either younger men or women to engaging in recreational activities with friends when spouses were not present. On the whole, younger husbands, compared to older ones, show up as more flexible in their family roles (*cf.* Crysdale, 1968).

THE IMPACT OF CHANGE ON FAMILY LIFE

The most striking features of the effects of changing sex roles in society on marriage are that the psychological ones appear to be the most profound; they are experienced quite differently by women and men; and they have varying consequences for couples in the middle and working classes (*cf.* Nett, 1976b; 1977). Furthermore, spouses in rural families and of certain ethnic backgrounds, especially those grounded in strong religious traditions, appear more resistant to changes in roles as well as experiencing more anxiety and ambivalence.[7]

Less well known is the impact on children of the simultaneous existence of sex-role differentiation and the currents of thought which promote androgyny.[8] Some more or less answerable questions which arise are the following: how do sex-role orientations differ between the generations within the family? How do parents and children perceive the ideal marriage relationship? What is the effect of maternal employment outside the home on sex-role stereotyping? And what are the sources of sex-role adaptations in children and adolescents?

What Do Children Think?

Lambert (1971) surveyed children aged ten to sixteen years to determine the degree to which they think of the sexes as being very different from each other. One of the most significant findings of the study was that boys, at all ages, in both language groups, think of the sexes as being very different whereas girls see them as being more similar. This was true whether the measure of sex role was behaviour, jobs, authority relations, or femininity. The difference was largest among the older French-Canadian children.

Carisse (1976), summarizing the findings of Minard's study of Montreal French secondary students, also reports marked sex-role stereotyping by age sixteen and seventeen.[9] The boys and girls had strongly interiorized the cultural image of their own sex role, of which they had a more vivid impression than that of the opposite sex; the boys adhered more easily than girls to the ideology of the supremacy of men; and finally, the children's agreement with regard to traditional family roles in the sexes was striking.

Generational Differences

We turn now from young persons' associations of specific jobs in the family with sex to more interactional aspects of the marital role, such as decision-making, helping or sharing, and giving in during arguments, etc. Larson (1977) found differences between members of families by sex and generation. In general the most agreement on these matters was found between parents, who also assigned little importance to the sub-missiveness of wives. Sons supported a more traditional view. Daughters were distinctly opposed to role segregation in marriage, whereas other members of the family were undecided on this item. Daughters also, regardless of age, were more in agreement with their mothers, and the most disagreement occurred between fathers and older sons, and in older sibling dyads. Older sons were distinctly less egalitarian than both younger sons and daughters.

In these same families Larson also found differentiated abilities to predict the ideal marriage-role response of *others* in the family. Children expected their parents, especially fathers, to be more traditional than they were, older sons were more imperceptive, and older daughters were most perceptive. When considering family constellations, he found "the greatest degree of ambiguity, imperceptiveness, and accordingly confusing interaction lies within family units . . . made up of one or more sons" (Larson, 1975: 234).

Another interesting two-generation study is that of Simmons and Turner (1976) comparing fertility ideals and sex-role attitudes of women and their adolescent children aged 12 to 19 years of age. No aggregate mother-daughter differences in the sex-role stereotypes or sex-role self-concept scores were found, which led them to conclude that these aspects of gender are changing less quickly than popular discussions have indicated. However, the younger generation is much less traditional with regard to sex-role standards, i.e., statements of how men and women should ideally act.

The Effect of Maternal Employment

Mothers working outside the home as an influence on children's sex-role attitudes and standards has been an issue since the increase in labour-force participation of married females, the polemics of feminism which centre around the androgynous personality as the healthy one, and the increased recognition of the limitations of the domestic model for achievement motives in daughters (*cf.* Ambert, 1976: 73).

Simmons and Turner (1976: 266) found mothers important as models in their children's gender learning and attitudes to wife employment, although not directly as the result of maternal employment. They found statistically significant correlations between mothers' behaviour and children's attitudes to sex role among children who strongly believe their mothers to be good models. They also found evidence of children rejecting their mother to the point where she serves as a counter-model.

More directly studying the effects of maternal employment, Gold (1976) corroborated her prediction that the nursery-school children of working mothers would have a broader concept of sex role than the children of homemaking mothers. The children's perceptions of their mothers were not related to the mother's employment status, but fathers were perceived more negatively by their sons if the mother was employed. In another study Gold (1977: 104) concluded that maternal employment is more strongly associated with the development of ten-year-old boys than of girls the same age. Furthermore, she stated that "fathers have an important influence on the development of children of employed mothers. More participation in family and household activities by the fathers is linked favourably with the children's adjustment and academic development."

Older children of employed mothers also seem to be different in interests and activities from children whose mothers are not employed outside the home, and to be affected differently according to their sex. In Propper's (1972) study of Grade 9 to 12 students, girls of employed mothers indicated fewer memberships in clubs, organizations, and teams at school. More boys of working mothers were found taking lessons in dancing, dramatics, speech, art, or music. Similarly to Gold's nursery-school children, the mothers' employment status appeared to affect the adolescent sons' relationship to the father, since a higher proportion of boys of non-employed mothers reported admiration for their fathers compared to boys of labour-force mothers.[10]

The results are consistent with those of the American study of Douvan (1963). They are also interesting in view of Kelly and Worell's (1976) study which shows that androgynous traits in male university students are associated with *both* parents behaving in a warm, involved manner with the son. They conclude as follows:

The presence of parents who model and reinforce cross-typed characteristics is related to non-traditional roles in children. The likelihood of an andro-gynous orientation is especially enhanced when the *same-sex* parent exhibits cross-typed characteristics. Thus the androgynous male describes a history of exposure to parents (and hence, role models) who demonstrably expressed warmth and affection. The androgynous female reported close interaction with a mother who was capable of both conventional maternal affection and un-conventional encouragement of curiosity.

Other studies have also emphasized the non-sex-differentiated treat-ment of children for the positive effects on girls, who are thus permitted to engage more freely in behaviour which will better satisfy their achieve-ment needs. Kimball (1976) was surprised to discover little difference in the fear of success, between Grade 8 Canadian girls and boys. She speculates that the similarity of their conflicts about success is due to the changing societal evaluation of achievement orientation as a character trait. It may well be the result of changes in gender-socialization patterns.

In this section we have addressed ourselves only to those questions for which Canadian research provides some answers. Many other queries are raised. Some are about the way boys and girls perceive the relative power of the mother and father, how it varies with age and adolescent work experience, and whether its sources are personal, stereotypical, or occupational.[11] Questions about both unintentional and purposeful androgynous training by parents and grandparents, and in single-parent households are perhaps among the most interesting, but not yet in-vestigated.

SUMMARY AND CONCLUSIONS

To what conclusion has our examination of the few scattered and merely suggestive materials on sex roles learned in the Canadian family led us?

In many respects socialization of children in the family is still clearly differentiated by sex in most segments of the society. Undoubtedly such factors as rural or urban residence and ethnic background, social class, religious affiliation, the labour-force status of mothers, the sex of the parent in one-parent households, and other variations, contribute to diversity of pattern.

Sex-role stereotyping and images do not differ markedly between the generations. Parents appear to be quite successful in passing on to their children their own beliefs as to what women and men are like and how they behave and what they do. Indeed, in some respects adolescents adhere more closely to the stereotype than adults. Perhaps this is due to the fact that activities and interests of youth vary more by sex, whereas in adults there is more convergence, at least in the household and family interests.

A greater difference exists between the generations and between the sexes on sex-role orientations, including ideal marriage roles, than on sex-role stereotypes. Some studies show parents holding more egalitarian ideals and others find children more liberal. Age may be a factor as well as sex, and sibling position. Males appear consistently less egalitarian than females, with adulthood and marriage having somewhat of a liberating effect on both their standards and their perceptiveness of the sex-role orientations of others in the family.

The effect of differential reinforcement, modeling, and identification by children with same-sex and cross-sex parents is far from clear. It is fairly obvious that by high-school age children's interests and activities are polarized by sex, that girls are less oriented toward occupational achievement, and that both girls and boys have rather firm notions of their own sexual identities in stereotypical terms. To the extent that some undifferentiated gender adaptation (psychological androgyny) occurs, it may be attributed to identification with both parents. Maternal employment has differential effects on boys' and girls' sex-role orientations and identities, but not independently of the role of the father in the family.

The Canadian materials add to the already mounting evidence that males may be more vulnerable psychically to changing ideologies and to changed roles in the family (i.e., mother employed outside the home). Canadian males sit rather easily in their position of supremacy and headship in the family, and find it hard to totally reject a chauvinist complex of attitudes. While all sons are less sensitive to the ideological positions of others in the family they grow up in, the traditionally favoured position of eldest son seems especially handicapping psychologically and a probable liability to social integration into the family.

Not as evident, but something to be considered, is the apparently androgynous element in the feminine experience of changing sex roles. Girls and women identify as feminine, they place value on their work at home, and they want to be protected; at the same time they reject the homemaker role as the sole source of satisfaction and consider that they are strong and capable. Sometimes interpreted as "ambivalence", or wanting to have their cake and eat it, these so-called inconsistencies are entirely compatible from the androgynous view. The fundamental belief of the ideology is that all human beings, regardless of sex, have the same basic needs which must be met in order to achieve good mental health and happiness. A non-polarized view of gender provides roles which legitimate the expression in one person, of either sex, of tenderness and strength, of nurturance and achievement, and of receptiveness to intimacy and assertiveness.

In summary, the gaps in the Canadian research on learning sex roles are numerous and wide, but then again the scant materials point to a picture of moderate change from family socialization to sex-role orientations and adaptations.

Notes

1. The exceptions are those rare instances where a child is born hermaphroditic, and those other cases of sex change surgically.

2. The use of the words "gender" and "sex" is very confusing at the present time. Oakley (1972) has used the term "sex" to mean biological and anatomical characteristics and "gender" to refer to cultural associations. Stoll (1974) reverses the meanings. Vaughter (1976) indicates that there appears to be a developing consensus on the former usage, with sex equal to biological

and gender to learned traits.

3. Boyd (1976) believes the egalitarian response was inflated by the hypothetical situations. The female physician was already present in an emergency situation, and a female was to be considered for Prime Minister *if* the party were to choose a woman and *if* she were qualified.

4. See Kimball (1975) for an excellent discussion of the socially acceptable ways women channel the expression of aggression while playing the traditional feminine role.

5. In the psychoanalytic theory the

"myth" is an essential part of the human condition, and thus can never be dispelled. It is the basis for the Oedipus complex, the resolution of which results in the socialized (i.e., civilized) person of both sexes. It is myth not because it is untrue, but because the power of the father is perceived at the *unconscious* level by both the infant girl and boy who must, in different ways, come to grips with the reality of societal restrictions on their infantile fantasies. It is grounded in the cultural universal of the incest prohibition.

6. The tendency for sociologists to study occupational mobility and educational aspirations along father-son lines is a somewhat unrealistic approach in light of the greater association reported in *Perspectives Canada* (1975) between mother's educational level and son's education than between fathers and sons.

7. This is in contrast to generational change reported by Simmons and Turner (1976: 267) as appearing "to be taking place in families where the mother belongs to an ethnic-religious group which is relatively 'traditional' in sex-role standards and in its family-size ideals."

8. Psychological androgyny, sometimes called "sex-role transcendence", refers to a personality organization which makes it possible for persons of either sex to simultaneously endorse both masculine and feminine characteristics about themselves, or to behave "instrumentally" and "expressively" as the situation requires, instead of stereotypically and rigidly.

9. Vernon (1972) reported interest factors which are bipolars and which divide up the adolescent girls and boys. In boys Science interest and Concept Maturity contrasted with Art interest and Divergent Thinking, Literary Creativity, and Sociometric popularity in girls.

10. It should be noted that two-thirds of the mothers were reported by their children as taking employment because of economic reasons. An equal proportion of employed and non-employed mothers—one-fourth —were reported by their children as disliking housework.

11. Eichler (1976) informs us that adults rank the prestige of the occupation of housewife as medium on the scale, but there are no comparable rankings for children. Baxter (1976) reports that the perceptions of adolescent boys of occupational prestige are similar to adults, but she did not include girls in her sample.

SELECTED BIBLIOGRAPHY

AMBERT, ANNE-MARIE. *Sex Structure*, second ed., Don Mills, Ontario. 1976

BOYD, MONICA. "Equality Between the Sexes: The Results of Canadian Gallup Polls, 1974   1953–1973", paper presented at the Annual Meeting of the Canadian Sociology and Anthropology Association.

ELKIN, FRED and GERALD HANDEL. *The Child and Society: The Process of Socialization*, 1972   second ed., New York.

LAMBERT, R. D. "Sex Role Imagery in Children: Social Origins of the Mind", *Studies 1971   of the Royal Commission on the Status of Women in Canada*, No. 6, Ottawa.

NETT, E. M. "The Social-Psychological Effects on the Family of the Women's Move- 1976   ment", *Canadian Home Economics Journal*, Vol. 26, pp. 12–19.

PYKE, S. W. "Children's Literature: Conceptions of Sex Roles", in E. Zuric and 1973   R. Pike, eds., *Socialization and Social Values in Canada*, Toronto.

Women in Canada, second ed., Toronto. 1976

Kinship Networks

G. N. RAMU

By virtue of birth into a family, whether it is single-parent, nuclear, or extended, almost everyone inherits a group of relatives. Upon marriage, we acquire additional relatives thus forming an extensive network of persons to whom we are related through blood (consanguinal) or marriage (affinal). The term "kinship" refers to such a collectivity as well as to "a structural system of relationships in which individuals are bound to one another by complex interlocking and ramifying ties" (Murdock, 1949: 92). The notion of a kinship *system*, which is often found in sociology and anthropology texts, is comprehensive and includes not only a group of interrelated persons, but socially defined interrelationships, rights and obligations entailed in various kinship statuses, and normative codes of behaviour.

Generally, sociologists study only an aspect of kinship systems, e.g., the social importance of kinship networks in urban industrial societies such as Canada and the United States. Some of the questions they raise are: What is the nature of urban kinship systems? How do they differ from less advanced societies? Who are the most important kin for routine interaction and mutual aid? What are the bases for such sustained relationships? Is there a "functional fit" between certain kinship systems and urbanism and industrialism? In this chapter we will attempt to answer some of these questions in the light of Canadian data.

We shall use the term *function* to signify a task or a duty performed by the *kinship network* in the interest of its members and the society. By kinship networks, we understand formal and informal ties among such relatives as parents and their adult children, siblings, grandparents, uncles and aunts, to name a few. The kin-family network is composed of nuclear families bound together by affectional ties and choice. Members of such networks volunteer to help rather than direct activities. They perform supportive rather than coercive roles (Sussman and Burchinal, 1962: 320). In essence, kinship network is ego-based, voluntary, and depends on mutual interest, affection, concern, and often, aid.

In the subsequent discussion, we shall first outline the main theoretical issues on the relationship between urbanization and kinship. The main question here is whether extensive kinship networks can be identified and function in industrial societies. Second, we shall summarize the major findings about kinship ties in urban Canada. The concluding section summarizes the main points and offers a set of open questions about research on urban kinship in Canada.

A THEORETICAL OVERVIEW

Prior to the mid 1950s most sociologists assumed that urbanization and industrialization minimize the social and personal significance of kinship. To be successful in an urban milieu, it is imperative that one cultivates certain characteristics, such as individualism, achievement-orientation, aspirations for social mobility, and extensive ties with non-kin. Park (1928) noted that in cities, old clan and kinship groups are broken up and are replaced by social organizations based on rational interests and personal choice. Wirth (1938: 12) affirming Park, states that

The bonds of kinship . . . and sentiments arising out of living together for generations under common folk-tradition are likely to be absent, or at best, relatively weak. . . . The family as a unit of social life is emancipated from the larger kinship group characteristic of the country and individual members pursue their own diverging interests in their vocational, educational, religious, recreational, and political life.

Consequently, the nuclear family and not the extended family or the lineage, becomes the most important kinship unit in urban milieu. This distinguishes urban from primitive, or peasant kinship systems.[1]

Parsons (1943), in a theoretical discussion of the nature of urban kinship systems, argued that extended kinship elements do not form firmly structured units of the urban social system. Instead (as we already indicated), the basic unit of kinship is the nuclear family consisting of husband, wife, and their unmarried children living separately from and independent of any extended kin. Such an *isolated nuclear family* is structurally suitable for meeting the demands of an urban industrial society. Parsons further suggests that any significant deviation from such a nuclear unit would result in a "reduction in the productivity of our economy and drastic limitation on the realizeability of our democratic values" (cited by Irving, 1972: 5).

In essence, most sociologists emphasized that the demands of urbanization and industrialization call for a family pattern in which nuclear family units operate independent from one another, and isolated from each other.

In the latter part of the 1950s research in Canada, England, and the United States demonstrated that contrary to such formulations, kinship networks are viable in modern industrial societies. For example, Firth (1956). Young and Willmott (1957), and Bott (1957) found extensive extended-family ties among the working class in England that were expressed by frequent visits, mutual aid, and affection. Garigue (1956), in a study of French Canadians in Montreal, found extended-kin ties comparable to those found in England. We shall say more about Garigue's study later in this chapter. In a cross-cultural analysis of family patterns, Goode (1963: 75) asserts that

no matter what index is used, the family in the most industrialized nations has not taken on the supposed characteristics of an isolated nuclear-family system. The extended kin network continues to function and to include a wide range of kin who share with one another, see one another frequently, and know each other. . . . the frequency of social participation between the average modern nuclear family and its relatives may not have been reduced at all.

Further, research in the United States by Sussman (1953, 1959, 1965), Litwak (1960abc), and Adams (1968), to cite a few, has led to a reconceptualization of urban kinship. Sussman's studies revealed that there is an established pattern of mutual aid among various kin, especially among parents and their adult children. Such aid ranged from large gifts such as furniture and financial aid toward the down-payment on a house to such trivial services as lawn-care (if proximity permits) while the children are on vacation. The aid was given very frequently by parents during the early years of marriage when the couple had limited resources and growing expenditures. The parents, in turn, expected their children to show a certain degree of affection and concern, attention, and inclusion in some of their activities. Sussman and Burchinal (1962: 332) concluded that parental aid for the most part: (a) was given voluntarily and was based on feelings and sentiments between parents and children rather than upon legal and cultural norms; (b) was intended to assist rather than to direct the achievement of occupational goals of family members receiving aid; (c) weakened the financial autonomy norm of the nuclear-family unit without replacing it; and (d) was available for an increasing number of families because of higher incomes, retirement programs, more middle-aged women returning to the labour market, and new norms for a post-parental period in which there were emerging identifiable grandparent roles.[2]

Litwak (1960abc), in an effort to conceptualize the nature of a modern urban kinship system, argues that the nuclear family is not necessarily isolated from the rest of the kinship system. Instead, there emerges a *modified extended family* which can be conceptually juxtaposed between the *classical extended family* found in traditional societies such as India and pre-modern Japan, and the isolated nuclear family which Wirth, Parsons, and others proposed. The modified extended family, Litwak argues, is functional for modern industrial society because its existence does not depend upon geographical and occupational proximity. Through reciprocal aid, communication, and identification among its members, the modified extended family encourages mobility and, therefore, remains a positive force for industrialization and urbanization.

Undoubtedly the research studies by Sussman, Litwak, and others, compelled a re-evaluation of previous theories on the structural isolation of the nuclear family. Such a reconsideration has led to a general understanding that extended-family networks, and urbanization and industrialization are not antithetical. In fact, extended-family networks are useful in that they enable the members of the neolocal nuclear family to adapt successfully to life in modern industrial settings. On this premise, Sussman asserts that "the isolated nuclear is a myth. . . . It does not merit any further attention of the field, and I, for one, refuse to waste any more time even discussing it" (Quoted by Rosow, in Shanas and Streib, 1965).[3]

In sum, empirical studies of kinship in England and the United States demonstrate that: (a) there is a widespread persistence of kin networks; (b) the kin network includes nuclear families that are residentially separate but maintain strong affective ties; (c) the most important members of the kin network are parents and their adult offspring, siblings, grandparents, uncles, aunts, and cousins; (d) there is an extensive but varying degree of kin interaction through face-to-face visits, exchange of greetings, letters, and telephone; finally (e) there exists a fairly institutionalized exchange of financial and material aid, and services.

With these theoretical perspectives in mind, our next task is to ascertain what is known about urban kin networks in Canada.

URBAN KIN NETWORKS

The study of kinship networks in Canada is still in a state of pre-infancy. There are at present not more than six studies which specifically deal with kinship networks in urban Canada. The focus of these studies is directly or indirectly related to the issues of kinship which surfaced in the United States in the early 1950s. In the following paragraphs we will outline the nature of these studies and their essential findings. Later we will present some of the specific issues which emerge from these findings.

Montreal Study of French Canadians   The pioneering work on urban kinship in Canada was done by Garigue (1956) who, following his collaborative research with Firth (1956) in England, attempted to explore the extent to which French Canadians in Montreal maintain close ties with their extended kin. The data were collected from 52 persons in 43 households between 1954 and 1955. The major findings were that "the urban French-Canadian kinship is a variant of that generally reported for western societies. It is a patronymic bilateral structure with two major dimensions of lateral range and generation depth" (Garigue, 1956: 263). The French Canadians maintained very close ties with their immediate relatives, visited them frequently, and exchanged goods and services. On the basis of his data, Garigue (1956: 272) concludes that there is

no trend toward transformation of the present French-Canadian urban kinship system into the more restricted system reported for the United States. . . .
Far from being incompatible, kinship and urbanism among French-Canadians seem to have become functionally related. Each urban domestic family, each household, each person, is normally part of system of obligations arising from the recognition of kinship ties.

Garigue's study is clearly dated and a generation has since passed. In the mid-fifties, various economic, social, and legal changes have undoubtedly left serious impressions on urban kinship networks. Therefore, the student must be careful not to interpret the findings as representative of the contemporary situation in Montreal.

Hamilton Study In the summer of 1962, 327 heads of households in a working class area of Hamilton, Ontario, were interviewed for a kinship study by Pineo (1976). The respondents were of British, Sicilian, Italian, and East European origins. The major findings were that: (a) an extended family exists among the respondents; (b) there is a pattern of frequent visits; (c) although the over-all relationships are bilateral in character, meaning that the kin relations occur without any distinction or discrimination between wife's and/or husband's relatives, as well as relatives of both parents, the patrifocality is fairly common.

Montreal Study of Italians During 1964–65, using observation and interview techniques, Boissevain (1976) studied family and kinship patterns among the Montreal Italians. The number of persons interviewed was 261. The study revealed that: (a) the nuclear family, characterized by neolocality and bilaterality, was central to the Italian social structure; (b) there the majority of interrelated nuclear families live near one another; (c) Italian Canadians and their relatives not only saw each other a great deal but; (d) that neighbourhood and friendship groups were often part of kinship network; and (e) the kinship networks played an important role in their marital arrangements.

Montreal Study of English Canadians In 1961, Osterreich (1976) studied the genealogies of forty-five English Canadians of lower- and middle-class origins who were Montreal suburbanites. The focus of the study was to assess the impact of geographic mobility on kinship networks. The essential findings were that: (a) geographic mobility did not have a significant influence on either their knowledge of kin or on the frequency of contact; (b) extension of mutual aid was not dependent upon geographic proximity but services were; (c) kin orientation and commitment were not dependent upon geographic proximity but rather on genealogical closeness; and (d) the kinship network fell within Litwak's conceptualization of the modified extended family.

St. Boniface Study   In 1962, Piddington (1973) collected sixteen genealogies from French Canadians in St. Boniface, a suburb of Winnipeg. In essence, he found that kinship networks, in terms of visiting and affective ties, were not restricted by geographic proximity and convenience of access, but by strong kinship bonds characteristic of French Canadians. He also found that intermarriage of kin was common and kinship served as a source of support for the continuity of the French-Canadian culture. We will have more on Piddington's study later in this chapter.

Toronto Study   Irving (1972) studied kinship patterns among fifty-four Canadian-born Protestant couples of British origin. The respondents were chosen from the world of clients who used Metropolitan Toronto Family Service Agencies. In particular, the study focused on three aspects of urban kinship networks: patterns of interaction; helping practices; and kin conflicts. Irving (1972: 91–93) established that parents and parents-in-law are a highly significant part of the social environment of young married couples, and that relationships between the marital couple and their parents and parents-in-law are not random or uniquely determined, but are patterned. Further, it was found that extension of aid was not only common but expected. Finally, Irving found that there was a structural predisposition to strain in certain kinship statuses. For example, wives had the most conflict with their mothers-in-law; husbands had the most with their own mothers, and next with their mothers-in-law.

In sum, empirical evidence from the selected summarized studies[4] demonstrates, that in urban Canada there is a widespread persistence of kinship networks and this is consistent with the findings of Sussman and others in the United States. Canadian kinship is bilateral with both parents' lines receiving equal recognition with regard to descent and inheritance. One's kinship universe is composed of both relatives by blood and relatives by marriage. Further, kinship networks with various degrees of group significance are found in virtually all research settings. In the next section we will elaborate on these points.

Some Aspects of Kinship Networks

One of the characteristics of urban kinship networks is its voluntary basis. Kinship bonds are established and maintained in a context relatively free from normative pressures or a sense of strong obligation. Although one recognizes and maintains a formal relationship with a wide group of relatives, one tends to be selective as far as close ties are concerned. In this section, we shall examine the nature of such selective ties in the research settings discussed previously.

KINSHIP RECOGNITION

At the beginning of this chapter, we stated that we inherit a group of consanguinal and affinal kin. In this group, one can identify at least three categories based on the amount of knowledge one has about these, the interaction, and affection. These can be broadly categorized as *nominal*, *effective*, and *intimate* kin (Firth, 1956). Nominal kin are those whose names and "whereabouts" one clearly knows but with whom one has little formal or informal contact. Effective kin are those with whom one maintains certain ritual ties, such as the exchange of greetings on holidays or mutual attendance at weddings and funerals. Intimate or core kin are those with whom one maintains a close and continuing relationship, such as those demonstrated by Garigue, Irving, and others.

Many studies of urban kinship assume that there is little emphasis on residential propinquity (i.e., kin living with or near each other) and that since kinship is divorced from social, economic, and political functions, individuals tend to *recognize* a relatively small number of kin—whether nominal, effective, or intimate. The size of an individual's kinship universe is usually taken as an indicator of the significance of kinship. Although size alone is a crude measure of the social significance of kinship, available evidence indicates that kin recognition is extensive in modern societies (Firth, 1956; Young and Willmott, 1957).

In Montreal, for example, the range of kinship recognition among French Canadians in terms of the mean genealogical knowledge that a respondent had in 1954–56 was 215 persons (Garigue, 1956: 264). This included, presumably, all relatives irrespective of the level of ties. "The most extensive knowledge was usually concentrated into the generations of ego and his parents, which together included from one-half to two-thirds of the persons known" (Garigue, 1956: 264). A study of Anglophones found that an average of about 60 relatives was recognized

(Osterreich, 1976: 534). Among the Montreal Italians, effective recognition for the purpose of mutual aid and friendship goes only as far as first cousins. This means that the kinship universe among the Italians constitutes primarily intimate kin (Boissevain, 1976: 287).

The variance in the number of recognized kin could stem from the non-randomness of the samples, dated evidence, ethnicity, and other factors. Yet, the extent of kin recognition does give a rough indication of the significance attached to kinship networks in a society or a group. Accordingly, the French Canadians seem to recognize a larger number of kin than any other group and hence seem to attach greater significance to kinship.

Pattern of Interaction

If the range of kin that Canadians recognize is between 60 to 215, they do not, and possibly cannot, interact with all of them on an equal basis. For example, among French Canadians in Montreal, personal choice as opposed to either residential distance or degree of relatedness was the salient criterion for sustained interaction (Garigue, 1956: 264). Besides such a choice, the nature and degree of interaction is to a large extent determined by distance, sex, and class factors.

Visits, Telephone Contacts, and Exchange of Letters

The inner core of the intimate kin group in Canada, as elsewhere, consists of parents, parents-in-law, and siblings (and occasionally cousins). Relationships with parents and parents-in-law are characterized by feelings of affection, concern, obligation, and loyalty. Relationships with brothers and sisters are based upon a sense of friendship, affection, and mutual compassion. Ties with other relatives are formal and ritualistic.

The pattern of contacts, according to most studies, is a function of physical and kinship proximity and personal preference. Among the Montreal Anglophones, "Biological and geographical distance of relatives were found to affect the contact ratio. [Those studied] . . . were in touch with parents and grand-parents and almost all siblings. . . . The contact ratio was higher for relatives who lived in Montreal or within 200 miles of the city than for others. . . . Face-to-face contact occurred with much greater frequency among people who had relatives in Montreal" (Osterreich, 1976: 536). In Hamilton, sixty-eight per cent of the respondents had close contact with at least one relative (Pineo, 1976).

In Toronto, it was common among the young married couples to drop in, unannounced, on their parents and parents-in-law but the older generation gave prior notification. Such visits took place at least once a week depending upon whether these kin lived in the same neighbourhood or within the metropolitan area (Irving, 1972: 42–51). The French Canadians in Montreal and St. Boniface not only visited their intimate kin very frequently but tended to use such occasions to reinforce their affective ties (Garigue, 1956; Piddington, 1973). Among the Italians different kinship ceremonies provided an opportunity for the meeting of various kin and for the exchange of information about mutual kin (Boissevain, 1976: 289).

Canadian data, in general, suggest that when the degree of kinship is remote the respondents tend to attribute their infrequent contacts to geographical distance. Most of those who are generally visited, regardless of geographic distance, included such intimate kin as parents, parents-in-law, and such others.

Besides routine visits, it is a general practice among close relatives to "get together" during Christmas and Thanksgiving, at the birth or death of close relatives, and at other ritual and symbolic events. Telephone calls and letter-writing have also become means of "keeping in touch" with intimate kin who are geographically dispersed. In essence, most studies conclude that although there is considerable interaction among kin in urban contexts, it is confined to a small group of preferred blood kin and relatives by marriage.

Initiation and Management of Kinship Ties

It is often suggested that in urban kinship networks, effective relationships are initiated and maintained by females. For example, the mother-daughter bond is reported to be especially strong (Young and Willmott, 1957; Adams, 1968). Among the French Canadians, for example:

Women are more active within the kinship system than men, and this fact combined with their primary role as wives and mothers gives them a great deal of influence and supplies the continuity of the kin group. . . . Urban French-Canadian men and women not only give different stress to kinship, but also have different roles. Men, for instance, reported that they usually thought of their kin group in terms of their male relatives; their knowledge of their female relatives was more restricted. Women seemed to have greater awareness of the kin group as composed of both sexes. Not only was their knowledge of the total kin group greater, so that in a number of instances wives knew more of their husbands' kin than the husbands themselves did, but they also had much greater knowledge of the affairs of the kin group (Garigue, 1956: 263, 266).

In the French-Canadian case, there is clear evidence of matrifocality. The females not only maintain extremely close relationships with their mothers but also demonstrate a knowledge of and a capacity to maintain extensive kinship relationships. The mother-daughter relationship is, perhaps, the closest, both affectively and interactionally and this is true regardless of their relative socio-economic status (Adams, 1968: 308).

In Hamilton, however, a different type of relationship was noted. "The first indication that matrifocality is not the pattern . . . is that proportions reporting at least weekly contact with kin were virtually identical for men and for women" (Pineo, 1976: 549). Moreover, the Hamilton respondents maintained contact outside the household more frequently with the husband's parents than the wife's (Pineo, 1976: 550). Among the Toronto English Canadians, a similar equivalence of kin lines was observed:

Contrary to the findings of other studies there was no significant difference between husbands and wives in the frequency of face-to-face contacts with parents . . . . Perhaps the main reason for the rather unusual finding of minimal differences between husbands and wives with regard to the frequency of visiting was that . . . societal ideal of bilateral symmetry was realized in this sample in relation to proximity to parents (Irving, 1972: 54–55).

The differential patterns such as the ones stated above are indicative of the nature of urban kinship networks. The maintenance of interpersonal relationships depends upon personal preferences, resources, and physical proximity. The lack of normative prescriptions concerning with whom ties should be kept enhances the flexibility of urban kinship.

Mutual Aid

One of the implications of the structural isolation hypothesis is that urban societies emphasize individualism, autonomy, and self-reliance on the part of individuals. This means that kinship has little objective significance or subjective relevance. In addition, the emergence of professional day-care and health-care centres, commercial banks with liberal lending policies, instant credit, varieties of recreational agencies and voluntary associations has tended to minimize the role of kinship in one's life. Although this is true for first-generation immigrants or those whose parents and other significant kin are not affluent enough to give support in times of need, among those who have the resources and inclination there clearly exists a well-established practice of exchanging goods and services.

The significance and continuity of urban kinship networks can partially be explained by the fact that mutual aid continues to be an important value and function. In the words of Sussman and Burchinal (1962: 321), "The lifelines of the network are help and services exchanged among members of nuclear families related by blood and affinal ties. Help, services, and social interaction characterize the activities of this interdependent kin family network." In Canada, there is considerable evidence suggesting the prevalence of mutual monetary assistance and the exchange of various forms of service. Osterreich (1976) and Irving (1972) found that among English Canadians an exchange of goods and services was common. In many cases, when a young couple plan to buy a new home or furnishings, the parents provide funds either for down-payment or the total cost, if they are able. Such assistance is usually given to newly married couples who do not have savings of their own. After five or more years of marriage such help is seldom sought or given with the exception of gifts to grandchildren (Irving, 1972: 79).

Very often the parents or the adult children tend to be discreet in extending a helping hand lest this be seen as an infringement on the financial autonomy and self-reliance of the recipient. Therefore, aid is often disguised in the form of gifts offered on ceremonial or festive occasions such as birthdays, graduation, anniversaries, or Christmas. What is important here is that "the vast majority of these acts of filial and kin responsibility are carried out voluntarily or on the basis of affection rather than because of a compulsion to do so emanating from the legal system" (Nye and Berardo, 1973: 416).

MOBILITY AND KINSHIP NETWORK

The sociological analysis of the relationship between mobility and kin networks takes into account at least two dimensions. First, what is the impact of geographic and social mobility on the extended-kin network? Does the combined impact of such experiences attenuate kin networks? Second, how do extended-family ties determine mobility patterns? Does commitment to one's kin reduce the prospects of geographic or social mobility? In this section, we will briefly address these questions.

Geographic Mobility and Kinship Ties

Canadian census data clearly demonstrate that "one of the direct means available to an individual for coping with inequities between the size of the labour force population in any area and the number of opportunities for earning a livelihood, is migration" (Kalbach and McVey, 1971: 82). According to the 1961 Census, 42.3 per cent of the population changed residences within Canada, with most of these moves being intraprovincial, from one municipality to the other and involving a rural-urban shift (Kalbach and McVey, 1971: 83). Increased urbanization and industrialization in Canada, offers a wide variety of opportunities for occupational mobility and temporary residence for a large number of Canadians.

The Canadian evidence on the relationship between geographic mobility and kinship is sparse. The only study which deals primarily with this issue was conducted by Osterreich (1976) in Montreal. In general, she found that geographic mobility did not have a significant influence on the overall kinship networks and that the families involved conformed to Litwak's modified extended-family pattern. She found that the mobile respondents knew more relatives (median 64) than the non-mobile (median 49.5). However, the pattern of contacts (face-to-face visits, telephone calls, and letters) depended upon the geographic proximity, in that non-mobile respondents demonstrated a higher frequency than mobile. Osterreich (1976: 539) also noted that "dependence on relatives for help was not general among these respondents; some forms of help were much more common than others, and, moreover, geographic mobility reduced the dependence on relatives for aid." In short, "the respondents in this study whether mobile or non-mobile reported essentially the same kinds of relationships with kin" (Osterreich, 1976: 543).

Both Garigue (1956) and Piddington (1973) concluded that geographic proximity was not a critical factor for the maintenance of close ties among intimate kin (Garigue, 1956: 267). "Only when the degree of kinship was more remote did informants remark that geographical distance influenced contacts. Besides degrees of kinship and geographical location, personal preference was an important factor in contact." Piddington (1973: 126) found that among French Canadians, genealogical closeness rather than geographic proximity and convenience of access, determined the strength of kinship bonds.

There is a paucity of Canadian data on how class and the occupational status of geographically mobile persons affects kinship contacts and sentiment. Further, the patterns of migration from farm to city, between cities, or distance travelled are likely to affect relationships between families differentially. But we cannot say precisely how.

Social Mobility and Kinship Ties

Individuals seeking increased economic and occupational opportunities move where these are perceived as available. Cities are the centres of modern industrial and bureaucratic establishments and with their pervasive ideology of equal opportunity they are magnetic forces for qualified, competent, and achievement-oriented persons. As a result, the pattern of internal migration has been in the direction of urban centres from rural areas. This is evident from Canadian census data which suggest that in 1871, roughly 82 per cent of the population was rural; a century later, it dwindled to 24 per cent of which only 6.6 per cent was *rural farm* population. In 1871 there were no cities of 100,000 population in Canada. By 1971, there were nineteen of these and such a growth of urban centres represents not only a high degree of urbanization but also their social and economic importance.

A common assumption is that upward mobility requires individuals and families to radically change their patterns of values, attitudes, and roles. There should be considerably less attachment and obligation to their extended families. Instead, they should subscribe to values and norms associated with modern industrial systems—individualism, secularism, and rationalism. Consequently, the extended family can become an impediment to one's aspirations. However, as Goode (1966) and Tavuchis (1976) argue the relationship is far from clear, and that such premises are based on inadequate data.

Although we lack firm evidence on the relationship between occupational mobility and kinship ties in Canada, non-Canadian data indicate that extended-family networks and occupational mobility are not intrinsically incompatible. To the contrary, extended kin, depending on their ethnic and class status and degree of kinship solidarity, may effectively contribute towards the upward mobility of individuals (Litwak, 1960; Adams, 1968; Tavuchis, 1972).

Kinship and Multi-Culturalism

There are indications that in Canada many groups such as the Italians, the Dutch, the Hutterites, and the French Canadians, to name a few, depend on kinship networks, ceremonies, asd rituals to foster their cultural identities (Boissevain, 1976; Ishwaran, 1977; Piddington, 1973, 1976). For example, among the Italians, kinship ceremonies and rituals reinforce the Italian identity and as Boissevain (1976: 290) puts it, "Kin relations are almost couched in the idiom of Italian culture." Both Garigue and Piddington consider that kinship is central to the cultural complex of French Canadians. "The[se] ideals about family and kinship were not isolated but were part of a cultural complex system of education, membership in the Catholic Church, and various political theories about the status of French-Canadians in Canada. To be a member of French-Canadian kinship group implied attitudes and beliefs about some or all of these" (Garigue, 1956: 273).

Piddington notes that kinship among Franco-Manitobans plays an integrative function.

The French-Canadian culture continues to survive, though in a variety of new forms which are themselves constantly changing. In this process of survival, kinship plays an important part. It serves to integrate the local community by providing a complex set of interlocking kinship relationships.

These provide channels through which significant social activities can be organized; in particular they facilitate marriage between kin which, in turn, strengthen the system. . . . The material from St. Jean Baptiste suggests that over the whole of Canada . . . there spreads a network of recognized kinship relationships which helps to keep French-Canadians aware despite geographical dispersion, of their identity as a distinct ethnic group and of the advantages of belonging to such a group (1976: 571).

Thus kinship among some groups serves as a source of cultural identity and stability. By providing structured opportunities for sustained interaction, ethnicity is reinforced. However, what we do not know is whether or not this interrelationship is commonly found among ethnic groups other than those mentioned.

CONCLUSIONS

Sociological research of urban kinship networks in Canada is minimal and unsystematic. The present state of our knowledge on this issue is confined to about six studies that deal directly or indirectly with the major theoretical issues generated in Britain and the United States. What is known and what is problematic about this area may be summarized as follows:

What is Known

1. Urban Canadian kinship networks are created and consist of interpersonal ties between an individual and his/her blood kin and affines, and between nuclear families. The neolocal nuclear family is the basic unit of kinship.
2. The nuclear family is *not* structurally isolated as suggested by Wirth, and Parsons. Close ties exist between intimate kin and most studies reveal that a high degree of kinship solidarity is common among Canadians.[5] Consequently extra-nuclear family ties in Canada generally conform to Litwak's (1960) concept of the modified extended family.
3. Interrelated urban families maintain contacts through frequent mutual visiting, telephoning, writing, and helping. The frequency, effectiveness, and subjective salience of such contacts hinges not on geographic prox-

imity but on the degree of genealogical relatedness. Further, although females typically serve as the focus and point of articulation of the web of kin ties, the cultural ideal of bilaterality is realized by the equal recognition of both maternal and paternal blood kin as well as affines. 4. A strong sense of mutual concern and welfare among intimate kin is evident from the reciprocal aid and services that are voluntarily given.

Open Questions

1. There is a lack of clear evidence on the relationships between social and geographical mobility and kin networks. The only study available focuses mainly on the impact of geographic mobility on extended-family ties. What we do not know is the role of class and occupational mobility in the maintenance or attrition of kinship ties. What is the initial state of contact between geographically dispersed, and occupationally and socially divergent but interrelated nuclear families?

2. Although there are scattered findings on mutual aid, we lack information on the details and specifics. What is the nature and extent of financial aid? How frequently does one give or receive aid? Is the extent of aid a function of one's class? Do children reciprocate when the parents are in need of such aid in their old age? The Canadian data do not even marginally deal with these issues.

3. The role of kinship networks in the maintenance of ethnicity is unclear. There is limited evidence to suggest that kinship serves as a source of integration among some minorities, but comparative data are needed before valid generalizations can be made.

Notes

1. Schneider (1968: v) distinguishes between contemporary western and primitive kinship systems as follows:

The kinship systems of modern, western societies are relatively differentiated as compared with the kinship systems found in many primitive and peasant societies. By "differentiated" I mean simply that kinship is clearly and sharply distinguished from all other kinds of social institutions and relationships. In many primitive and peasant societies a large number of kinds of institutions are organized and built as parts of kinship system itself. Thus the major social units of the society may be kin groups—lineages, perhaps. These same kin groups may be property-owning units, the political units, and so on. Thus, whatever a man does in such a society he does as a kinsman of one kind or another.

2. Drawn from Irving (1972: 23).
3. Such a categorical assertion by Sussman does not seem to have any bearing on the persistent character of controversy in kinship research. For example, Litwak's views have been questioned by Reiss (1962), and Robins and Tomnec (1962) who maintain that geographical propinquity is an important factor in maintaining intimate relations. Tavuchis (1972: 40) casts further doubt when he notes "that Litwak's data do not refer specifically to the effects of mobility on extended kin ties but rather suggest that individuals with strong extended kin ties are not necessarily hampered with respect to geographical or occupational mobility. This is an analytically and empirically different question, we would argue, from the effects of mobility on family relationships although certainly pertinent in other contexts."

Gibson (1972) has offered an excellent critical commentary on the theoretical formulations of Sussman, *et al.* Gibson's main argument is that the conclusions drawn by Sussman and others are not valid because these scholars have not clearly conceptualized the nature and patterns of urban kinship networks, the sampling procedures are not scientific enough to permit generalizations, and, finally, there is a certain amount of exaggeration of the significance of kin in urban setting in their writings. Gibson, on the basis of his study of 486 disabled men and their families, in which there was a need for aid from kin, argued that the Parsonian notion of the structural isolation of the nuclear family was still valid. Adams (1968) also suggests that the emphasis should be placed on "relative" rather than "isolated".

The interested student is referred to Morgan (1975: Chapter 2) for a detailed overview of sociological literature on urban kinship.
4. The studies cited here are chosen from a variety of published sociological materials. We have not included those studies in which the kinship network is not the major unit of analysis. There are innumerable studies in which kinship has received incidental reference (e.g., Seeley, *et al.*, 1955; Kohl, 1976; Ishwaran, 1977). We have used some of these studies, nevertheless, where they are pertinent to our discussion.
5. A negative case to this generalization can be found in a study of a Toronto suburban life where nuclear family seems to be structurally isolated (Seeley, *et al.*).

SELECTED BIBLIOGRAPHY

BOISSEVAIN, J. "Family and Kinship among Italians of Montreal", in K. Ishwaran,
1976   ed., *The Canadian Family*, Toronto.

FIRTH, RAYMOND. *Two Studies of Kinship in London*, London.
1956

GARIGUE, PHILIPPE. "French-Canadian Kinship and Urban Life", *American Anthro-*
1956   *pologist*, Vol. 58.

IRVING, HOWARD. *The Family Myth: A Study of Relationships Between Married*
1972   *Couples and Their Parents*, Toronto.

LITWAK, E. "Occupational Mobility and Extended Family Cohesion", *American*
1960   *Sociological Review*, Vol. 29.

——. "Geographic Mobility and Extended Family Cohesion", *American Socio-*
1960   *logical Review*, Vol. 30.

OSTERREICH, HELGI. "Geographic Mobility and Kinship: A Canadian Example", in
1976   K. Ishwaran, ed., *The Canadian Family*.

PARSONS, TALCOTT. "The Kinship System of Contemporary United States", *Amer-*
1943   *ican Anthropologist*, Vol. 45.

PIDDINGTON, R. "The Kinship Networks among French-Canadians", in G. L. Gold
1973   and Marc-Adelard Tremblay, eds., *Communities and Culture in French Canada*, Toronto.

PINEO, PETER C. "The Extended Family in a Working-Class Area of Hamilton", in
1976   K. Ishwaran, ed., *The Canadian Family*.

SUSSMAN, M. "Relationships of Adult Children with Their Parents in the United
1965   States", in E. Shanas and G. Streib, eds., *Social Structure and the Family*, Englewood Cliffs, New Jersey.

NICHOLAS TAVUCHIS

More than a decade has passed since the publication of Elkin's, *The Family in Canada*. In this invaluable compendium the author charted trends of research, took inventory of extant sources and studies, and delineated the gaps in our knowledge of this institution. After surveying empirical studies of a variety of ethnic groups, Elkin came to the following conclusion:

it is apparent that valid information on ethnic and immigrant groups is meager. For most groups, the authors have been primarily interested in historical studies and secondarily in folklore and demography. Relatively little has been written on family patterns, family variations or family problems. Undoubtedly, considerable changes have taken place, but what they are and how they have affected family relations, we do not know. This is an important neglected area in Canadian ethnic group research" (1964: 64).

Given the centrality of ethnicity in Canadian history, this is, to say the least, a curious state of affairs. For as Kralt (1977: 1) reminds us, "With the exception of some 300,000 of Canada's Native Peoples, today's entire Canadian population consists of immigrants and their descendants." No doubt, many individuals are only dimly aware of their ethnic roots or choose to retain only selected and superficial vestiges of this once primordial social identity. For others, however, conscious or latent facets of ethnicity continue to shape their lives from birth to death. Whatever the contemporary meaning and relevance of ethnicity—and there is much disagreement on this issue with some observers proclaiming its waning and others its resurgence—any failure to consider ethnicity as it is manifested in the family, impoverishes our understanding of both social phenomena.

Our primary purpose in this paper is to see how far we have come

*I wish to acknowledge my indebtedness to my friends and colleagues, professors Charles David Axelrod and G. N. Ramu, for their helpful comments on earlier drafts of this chapter.

since Elkin's evaluation. This will entail an exploration of what is known and unknown or problematic about ethnic families in Canada, based mainly on selected sociological and anthropological materials. Our point of departure will be a brief discussion of the socio-psychological concept of "ethnic group" and the relationships between the family and ethnicity.

ETHNIC GROUPS AND ETHNICITY

The term "ethnic group", as it is conventionally defined and used here, refers to those who conceive of themselves, and are so viewed by others, as sharing a distinctive social and cultural heritage that is passed on from generation to generation. This sense of a unique identity may be based upon the criteria of racial, religious, or national origin, or some combination of these social categories (Gordon, 1964: 27; Shibutani and Kwan, 1965: 47; Mindel and Habenstein, 1964: 4). The extent to which individuals identify with and participate in socially significant activities of the ethnic community is influenced by a host of psychological, sociological, and historical variables. (The same may be said for differences in commitment between ethnic groups.) Our guiding premise is that the family setting is a major sociological determinant in patterning attitudes and behaviours and is a primary institutional bridge between individuals, and ethic groups, and the wider society.

Although the range of ethnic groups in Canada is as varied as its geography, certain dimensions of ethnicity have historically been more conspicuous than others. In order to keep this discussion within a manageable scope we have focussed upon European national ethnic groups for which data are available. The decision does not mean to deny the importance of race and religion but to have included all ethnic groups would require a volume in itself.

THE FAMILY AND ETHNICITY

Any group bent on preserving the integrity of a distinctive cultural legacy is faced with the crucial and perplexing problem of effectively socializing a next generation to its beliefs and practices. This sociological truism underscores the strategic significance of the family—whatever its form or structure. For it is this institution that is ultimately and inextricably linked to the vitality and persistence of ethnicity, insofar as it is able and willing to foster allegiance and conformity to traditions.

In this respect, the family is the first line of defense against potentially erosive and competing assimilative pressures. As Kalbach (1974: 2) suggests, such influences are especially pervasive in urban-industrial societies which stress rationality and impersonality:

Developments in modern society have made it difficult for groups to remain regionally and culturally isolated. Increased mobility, rapid growth, and social change in general, have brought diverse cultural groups into increasing contact with the larger regional and national system. Under modern conditions, it becomes increasingly difficult to maintain strong ethnic identities arising from different cultural experiences. Educational opportunities and experience have become increasingly standardized throughout the country, and the effects of mass production and distribution, as well as the mass media have contributed to an increasing similarity of life styles from one end of the country to the other.

A similar thesis stressing convergence is advanced by Goode with specific reference to the family (1963: 1):

For the first time in world history a common set of influences—the social forces of industrialization and urbanization—is affecting every known society. Even traditional family systems in such widely separate and diverse societies such as Papua, Manus, China, and Yugoslavia are reported to be changing as a result of these forces, although at different rates of speed. The alteration seems to be in the direction of some type of conjugal family pattern—that is toward fewer kinship ties with distant relatives and a greater emphasis on the "nuclear" family unit of couple and children. . . . we are witnessing a remarkable phenomenon: The development of similar family behaviour and values among much of the world's population (emphasis in original).

In addition to these twin forces, another element that cannot be ignored in the Canadian context is linguistic homogeneity. Although there are variations between older and more recent ethnic groups in retention of their mother tongues, the increased dominance of English is clear: "By far the major language transfer in Canada has been from all languages (including French mother tongue) to English home language" (Kralt, 1977: 37).[1] Similar trends were found in a study of the ten largest non-official language groups in five metropolitan areas (O'Bryan, Reitz, and Kuplowska, 1976). If we accept the axiom that language is the lifeblood of ethnicity and is nourished within the family, these patterns have profound implications for the future of ethnicity.

Each ethnic group evolves different sets of responses to alien influences which are filtered through the family. As Mindel and Habenstein (1976: 7) put it, "One of the most significant ways in which an ethnic culture is expressed is through those activities that we identify as family activities. . . . If traditional ethnic values are to be found anywhere, they will be found in the family."

Having set down some of the general issues and before proceeding to specific studies, let us try to locate some of the broad contours of ethnicity in Canada by examining some demographic trends. This account will necessarily be abbreviated and those interested in more detailed expositions are referred to several reports that draw upon the census and vital statistics (Kralt, 1977; Kalbach, 1976: 11–76; Kubat and Thornton, 1974; Kalbach and McVey, 1971; Kalbach, 1970).

ETHNIC DISTRIBUTION

The population of Canada rose from approximately 3.7 million in 1871 to 21.6 million in 1971. The ethnic distribution has been relatively stable over this period with immigration peaking between 1900–30 and after the Second World War. Although the proportion of persons identifying themselves as British (English, Irish, Scottish, and others) has declined from a high of 60 per cent in 1871 to 45 per cent in 1971, this census group[2] is dominant in all regions except Quebec and the Prairie provinces.

Despite recent decreases in fertility and the absence of significant immigration, Canadians of French origin are concentrated in Quebec (79 per cent) and account for about 29 per cent of the population—the position they have historically maintained. The residual category "All Other" includes European other than British and French, Asiatics, Native Peoples, and others. The largest European ethnic groups in 1971 were the Germans (6 per cent), Italians (3.4 per cent), Ukrainians (2.7 per cent), Dutch (2 per cent), Scandinavians (1.8 per cent), Jews (1.4

per cent), and Poles (1.5 per cent). During the intercensal decade 1961–71, the largest increases were recorded by East Indians, Italians, Greeks, Jews, Portuguese, and Chinese. If these trends continue "it appears likely that the ethnic origins of the population will probably be divided between the 'French' ethnic group and 'All Other' ethnic groups each having about 30 per cent of the total population and the other 40 per cent being of British origins" (Kralt, 1977: 5).

At first glance, these figures support the image of Canada as a multi-ethnic society. What they do not reveal, however, is that the influence of the English extends far beyond their numerical superiority into every major institution (Porter, 1965; Forcese, 1975). This fact, along with their linguistic hegemony, raises two important questions that are related closely to the notions of convergence and homogeneity. To what degree do the family patterns of this dominant group serve as models for other ethnic groups to emulate? Second, is there anything distinctively "English" or "Anglo" about such configurations or do they represent the Canadian version of the global trend toward a conjugal form of family organization? Obviously, we cannot begin to address these issues without first looking at specific studies of family patterns among various ethnic groups.

ETHNIC FAMILY PATTERNS

English

We are virtually ignorant of English-Canadian family patterns. Because of the lack of studies at the time, Elkin did not even include those of English origin in his survey of ethnics and even a cursory examination of the literature indicates that the situation has not changed significantly since then.

One of the earliest and most frequently cited studies on English Canadians, *Crestwood Heights* (Seeley, Sim, and Loosley, 1956), was based on research conducted after the Second World War. The authors of this detailed analysis, spanning five years of interviews and observations, describe and dissect the social life of an affluent, upper-middle-class Toronto suburb which was predominantly English but with a substantial Jewish minority. The picture that emerges depicts the stereotypical isolated nuclear family of a socially mobile community based on romantic love between spouses with minimal ties with other kin. Within the small family unit the husband's primary function is to earn an income and the wife's to express the family's social position by keeping the home running smoothly through her roles as social director, child-raiser, and consumer. Ideally, an egalitarian atmosphere prevails and there is an emphasis on the development of individuality, autonomy, respectability, and achievement. Children are an important focus during their tenure in the household and the philosophy guiding their nurture is sensible and balanced—neither over-solicitous nor over-protective. Fathers are mildly patriarchal by the standards of previous generations and mothers the emotional hub of the family and marriage. Daily routines and tasks in the home reflect the economic division of labour and are divided into masculine and feminine spheres.

All this is not to suggest that strains are absent. For example, women tend to rely heavily on a variety of "experts" for guidance in such matters as child-rearing, education, etc., whose approaches are viewed with scepticism by men. This is illustrative of numerous other cleavages in the belief systems of men and women. Although feminist ideals did not become articulated until many years after this study, the seeds of the ideology and the "problem" are clearly delineated by the authors.

Despite its vintage, *Crestwood Heights* has become a minor classic and illuminates two issues that continue to concern family sociologists. First, Seeley, *et al.*, found no consistent differences in the family relations of Jews and Anglos. This suggests that at a particular class level ethnicity is neither salient nor consequential. Second, Larson (1976: 59–60) and others postulate that the family described in this report represents the ideal-typical Canadian family that later generations of ethnics approximate. As we shall see, existing studies support this position. However, we would add that there does not appear to be anything specifically "Canadian" about this model and that its essentials conform to the global conjugal form that transcends national boundaries. Although lack of comparative materials at the time made it difficult to substantiate the impression of apparent convergence, this same point is cogently made by Riesman in his introduction to the book: "In fact, there is almost nothing in the book which strikes me as peculiarly Canadian, although when I visited Crestwood Heights during the course of this research I felt

I was in the presence of three provincialisms: towards London, towards Hollywood–New York, and towards Tel Aviv" (1956: xi).

No comparable work has appeared since *Crestwood Heights* was published. Instead, the literature on English Canadians consists of a handful of studies dealing with specific aspects of family and kinship (e.g., Osterreich, 1965; Pineo, 1968; Irving, 1972. For detailed discussions of these and other works see Chapter 6). These investigations reveal that urban English Canadians of all classes, like their counterparts in the United States and Western Europe, participate in extensive-kin networks involving mutual aid, affection, and frequent contact despite geographical and social mobility. If these ties are not as elaborate as those found in pre-industrial societies, they are still more prevalent and socially significant than those in *Crestwood Heights*.

Larson (1976: 61) has summarized a number of surveys conducted during the past few years on college students' attitudes toward courtship, marital roles, sex, children, divorce, the employment of women, etc. The most striking differences were between the sexes with women being significantly more egalitarian and less conservative in their views than men—a pattern adumbrated, as we have seen, in *Crestwood Heights*. Larson cautiously concludes that, "collectively, these papers appear to document both the persistence of middle-class Anglo-Saxon traditions and the emergence of considerably more liberal attitudes and behaviours" (1976: 61). Precisely what these traditions are, however, remains unclear since we lack a firm empirical base and time trends on English-Canadian families.

French

As compared with English Canadians, the corpus of works on French Canadians is richer though not as substantial as we would desire. A major impetus for the studies that have appeared over the past two decades has been the seminal research of Garigue (1962, 1968, 1976) which focused on the effects of urbanization on the kinship patterns of the French in Montreal. In addressing this question Garigue's accounts of urban French-Canadian families have become the standard references for this ethnic group.

In contrast to the atomistic portrait of English Canadians painted in

Crestwood Heights, Garigue's first work stressed the resilience, salience, and adaptability of family and kin ties among the French. The unique social and demographic contexts of socialization within the family also diverge from the English model (1976: 229):

The fact that a French Canadian is normally socialized in a large household conditions him at an early age to multiple kinship obligations. The socialization is carried out in a world in which authority is male and narrowly defined and emotional needs are satisfied through sibling, cousin, mother-child, grandmother, and aunt relationships. The pattern is continued in adult life, but with greater freedom since each person can have a wider range of personal preference.

These patterns, together with the stress on pre-marital female chastity, maternity, a marked division of marital roles and authority, and the structural importance of females in maintaining and managing relations with kin, comprise a set of family ideals defined as peculiarly French Canadian. Garigue also notes the interlocking nature of family and ethnicity (1976: 299):

These ideals about family and kinship were not isolated but were part of a culture complex which included the French language as spoken in Quebec, a specific system of education, membership in the Catholic Church, and various political theories about the status of French Canadians in Canada. To be a member of a French Canadian kinship group implied attitudes and beliefs about some or all of these.

Subsequent investigations have challenged (Rioux, 1959), confirmed (Carisse, 1964; Tremblay and Laplante, 1971; Moreux, 1973; Piddington, 1976), and modified (Hobart, 1962; Tremblay, 1973; Carisse, 1976a) various facets of this view of French-Canadian family patterns. Rioux argued that Garigue had underestimated the effects of urbanization on kinship because its impact had just begun to be felt. His critique is not especially convincing and although his discussion of French-speaking Acadians whose genealogical knowledge was staggering compared to Garigue's informants is fascinating, it does not, as he contends, invalidate the latter's findings concerning the viability of kinship in an urban context.

Piddington's study of a small French-Canadian community in Manitoba and the work of Tremblay and Laplante on Acadians in Nova Scotia both indicated that the patterns outlined by Garigue were also evident in rural settings. Piddington's data on kinship recognition, intermarriage of relatives, mutual aid, etc., again highlight the interconnections between the family and ethnicity (1976: 574):

The material from St. Jean Baptiste suggests that over the whole of Canada and large areas of the U.S.A. there spreads a network of recognized kinship relationships which helps to keep French Canadian aware, despite geographical dispersion of their identity as a distinct ethnic group and the advantage of belonging to such a group.

In this theoretical assessment of traditional and contemporary authority models in French-Canadian families, Tremblay (1973) corroborates and extends the observations of Garigue and others. He finds evidence of a subtle but definite shift toward a conjugal form of family with an emphasis on individualism, behavioural and ideological autonomy of the nuclear-unit form from the wider kin group, expansion of feminine roles, and the democratization of marital and parent-child relationships.

Moreux's study of a Montreal suburb and Carisse's report on working-class families indicate that the pace of change, especially with respect to the traditional status of women, has been slow and that these families generally conform to the patterns found by Garigue.

What conclusions, however tentative, may be derived from these and other inquiries? First, it appears that the family structures and processes recognized as distinctly French Canadian continue to shape and dominate the lives of many members of this ethnic group and are resistant, if not totally immune, to novel influences and ideas. Nevertheless, there is increasing evidence of change and strain at various points in the traditional system and particularly among the educated, women, and the middle classes. The pivotal role of women in effecting social change is also suggested by Carisse's study of innovative women in Quebec (1976a) and Hobart's findings that French-Canadian females were more egalitarian and permissive in their attitudes toward marriage (but not pre-marital intercourse) than English males and females and French male students (1972: 192). Moreux also alerts us to strains that are likely to accompany changes:

Among the low-income families where the father is absent most of the time and less sensitive to the attacks on his pride or less aware of modern themes, one finds a better equilibrium. He will be more willing to take a back seat or will not be aware that he plays a secondary role. Generally speaking family conflicts are at their highest in bourgeois environments where links with relatives are weak, and where the father has more difficulty relinquishing his ideal role (1973: 76).

Second, Garigue has pointed to the importance of large families in the perpetuation of family ideals. What effects the decreased birth rate will have, or to what extent these will be offset by a resurgence of ethnicity in Quebec, remain to be seen.

Finally, there are signs that family relationships once viewed as deviant and "un-French" are beginning to be accepted as legitimate variants. In discussing such alternatives, Larson (1976: 64) writes, "There is evidence of a professional family with democratic and egalitarian intra-family relations. . . . If such a family exists, it is clearly distinct from the matricentric family and might be thought of as marriage-centric. It is closer in many respects to the emergent English Canadian family than to the common ideal-typical middle-class family system."

Germans

Persons of German origin are a large and heterogeneous population concentrated mainly in the less urbanized areas of Ontario and the Prairies. We are not aware of any comprehensive sociological study of this group. There are, however, numerous reports on German-speaking subgroups such as the Hutterites (Hostetler and Huntington, 1967; Hostetler, 1974; Peter, 1976) and to a much lesser extent on Mennonites (Francis, 1955).

Among other reasons, Hutterites have been the focus of considerable interest because of their extraordinarily high birth rate, distinctive communal social organization, and ability to flourish in a society that clashes sharply with their beliefs and practices. Hutterite colonies are located primarily in isolated rural areas in the Prairie provinces, the Dakotas, Montana, and Washington, and the group is estimated to number over 22,000. Family patterns are finely attuned to fundamentalistic Christian values which stress reconciliation with God through the merging and subordination of individual identity to the community. As mirrored in the family, such commitment entails strict age and sex distinctions expressed in the authority of elders and males. Socialization is strictly controlled and involves clearly marked stages explicitly geared to progressive de-individuation and the inculcating of appropriate gender- and age-linked attitudes and behaviour. The efficacy of this process is aided by isolation from alien influences during the formative years, distinctive language and dress, and an uncompromising belief in the rectitude and desirability of the Hutterite way.

Specific family patterns deviate from those of wider Canadian society at virtually every point. Hutterite kinship is technically bilateral but with a strong patriarchal bias, patrilocal, colony exogamous, and endogamous within the three historical branches. Courtship is formally free but clearly restricted by communal norms and limited opportunities. The primary purpose of marriage is procreation and the channelling of sexuality. Romantic and affective ties between spouses are weak and their potentially disruptive force is deflected to other communal and kinship relations, e.g., sibling groups. Finally, "Hutterites have maintained the extended family. Three, sometimes four generations live in the same community although the members of an extended family might not necessarily live under the same roof" (Peter, 1976: 291).

The sources cited affirm the role of the family in perpetuating a distinct religio-ethnic culture among the Hutterites. Similar claims about the approximately 175,000 Mennonites in Canada have more often been asserted than demonstrated. Studies by Maykovich (*née* Kurokawan) on socialization (1971) and mental health (1976) in three Mennonite Orders of varying orthodoxy in Ontario raise some question about the stereotype of a solitary, culturally unique, and harmonious family system. Maykovich found clear variations in the adherence to and effectiveness of different modes of induction procedures, e.g., consistency of discipline, authoritarianism, etc., between the groups. In addition, there were patterned variations in the psychological adjustment, value conflicts, and degree of self-esteem among Mennonite children. In a related study (1975), the author compared the success values of Japanese, Italians, and Mennonites as revealed by educational and occupational aspirations. Unlike their orthodox counterparts, progressive Mennonites resembled the other two ethnic groups in having high aspirations for their children, pressuring them to achieve, placing a high value on education, and so on. Apart from these works on Hutterites and Mennonites, we know little about the family patterns of other German Canadians.

Italians

The overwhelming majority of Italians are found in the urban centres of Quebec and Ontario and are recent immigrants, i.e., persons or their parents who came to Canada after the Second World War (Kralt, 1977: 16, 19). General descriptions of this group have been provided by Hobart (1966), Richmond (1967), and Jansen (1971).

The small number of works on Italian-Canadian families are contradictory and equivocal. On the one hand, Jansen found that first-generation immigrants in Toronto were occupationally, residentially, and linguistically segregated and had minimal contacts beyond primary groups based on kinship, village, or regional affiliations. Similar patterns are reported by Boissevain (1976) for Italians in Montreal. The maintenance and commitment to traditional Italian family values predicated on strict rules of inclusion and exclusion with regard to obligations and loyalties, shields the individual and family from the strains of acculturation but also retards the rate of absorption into the larger Canadian society.

On the other hand, this socio-cultural insularity is not manifest with respect to the intermarriage of males or in the socialization of later generations. Despite the ambiguities in interpreting the sociological meaning of ethnic intermarriages,[3] a high incidence among Italian males has been noted (Hobart, 1966; Kalbach, 1974; Boissevain, 1976) and attributed, in part, to the differential rearing and treatment, e.g., stricter and more protective attitudes toward females. Detailed analyses of socialization (Danziger, 1971, 1975, 1976; Maykovich, 1975) have compared Italians who were more or less acculturated (as measured by language competence and length of residence in Canada) with native-born Canadians and other ethnics. The findings show that a large proportion of immigrant parents, acculturated and unacculturated, had high (if unrealistic) aspirations for their children, were as supportive as other groups, and were more conservative in rearing females than males.

Although admittedly exploratory, these works provide a firm point of departure for understanding change and stability in the family patterns of Italian Canadians as compared with other ethnic groups.

Ukrainians

To date, there is only one study (Hobart, 1976) of any sociological import on Ukrainian-Canadian family patterns and these data were collected over fifteen years ago. Hobart examined attitudes toward family size, marital roles, and child-bearing among a sample of three generations in Edmonton, Alberta, and surrounding rural communities. In summarizing the results, Larson (1976: 352) observes that:

The patterns of the first generation closely reflect those of their native country. Those of the third generation, in contrast, closely approximate those of the ideal-typical English Canadian family: small families, maternal employment, egalitarianism in marital and parent-child relationships, values supportive of divorce and intermarriage, and weaker kin orientations.

He further notes that because there are no comparisons with other ethnic groups, it is difficult to point to any unique characteristics of Ukrainian families. We would agree and add two further comments. First, since we do not have reliable information on the family patterns of the first generation in Canada *or* Europe, intergenerational comparisons are, at best, problematic and speculative. Second, despite the absence of comparable studies, it is apparent that the direction of changes parallel those referred to earlier by Tremblay in his discussion of emergent French-Canadian patterns. Thus, Hobart's study, with all its methodological problems, provides further evidence for the thesis of convergence.

Dutch

The Dutch live primarily in Ontario and the Prairie provinces and are less urbanized (65 per cent) than the national average (76 per cent). Compared with all other European ethnic groups excepting the Hutterites, they have the highest fertility as measured by the average number of children born to never-married women (Kralt, 1977: 15, 19, 56). Our knowledge of this group is limited to a single monograph on a small, self-contained farming community in rural Ontario based on field work conducted between 1965 and 1971 (Ishwaran, 1977).

A singular feature of this ethnography is the author's consideration of the historical roots of the migration including conditions in the Netherlands and the development of the community in Canada over time. Ishwaran discerns several configurations that set these Dutch apart from their neighbours and wider Canadian society. Although the effective social unit is the nuclear family, ties between families and more distant kin in Canada and the Netherlands are strong and active. The close institutional ties between the family and religion are expressed in ideals and practices that accentuate male authority, maternal and domestic roles of women, rigid socialization that is sex-based, the structural importance of he eldest child as a parental surrogate, extended-kin ties, and extremely conservative attitudes toward intermarriage, sex, contraception, and divorce. To the extent that this combination of values is realized in conjunction with the Dutch language and other customs, the community's concept of "Dutchness" is reinforced and maintained.

Ishwaran indicates that the families of Holland Marsh had, at the conclusion of his research, been successful in implementing their ideals. Nevertheless, he also detected internal and external sources of potential conflict and strain that the community would have to confront in maintaining its cultural coherence and uniqueness. These included internal divisions related to regional origins in the Netherlands, the differential commitment to communal norms between generations, the increased use of English, the diffusion of competing values through the mass media, and economic problems arising from an increase in population, and a decrease in arable lands.

Jews

Data from the 1971 Census show that Jewish Canadians are concentrated in Montreal, Toronto, and Winnipeg. They have the lowest fertility and highest incomes of any group we have considered, are highly educated, and are primarily in professional, managerial, and technical occupations (Kralt, 1977: 14, 55, 66, 67).

Apart from such demographic profiles and historical descriptions of pre-migratory *shtetls*, i.e., small towns in Eastern Europe, factual accounts of Jewish family patterns in Canada are limited to excellent but unsystematic literary works (Richler, 1966, 1969) and unpublished theses and dissertations. One of the few published empirical studies available is by Kallen (1976) on a second-generation sample of adults in Toronto. She observes that the family in Canada carries on many of the same activities it did in the *shtetl* and serves as the focal point for more extended kinship relations and Jewish communal identity. The author goes on to explore the ways in which the family inculcates ethnic consciousness and the ideal of secular achievement through its stress on learning and formal education. The dominant familial motifs include an egalitarian marital ideology superimposed upon a sexual division of labour in domestic and occupational spheres, permissive and love-based child-bearing practices aimed at inculcating a high need to achieve, and concentration on the immediate family at the expense of more distant kin ties.

The relatively large family size and preferences (an average of 4.5 children) of this group are anomalies and probably reflect the high socio-economic status of the sample. Patterns conducive to preserving ethnic identity reported in other studies were also found in this community, e.g., residential segregation, low rates of intermarriage (Kalbach, 1974). Finally, Kallen noted a shift in the basis of ethnic consciousness from religion to various cultural aspects of Judaism and a strong identification, especially among the younger generation, with Israel. In sum, she views the family patterns of Toronto Jews as a mixture of traditional and modern influences which have been instrumental in the survival and success of this group in Canadian society. This research was conducted in 1967–68 and hence it is difficult to say how valid these generalizations are today.

Poles

Individuals of Polish descent are found mainly in Ontario and the Prairie provinces and numbered about 317,000 in 1971. According to a recent study of this ethnic group (Radecki and Heydenkorn, 1976: 128), "the family, . . has been almost totally neglected or ignored by writings dealing with the Polish group in Canada. Only one novel, based on research, deals extensively with Polish families in Canada."

In evaluating the changes that have taken place over time, the authors trace the evolution of traditional patriarchal- and extended-family patterns in Poland to the predominantly conjugal system characteristic of contemporary Canada. In Canada, traditional values, e.g., undisputed male authority, arranged marriage, large families, harsh child-rearing, care of the aged, etc., were undermined and altered by the absence of supporting institutions such as the church, geographical dispersion and isolation, and the exposure of the young to the Canadian educational system.

In a study of postwar immigrant families in Toronto (Radecki, 1970), it was found that the historical trend toward conjugality had accelerated. This was indicated by smaller family sizes and preferences, focus on the nuclear unit, rejection of traditional values by youth, working wives and their increased participation in decision-making, marriage based on personal preference, and the institutionalization of the aged.

The general trends noted by Radecki and Heydenkorn are summarized as follows:

New patterns of family interaction and new attitudes and beliefs are plainly discernible not only among the post-war immigrants but also among the whole Polish aggregate in Canada. Nuclear family orientations are slowly replacing the traditional extended family values. There is a generally greater permissiveness and very little authoritarianism on the part of the father; equally noticeable is the abandonment of previously rigidly held attitudes and values. It is likely that the Polish family in Canada is fast becoming indistinguishable from the Anglo-Saxon urban Canadian family, sharing many of its values and attitudes in parent-child and husband-wife relationships. The changes have taken place here while much traditionalism still seems to remain in Poland (1976: 137).

CONCLUSIONS

This all too brief sketch of ethnic families leads to a number of conclusions some of which are more secure than others. First, it is amply clear that adequate and systematic data, historical and contemporary, are scarce and there is little indication that researchers have given high priority to this area. To say that we know little is not to admit total ignorance but reminds us that caution should be exercised in interpreting current patterns or predicting future trends.

Second, the thesis of convergence advanced by Goode and others is, *with certain qualifications*, applicable to a large if unknown proportion of Canadian families and together with other changes in Canadian society suggests the waning importance of ethnicity. An extreme formulation of this position is exemplified by Kralt (1977: 81–82) concluding his careful examination of census materials on a variety of social and demographic characteristics of ethnic groups:

Although there are exceptions to the rule, it seems to the author that Canadian society is not the multi-ethnic society it is often conceived to be. . . . it would appear that the differences between ethnic groups are as much due to the time the individual has been exposed to Canadian society as to ethnic origin in and of itself. . . . With the almost universal adoption of the English or French language by nearly the entire population, it seems likely that Canadian society will effectively consist of two dominant groups with generally similar values, i.e., those values associated with urban, industrial societies. The impact of ethnic origin, as it has been characteristically understood and examined seems to be at an end. The only major exception to this generalization being the Native Peoples of Canada.

Our own reading of the fragmentary research available presses toward a similar judgment but with reservations stemming, paradoxically, from the very deficiences of the materials themselves. Aggregate demographic data, e.g., fertility, language loyalty, etc., are generated by complex family structures and processes that we are only beginning to explore, no less comprehend. Moreover, a crucial part of Goode's argument that has not been sufficiently appreciated, emphasizes that even if all family systems are moving toward some form of the conjugal pattern, the trend is not necessarily uniform, continuous, or simply a function of industrialization and urbanization. Changes in values and ideologies as well as commitments to existing family arrangements also affect the rate of change independently. With regard to the groups we have considered, signs of convergence are manifest in some instances, e.g., English, French, and questionable in others, e.g., Dutch, Italians, Hutterites. If those who predict the impending demise of ethnicity are even partially correct, then the latter groups represent isolated, rearguard pockets of ethnicity destined for cultural envelopment (or decimation) by the larger society. This may be so, but until we have more detailed and reliable reports over time, such pronouncements must be treated as hypotheses rather than accomplished facts.

Finally, there are sufficient traces of resistance to the pervasive forces of standardization and rationality in urban-industrial societies to give us some reason to believe that obituaries attesting the death of ethnicity may be premature. As Mindel and Habenstein (1976: 428) concluded after evaluating the current status ethnic families in the United States:

Somewhere between these great grindstones that would pulverize traditional family organization a type of family, once consigned to oblivion—being ground or melted down—persists: protean, adaptive, conservatizing, generating meanings, and forming a sense of identity partly from the realities of an earlier time, partly from the exigencies of the present. The bonds of ethnicity are reminiscent of the life forces of whose desert creatures that, buried in the earth for years, come "alive" again when it rains.

Precisely how closely this vision pertains to Canadian society will remain an open question until scholars from all disciplines (including writers and poets) begin to consider this subject worthy of their attention.

Notes

1. The extent to which this and other social trends will be affected by the political situation in Quebec remains to be seen.
2. The census definition of ethnicity is based on the country of birth of the nearest paternal ancestor born outside of North America. The question used to determine ethnicity in the 1971 census was: "To what ethnic or cultural group did you or your ancestor (on the male side) belong to on coming to this continent?"
3. See chapters 1, 2, and 22 for discussions of the role and significance of intermarriage. In one of the few published studies of the internal dynamics of intermarriage between English and French Canadians, Carisse (1976b) found that the cultural orientations of spouses, e.g., choice of community, relevant social networks, mass media, language, etc., generally mirrored English dominance in the wider society. This skewing was especially marked in a situation where the husband is English.

SELECTED BIBLIOGRAPHY

Canadian Ethnic Studies. Bulletin of the Research Centre for Canadian Ethnic Studies, University of Calgary.

GOODE, WILLIAM J. *World Revolution and Family Patterns*, Glencoe, Illinois. 1963

GORDON, MILTON M. *Assimilation in American Life*, New York. 1964

GREGOROVICH, ANDREW, ed. *Canadian Ethnic Groups Bibliography*, Toronto. 1972

ISHWARAN, K., ed. *The Canadian Family*, revised ed., Toronto. 1976

KALBACH, WARREN E. *The Impact of Immigration on Canada's Population*, Ottawa. 1970

KRALT, JOHN. *Ethnic Origins of Canadians*, Ottawa. 1977

LARSON, LYLE E. *The Canadian Family in Comparative Perspective*, Scarborough. 1976

MINDEL, CHARLES H., and ROBERT W. HABENSTEIN, eds. *Ethnic Families in America:* 1976 *Patterns and Variations*, New York.

TAVUCHIS, NICHOLAS and WILLIAM J. GOODE, eds. *The Family Through Literature*, 1975 New York.

JOHN F. PETERS

Divorce is of concern to any modern society for three very basic reasons. First, it is often viewed as a "failure" of one of the most fundamental institutions of our society, the family. Second, it invariably creates a trauma in the conjugal relationship, a relationship viewed culturally as supportive. Third, divorce is perceived as upsetting, at the least, and possibly detrimental to any children involved.

In modern society, divorce is a formal and judicial term. Only those individuals who are legally married can be legally separated. The term is not applied to the termination of cohabitation or a common-law union. Some countries such as Argentina, Columbia, Paraguay, the Philippines, and Spain have no legal provision for divorce. This does not mean that these countries have a higher percentage of "happy" marriages, but rather that political and religious influences have not permitted a legal dissolution of the marriage.

Where divorces are not permitted, usually only the husband can establish unions with other females, even if it is not a legally binding union (Goode, 1971: 303). Multiple-husband unions are usually not sanctioned, giving evidence of male power. In western societies where separation is common there are usually strong norms opposing the wife's cohabitation with a second mate, and much less sanction against the husband for similar behaviour. Furthermore, extra-marital sexual behaviour is thought to be more common with husbands than wives.

Most societies place a strong value upon marriage and family solidarity. This small-group and kin-bond solidarity is viewed as functional for the stability of both the society and its individual members. However, there are few, if any, societies, whether preliterate or modern, where marriage dissolution is not found. In a sample of forty societies, Murdock found only one, the Incas, where there was no provision for dissolving marriage (1950: 195–201). In an Eskimo tribe, women sometimes marry and divorce two or three times a year (Stephens, 1963: 234–35). Among the Navaho, only one in four were reported to have lived with the same spouse throughout their life. Murdock reports that among the Crow, "divorce is exceedingly frequent and a man subjects himself to ridicule if he lives too long with one woman" (1950: 198).

Divorce rates in modern countries have fluctuated considerably over the past decade. Generally industrialization is directly related to the divorce rate. Japan is one notable exception; its divorce rate declined with the introduction of industry. The United States currently has the highest divorce rate followed by the U.S.S.R., Denmark, and Western Germany. Canada's present divorce rate is rising and is currently about one-half that of the United States.

This chapter deals with divorce and marriage dissolution as it related to the family and the individual within the historical and socio-economic structure of Canadian society. The laws and social attitudes toward divorce have changed considerably in Canada in the past two decades. More changes are inevitable. First, we will offer a few theoretical perspectives, and this will be followed by a discussion of demographic and socio-psychological factors associated with divorce. The last section will focus on some legal aspects of divorce in Canada.

THEORETICAL PERSPECTIVES

Before discussing details pertaining to divorce in Canada it is appropriate to present a brief overview of the sociological perspectives related to this topic. This overview is somewhat selective, since an exhaustive treatment would entail much more detail than the limits of this chapter allow. The student will, however, find sufficient material to be sensitized to sociological explanations.

One way of looking at divorce is to relate background characteristics with divorce proneness (Goode, 1976: 538–39). Characteristics such as an urban background, marriage at a young age, short acquaintanceship, a short engagement, parents with an unhappy marriage, non-attenders of church, kin disapproval of marriage, dissimilar backgrounds, and disagreement of husband- and wife-role obligations yield a greater proneness to divorce. Most of the findings suggest that the relationship of these background characteristics toward marital instability are correct.

Another way of looking at unstable marriages is to focus upon the kind of relationship (Nye and Berardo, 1973: 497–500). Three types have been suggested; the aborted marriage, the mediocrely functioning family, and the interrupted functioning family.

Troubles in the aborted marriage are evident very early in the relationship. In some cases a normal sexual relation is not realized or the husband is continuously unemployed. In other cases the couple is not prepared to take on adult work roles and responsibilities normative to marriage. In other instances a spouse may, soon after marriage, realize that the partner is not the one with whom he/she wants to spend his/her life. The aborted marriage may be termed a non-marriage because marriage in the sociological sense never did exist. A set of functioning relationships necessary for a permanent marriage were never established (by the couple).

The second marriage type is the mediocrely functioning family. Familial roles and family functioning are present but only minimally so. The level of material well-being is often marginal. The home is not attractive; emotional needs are rarely met. There is bickering and quarrelling. Marriage is unrewarding and does not yield intense positive emotional effect. The marriage may last for years and should divorce occur, emotional disruption is minimal.

The third type of marriage, according to Nye and Berardo, is the interrupted functioning marriage. In this relationship the family functioned very well and was characterized by strong positive effects. The marriage was satisfying to both spouses. The satisfying marriage is interrupted; possibly because of the strong attachment of one spouse to a third person, alcoholism, or a priority of work over family.

Farber suggests a permanent availability model for contemporary society, in which a potential mate, whether single, divorced, widowed, or married, is theoretically available to any cross-sexed individuals (cf. Farber, 1964: 109–12). This model may seem appropriate in a society where divorce is on the increase and remarriage is common.

A marriage is based upon a voluntary association and when the commitment diminishes to the stage of greater commitment to another cross-sexed person, a new association may be established. Thus there is a sense of being permanently available. "All members of a society face a constant pressure to be highly competent in interpersonal relations if they wish to maintain their current marriage and remain in a favourable competitive position in the perennial marriage market" (Farber, 1964:

478). From this perspective, it appears that divorce is functional and remains as an inevitable part of the western marriage process.

A significant way in which to look at divorce, according to Levinger, is to view it as the final step in a process of estrangement (1976). Levinger borrows his construct from exchange theory[1] in which a relationship is viewed as an exchange between costs and rewards. Positive rewards would include love, material goods, services, status, and comfort. Dissatisfactory rewards could be discomfort, irritation, derogatory statements, no affirmation, or decreasing status. Relationships cost in time, in money, and in physical and mental energies. A relationship becomes strengthened as the rewards exceed or are weighted close to the costs. Costs which exceed the rewards result in fragmented or strained relationships.

Levinger's theory is based upon three basic concepts; attraction forces, barrier forces, and alternative attractions. These forces and/or alternatives have a bearing upon the actual choice of marital dissolution, combining psychological and economic variables.

Forces of *attraction* are those factors which give an individual second thoughts about severing the marital relationship. These attractions include the family income (for the high-income), home ownership, occupational status (usually that of the husband), ability to communicate with one another, sexual enjoyment, companionship, and esteem. *Barrier* forces are those factors encouraging the permanence of the existing relationship. These forces are numerous and include expenses of the divorce, separate living costs, obligation toward the marital bond, religious constraint, pressures from the primary group and community, and care of the children. When barrier forces are weak, alternatives which appear attractive will be investigated.

Alternative attractions are the pull factors to other options. This may include independence and a greater opportunity for self-actualization. For some it may mean alternate affectional rewards in a companion, possibly eventual remarriage. Many women in contemporary society are attracted to independent social and economic status.[2]

These perspectives provide us with clues to understand various forces that precipitate dissolution of marriage in our society. In the next section, we will outline the increasing divorce rate in Canada.

THE INCIDENCE OF DIVORCE

Divorce Rate

We have already indicated that a country's divorce rate is not necessarily a measurement of the marital satisfaction of conjugal members in that society. The divorce rate may be measured in one of several ways: *crude rate, refined rate,* or *annual rate.*

The crude divorce rate is based upon the number of divorces per unit of the entire population. This unit may be 1,000 (U.N. Demographic Year Book), or 100,000 as in Tables 8:1 and 8:2. The crude divorce rate is based upon persons of all ages. These people are "not at risk" in divorce, since only the married can opt for divorce. Such statistics would be somewhat unrealistic because of the age composition of some countries (such as 50 per cent of the population under fifteen years of age).

The refined rate relates divorce with a more specific population, usually women or married women over fourteen years of age. This measurement excludes the single, the widowed, and the divorced. It relates divorce more directly to those eligible for divorce.

Table 8:1   Number of Divorces and Rates per 100,000 population, Canada, 1947, 1957, 1968–76

Year	Number	Rate
1947	8,213	65.4
1957	6,688	40.3
1968	11,343	54.8
1969	26,093	124.2
1970	29,775	139.8
1971	29,685	137.6
1972	32,389	148.4
1973	36,704	166.1
1974	45,019	200.6
1975	50,611	222.0
1976	54,207	235.8

Source: Vital Statistics, Vol. II, Marriage and Divorce, 1976.

The annual rate may be presented as an absolute number of annual divorces: Canada, in 1976, had 54,207 divorces. Such a figure would not show a country's net population increase or decrease, the number of people in each age cohort, or the number of marrieds. Such a number, in itself, is rather unproductive for sociological analysis.

A measurement which the popular press frequently uses is a comparison of the number of divorces with the number of marriages in any given year. Canada would now have a ratio of 1 to 4, and in the United States the ratio would approximate 1 to 2. In some states the number of annual divorces exceeds the number of marriages. The press takes delight in such sensationalism and generally interprets such statistics as showing the increasing decadence of the family. The error of this measurement lies in the fact that while the number of those divorcing comes from a population who have been married two, ten, or possibly thirty-five years, those marrying represent a smaller population of nuptial ties in any one year. The composition of the two populations is different. The number of annual divorces could exceed the number of marriages.[3]

In Canada, the crude and refined rates for divorce are used. The crude rate is calculated against 100,000 population, and when used in comparison with other countries that use a base of 1,000 population the figure must be divided by 100 (U.N. Demographic Year Book). The refined rate is calculated on 100,000 married women over fourteen years of age. The annual rate is sometimes used to show the percentage increase or decrease from one year to the next.

Divorce Rate in Canada

Canada's divorce rate is now 236 per 100,000 population or a total of 54,207 for 1976 (Table 8:1). This represents an increase of 7.1 per cent over 1975. Canada's annual percentage increase has averaged almost 11 per cent since 1969. The divorce rate varies considerably from one province to another, but generally consistent patterns are seen. British Columbia has the highest provincial rate (333.7 per cent)[4] and Alberta a close second (309.9 per cent). These two western provinces historically have fluctuated with the highest divorce rates in Canada. Quebec's divorce rate (243.6 per cent) now exceeds that of Ontario's (224.9 per cent), a position it has held only since 1974. Until that year

Quebec's divorce rate was considerably lower than the Canadian average. Newfoundland is the province with the lowest rate (76.0 per cent). All provinces showed an increase over 1975's divorce rates except Manitoba (−2.5 per cent).

Table 8:2   Divorces by Provinces, in Number and Rate per 100,000 population, 1976

Province	Number	Rate
Canada	54,207	235.8
Newfoundland	424	76.0
Prince Edward Island	116	98.1
Nova Scotia	1,753	211.6
New Brunswick	938	138.5
Quebec	15,186	243.6
Ontario	18,589	224.9
Manitoba	1,941	190.0
Saskatchewan	1,207	131.0
Alberta	5,697	309.9
British Columbia	8,231	333.7
Yukon	67	306.8
Northwest Territories	58	136.1

Source: *Vital Statistics*, Vol. II, Marriage and Divorce, 1976.

Rises and declines in provincial rates should be looked at over the long term, especially where the frequency of divorce is relatively small. The province of Prince Edward Island is a case in point. In 1975 there were 75 divorces; in 1976, 116. This is an increase of 55 per cent. It would be unrealistic to establish this as a trend for P.E.I. with so few divorces over a short period of time, particularly when the previous year showed a decrease in the number of divorces.

Canadian divorce laws were altered considerably in 1968. In the following year the rate jumped in all provinces, and from 54.8 to 124.2 for all of Canada. The rate has consistently risen since that time, with the exception of 1971 (Table 8:1). It is significant to note that the years following the Second World War also showed a relatively high divorce rate, which later subsided.

Of all divorces registered in Canada in 1975, 5.5 per cent had had a previous divorce. Of the 197,585 marriages in the same year, approximately 11.5 per cent involved at least one divorced member. Remarriage is a common topic of discussion among the divorced, indicating that the institution of marriage is deeply imbedded with the culture of our society (see Chapter 9). However, the number of divorced who remarry is a small proportion of all annual marriages, and thus Farber's permanent-availability model is hardly applicable in Canada at this time.

Social and demographic variables related to divorce will be treated in the succeeding paragraphs.

FACTORS ASSOCIATED WITH DIVORCE

Age at Marriage

Studies on divorce consistently show a positive relationship between early marriage and divorce. This holds true in Canada as well. In 1976, 24 per cent of all brides and 7 per cent of all grooms who married under 20 years of age (*cf. Vital Statistics*, Vol. II, Remarriage and Divorces, 1976, pp. 25, 39). Forty-two per cent of all women and thirteen per cent of all men who divorced were first married under 20 years of age. Thus the proportion who divorce from this age cohort of marriage is disproportionately high. Those divorcing who were first married in the most frequently marriageable age cohort (20–24) represented 39 per cent of the women and 54 per cent of the husbands of all divorces, again a slightly larger proportion for those marrying at that age. Age at marriage is inversely related with the divorce rate.[5]

There are several factors which make early marriage susceptible to divorce. Restricted experience or romantic ideals void of realism before marriage do not form the building blocks for wholesome conjugal bonds later. A limited exposure to numerous interpersonal relationships in varied situations minimizes the coping facility of the young marrieds. A tiff or argument may readily be misinterpreted as lack of commitment or love.

The average age of husband and wife at time of divorce is 38.2 and 35.3 respectively. This age is gradually declining. Alberta has the highest percentage of husbands and wives divorcing under 20 and between 20–24 years of age (Peters, 1976a: 338).

Duration of Previous Marriage

On the average, marriages which terminated with divorce in Canada lasted approximately eleven years (Table 8:3). Divorces taking place after less than five years marriage duration comprise 16.7 per cent of all divorces, while marriages of less than ten years' duration comprise

Table 8:3   Divorces by Duration of Marriage and Median Duration of Marriage, Canada, 1976

	Divorces	Per Cent
Under 1 year	153	0.3
1 year	1,026	1.9
2 years	1,862	3.4
3 years	2,585	4.8
4 years	3,411	6.3
1–4 years	8,885	16.4
5 years	3,525	6.5
6 years	3,558	6.5
7 years	3,258	6.0
8 years	2,919	5.4
9 years	2,741	5.1
5–9 years	16,002	29.5
10–14 years	9,844	18.2
15–19 years	6,876	12.7
20–24 years	5,203	9.6
25–29 years	3,633	6.7
30+ years	3,548	6.5
Not Stated	67	0.1
Total	54,207	100.0

Source: *Vital Statistics*, Vol. II, Marriage and Divorce, 1976, Table 19, p. 41.

30 per cent of all divorces (1972–75). The modal year of marriage duration of the divorced is five years, though the years between four and nine years of marriage duration are each fairly comparable. Canada's duration of marriage for the divorced is somewhat higher than the sta-

tistics in the United States, a median of seven years in 1967. Many divorces in Canada are preceded by two and three years of separation, giving evidence of marriage breakdown long before the legal divorce. The trend between 1972 and 1974 has been a gradual decrease in the duration of marriage for those divorcing.

Rural-Urban Contrasts

Western societies generally show a higher rate of divorce in urban rather than rural areas. Urban communities demonstrate characteristics which are more vulnerable to divorce: secularism, anonymity, nuclear family, individual goals over collective goals.

This pattern is true for Canada as well. Generally the highly urban provinces show a higher divorce rate than the more rural provinces. Cities do show a higher divorce rate than the rural areas. Edmonton, Calgary, and Vancouver have a high divorce rate while cities in the east have a comparatively low divorce rate (Peters, 1976a: 343).

Income

U.S. studies show an inverse relation between income and divorce. Social workers in Canada have indicated to the author that this relationship has not been true in this country. They suggest that many resort to separation, sometimes termed "the poor man's divorce". The Taylor and Schacter recent research in Manitoba gives empirical evidence that there has been an increase in divorce concerning people on welfare, from both rural and urban areas since 1968 (1977). Increasingly, Canadians from lower-class families will be exposed to divorce, and will consider divorce as an option.

The preceding variables considered are consistent with Goode's comments of divorce proneness and background characteristics mentioned earlier in the chapter.

Children

Children were at one time considered to be a stabilizing influence upon the family. Current practice suggests that a broken home is no worse than that of a two-parent family where parents do not complement one another.

The number of dependent children involved in divorce cases is increasing—59,220 in 1976. Almost sixty per cent of all divorces involve children. The majority of these divorces concern one (22.6 per cent) or two (19 per cent) children. There is considerable variation in the number of dependents by province. The Yukon represents a high percentage of one-child dependent families in divorce while P.E.I. and Ontario have a high percentage of childless couples petitioning for divorce. If the wife petitions for the divorce she is more likely to be granted custody of the child(ren) than if the husband petitions. Petitioning wives gained custody in 88 per cent of the cases, while husbands were granted custody in 36 per cent of the cases in which they petitioned for the divorce (1972–75).

Petitioner

Females petitioned for divorce in 66 per cent of the cases in 1976. Such statistics should not necessarily suggest that wives are more irritable about conjugal relationships, or are to blame for divorce proceedings. In some cases the couple may find it more convenient for the wife to petition. In western society the wife is generally considered to have most at stake in the marriage. It is therefore conceivable that when proper consideration is not perceived as being received from the husband toward the children or herself she is more likely to initiate the divorce.

In Reed's (1975) study of almost 120,000 divorces between 1969–72 he found that 4.3 per cent or over 5,000 withdrew their petition. Wives were slightly more likely to withdraw their petition than husbands.

Alleged Grounds

Separation for not less than three years was the reason most frequently (1 per cent) used as grounds for divorce in 1976 (Table 8:4). This figure has been relatively stable during the past five years, but is expected to decline shortly, as a younger population with altered views concerning the sanctity of marriage seek divorce. Adultery is the second most frequent grounds stated for divorce (30 per cent). Other alleged grounds often used are mental cruelty (17.7 per cent) and physical cruelty (14.5 per cent). Mental cruelty as a ground for divorce is showing a gradual increase, and is expected to continue to rise gradually. Desertion for not less than five years is also showing a a steady decline—from 6.4 per cent in 1970 to 2.8 per cent in 1976.

Table 8:4   Alleged Grounds for Divorce by Type of Offence and Reasons for Marital Breakdown, Canada, 1976

Alleged Grounds	1976 Per Cent
Marital Offence:	
Adultery	30.4
Physical Cruelty	14.5
Mental Cruelty	17.7
Other	0.3
Sub-total	62.9
Marriage breakdown by reason of:	
Addiction to alcohol	2.5
Separation for not less than three years	31.0
Desertion by petitioner not less than five years	2.8
Other	0.8
Sub-total	37.1
Total	100.0

Source: *Vital Statistics*, Vol. II, Marriage and Divorce, 1976, Table 21, p. 42.

In some cases a combination of grounds might be used: mental and physical cruelty, adultery, and separation. At times, grounds are established to "fit" the law, or "fit" the disposition of the judge. Incompatibility is not acceptable by the law as grounds for divorce. In such instances mental cruelty might be used. However, this ground must be substantiated by a medical doctor and/or psychiatrist.

Reed's (1975) study carefully analysed the disposition of the almost one hundred cases which were withdrawn from the courts between 1969–72. The grounds of mental cruelty (3.9 per cent) were most likely to be dismissed by the court, while adultery was the most successful (0.8 per cent dismissed). Addiction to alcohol or drugs, mental cruelty, and physical cruelty were grounds which were most often discontinued by the petitioner (around 9 per cent). Adultery (4.9 per cent) and separation/desertion (2.4 per cent) were the least likely to be discontinued.

Reed's work also showed some interesting data on the alleged grounds for divorce and the duration of formal legal proceedings. The single ground of alleged adultery or imprisonment were more likely than others to be completed in less than three months' time. Petitions citing mental cruelty, addiction, or adultery in combination with another offence take more legal time.

LEGAL DIMENSIONS

Past and Present Divorce Laws

Unlike our neighbours to the south, the granting of a divorce is a federal matter firmly established in the British North America Act, but is administered by each province. Until 1968, there were no divorce courts in Quebec or Newfoundland. Application of injured spouses in these two provinces had to be made to the federal parliament and therefore limited the accessibility of divorce for much of the population.

Canadian divorce law finds its origin in the English Matrimonial Causes Act of 1857. Adultery was the only ground for divorce (except for cruelty in N.S.). Prior to 1925 a wife could not sue for divorce unless the unfaithful husband had committed some other offence such as desertion or extreme physical cruelty (Pike, 1975: 117–18). This practice, an obvious double standard, was rooted in the Victorian belief of woman as a husband's property. Laws prior to 1968 obviously encouraged many separation arrangements, or grounds for divorce, which could "fit" the legal system.

Along with other countries, Canada developed socially and economically in the mid-twentieth century, yet her divorce laws remained archaic. Canada was the last commonwealth country to establish a legal termination of marriage on grounds other than marital infidelity. England had extended its grounds as early as 1937. The government's conservative stance was due to "the perceived opposition of some of the organized religious groups to divorce law reform and the corollary perception of French-Canadian and Quebec opposition to similar changes" (Laroque, 1969: 2). It was feared that any attempt to amend the existing law "would disrupt delicate federal-provincial and English-French relations". The Pearson government finally made changes, but this was done only after the Canadian Catholic hierarchy accepted a principle that the church's specific beliefs might be incongruous with the "good" of the society.[6]

The divorce laws are again under review. The Law Reform Commission of Canada have made recommendations ranging from grounds for divorce, property, care of children, as well as the function of the family court. The current Canadian divorce law perpetuates a "fault culture" in which one party is seen guilty and the other vindicated (*Family Law*, 1976). The law provides adversary weapons to gain revenge on separations for such things as rejection, accumulated hostility, and disappointed expectations. Spouses are placed into an adversary polarization. The vital interests of one can only be defended by attacking the other. No form of reconciliation, assistance, or adjustment is encouraged. No form of amicable relationship is pursued. Fair and constructive arrangements with respect to property, finances, or children are impossible in the present system.

One alternative to the fault principle is the adoption of a failure principle. This principle seems viable in Canada, especially when 40 per cent of all annual divorces fall under the category of marriage breakdown. Many use the category of separation for not less than three years (Table 8:4). In the U.S. at least 24 states have some form of no-fault divorce.

Some countries provide divorce by consent (Netherlands, Sweden, Japan). Critics view such a law as making a marriage a private contract, rather than a public matter. One study has shown that possibly 40 per cent of divorces lack mutual consent (Glick, 1975: 22). Divorce by consent would discriminate against the non-petitioning spouse.

The Law Reform Commission proposes that marriage dissolution be granted when the husband and wife deem the relationship to have broken down. They do not advocate that a third party, such as the court, determine the status of the relationship. Matrimonial offence or fault should be inapplicable and only "marriage breakdown" be viewed as sufficient grounds for divorce. Adversarial pleading should be removed from the court. No act of living together or separately, should prejudice legal proceedings. Dissolution hearings by the family court should be heard whether one or both spouses consider the marriage as broken. In the case of children the commission recommends an assessment conference by the court which would include a support staff person or a community-based service. Consideration of financial provision, custody, care, and access to and for the children would be the concern of this assessment group.

Along with the Commission, the Canadian Bar Association (as early as 1973) and the Federal Advisory Council on the Status of Women (1976) recommended that separation or a waiting period, whether with or without children, living together or separately, be reduced to one year. Even if one spouse opposes divorce, a one-year period is deemed appropriate.

Should a one-year separation be accepted as grounds for divorce, the grounds of imprisonment, addiction to alcohol or drugs, unknown whereabouts, a non-consummation of marriage would no longer be necessary. There would be but one ground for divorce: a twelve-month period of separation or waiting.

Divorce and Division of Assets

Though the establishment of the grounds for divorce and the issuance of the decree of divorce absolute is a matter of federal legislation, it is the provincial law which determines the division of assets, support, and child custody. This presents considerable interprovincial variation.

In the much publicized 1974 Murdock case the Supreme Court of Canada rejected Irene Murdock's bid of half-interest in a prosperous Alberta ranch. Despite her help in building up this family asset during 24 years of marriage, the court ruled that the property was his since it was in his name. Irene Murdock has been able to gain $65,000 in court-ordered settlements since the Supreme Court decision. The provincial court decision would have been made differently had the case been reviewed in Quebec where all property is jointly owned by the spouses. Debate over the assets related to marital dissolution continues in law and in the courts.

Laws with respect to assets in the past favoured the husband. In other cases the "guilty" person or the "loose living" husband was more severely penalized with higher maintenance costs. Ontario's Attorney General appropriately commented that we need to "sweep away centuries of legal tradition and ramshackle[d] structures of marriage law".

Provinces are changing laws so they are much more egalitarian. Ontario distinguishes between family and business assets. Family assets would be split 50/50 according to discretionary powers of the judge. The Law Reform Commission in Saskatchewan proposes that a couple's home be co-owned, regardless of which spouse holds the title. The Ontario Act makes the new law of the division of assets applicable to common-law relations of longer than two years. This province's Law Reform Commission advocates that contracts be established between spouses at the time of marriage, and that these contracts be reviewed annually. Some counsellors suggest that the annual contract-renewing exercise would bring tensions heretofore not present.

Divorce- and family-law reform is essential to a society which has encountered numerous social, political, and economic changes. In many homes the attraction of career "success" has left much of the child-rearing responsibilities to one spouse. To many Canadians a decent living can only be achieved if both husband and wife work. In some provinces over 40 per cent of the married women are in the work force. Some couples choose voluntary childlessness. The feminist movement and human rights laws have also done much to alter the expectations of individuals in and out of marriage. The historical roots, religious beliefs, personal needs, and social status of Canadians yield a combination of varied ideologies, particularly when related to an institution as fundamental as the family. It is unlikely that any law would satisfy all people in our heterogeneous society.

Procedures for Divorce

An estimated 90 per cent of all divorces in this country involved a solicitor. Legal fees run from $450 to $1,000 in non-contested cases. To challenge the cost of legal fees, divorce kits are issued for around $100, and the British Columbia Court Registry has issued a practical divorce guide at cost.

After contact with a solicitor has been made, a petition for divorce is filed in the provincial court.[7] The person against whom the case has been filed is "served", and 20, 40, or 60 days are established to allow him/her to make pleadings. After the allotted number of days have passed, pleadings are considered and a date is generally set for court. Depending upon court activity, the court hearing may take place in one to three months' time.

In the event that the petition has not been dismissed or discontinued a *decree nisi* is granted on the divorce. After 90 days a decree absolute is granted, unless contested by the respondent (less than one per cent do).

For the four years succeeding the Divorce Act (1968), 16 per cent of all divorce petitions were terminated in less than six months, 77 per cent in less than twelve months, and 98 per cent in two years or less (Reed, 1975).

In Canada 10 per cent of all divorce action is contested (*Studies on Divorce*, 1975: 49). It is quite common for a judge to process fifteen non-contested divorce cases in a two-hour session; some taking as little as five minutes. In witnessing divorce courtroom proceedings students of sociology of the family have often voiced surprise that a marital bond could be legally terminated so quickly. The divorce petitioners have been witnessed to show relief and pleasure.

The high frequency of divorce cases which are non-contested, and the rapidity with which they are "resolved" in the courtroom raise questions about the purpose of radical law reform. Fault-finding and mud-slinging appear to be minimal, particularly where there is little or no property, and no children. Contested cases for child custody, visiting rights, or the division of a sizeable estate do produce a battlefront in and out of the courtroom.

CONCLUSIONS

Canadian research on divorce is very recent, but is increasing in interest as traditional views of the individual and the family are being examined. Social scientists in Canada are studying divorce from a legal, economic, psychological, and sociological perspective.

This chapter has looked at some theoretical perspectives, including that of divorce proneness, types of relationship termination, permanent availability model, as well as a marital dissolution orientation which is based upon attractive and barrier forces. These perspectives help us to comprehend the sociological factors in the divorce experience. Further theoretical work that can be applied to pre-divorce and post-divorce counselling would be readily received by the many who are evaluating their conjugal relationship.

There is an inverse relation between age at marriage and divorce, and a positive relation between larger urban centres and divorce. Similarly "frontier" communities characterized by economic opportunity and a rapid population boom show a high rate of marriage dissolving. Some pilot research suggests that divorce is increasingly being considered by lower-income families.

Canada's divorce rate has increased substantially in the past decade, and will continue to rise. The institution of the family is not seriously threatened. Many who have dissolved their marriage remarry. Social stigma against divorce as well as remarriage is disintegrating. Laws for divorce grounds, child custody, and the division of financial assets are being reassessed. Changes are being made to fit the perceived social needs of our society. The average age at first marriage is slowly climbing. More individuals are opting for singlehood. Marriage contracts have been recommended. Other changes are inevitable as some couples consider a childless marriages, and others opt for cohabitation.

Notes

1. This theory was developed by Thibaut and Kelly, 1959, and later by Homans, 1961, and Blau, 1964.
2. For a more detailed explanation of this theory read George Levinger's article, "A Social Psychological Perspective on Marital Dissolution".
3. For a more detailed discussion of this topic see John Scanzoni in *Sexual Bargaining* (1972), pp. 6–13.
4. Unless otherwise indicated, all statistics are for 1976.
5. Though the use of marriage and divorce in age cohorts in the same specific year is not a true comparison, the proportions indicated are worthy of note.
6. A more detailed discussion of social issues, social attitudes, and the history of Canadian divorce laws may be found in Pike's "Legal Access and the Incidence of Divorce in Canada", Laroque's "The Evolution of the Canadian Divorce Law", Deckert's and Langelier's, "A Comparative, Crosscultural Study of Divorced Canadians", Abernathy's and Arcus', "The Law and Divorce in Canada", and *Studies on Divorce*, 1975.
7. The author is indebted to W. Douglas Miller, Barrister, Solicitor, for assistance in the details regarding filing procedures.

SELECTED BIBLIOGRAPHY

Family Law. Law Reform Commission, Information Canada.
1976
Family Law Reform. Ministry of the Attorney General, Toronto.
GLICK, PAUL. "A Demographer Looks at American Families", *Journal of Marriage*
1975   *and the Family*, Vol. 37, No. 1 (February), pp. 15–26.
GOODE, W. J. "Family Disorganization", in R. Merton and R. Nisbet, eds., *Con-*
1976   *temporary Social Problems*, Chapter 10, New York.
Journal of Social Issues. Divorce and Separation edition, Vol. 32, No. 1.
1976
LEVINGER, GEORGE. "A Social Psychological Perspective on Marital Dissolution",
1976   *Journal of Social Issues*, Vol. 32, No. 1, pp. 21–47.
PETERS, JOHN F. "Divorce in Canada: A Demographic Profile", *Journal of Com-*
1976   *parative Family Studies*, Vol. 7, No. 2, pp. 335–49.
——, ed. *Divorce in Canada*, forthcoming.
PIKE, ROBERT. "Legal Access and the Incidence of Divorce in Canada", in *The*
1975   *Canadian Review of Sociology and Anthropology*, Vol. 12, No. 2
        (May), pp. 115–33.
Vital Statistics. Volume II, Marriages and Divorces, 1975, pp. 84–205, Ottawa.
1977
WUESTER, T. S. "Canadian Law and Divorce", in S. Parvez Wakil, ed., *Marriage,*
1975   *Family, and Society: Canadian Perspectives*, Scarborough.

Remarriage

9

BENJAMIN SCHLESINGER

On examining the literature dealing with the sociology of the family in Canada, and in the United States, one would realize that the study of second marriages is a neglected area. This type of family has been generally called "reconstituted families", "blended families" or "second marriages". In this chapter, we will refer to this family pattern as "reconstituted families (RF)". Thus, a reconstituted family "is a family composed of a man and a woman, at least one of whom has been previously married and has a child or children from that previous marriage" (Schlesinger, 1975).

There are innumerable types of such reconstituted families and these are: (1) divorced man remarried to a single woman; (2) divorced man remarried to a widowed woman; (3) divorced man remarried to a divorced woman; (4) single man married to a divorced woman; (5) single man married to a widowed woman; (6) widowed man remarried to a single woman; (7) widowed man remarried to a widowed woman; (8) widowed man remarried to a divorced woman; (9) father, father's own children, and new mother; (10) mother, mother's own children, and new father; (11) father, father's own children, and mother, mother's own children.

It is clear from this list that RF can develop into complicated relationships involving former spouses, former relatives, children living with other spouses, former spouses who remarried, and friends.

In this chapter, we will briefly present a few sociological propositions related to remarriage and then provide Canadian data on various patterns of remarriage. This will be followed by a general discussion of the significant sociological characteristics of remarriages and reconstituted families. The last section includes a brief summary and conclusions.

SOCIOLOGICAL PERSPECTIVES

There is no notable theoretical perspective on reconstituted families in general and remarriages in particular. An effort to draw a few basic propositions from various published sources has been made by Goode, *et al.*, (1971: 593–95). In what follows, we will summarize a few selected propositions from the inventory compiled by Goode and his associates. We assume that this summary would, at the least, provide a general sociological understanding of remarriage and related aspects.[1]

A high divorce rate in any culture will be accompanied by a high remarriage rate. As indicated earlier, wherever institutionalized opportunities for divorce exist, it follows that similar opportunities are made available for the remarriage of those who are divorced. This is further supported by the fact that *divorced persons are more likely to remarry than to remain unmarried and in contrast those who are widowed tend to remain so.* It has also been found that *there is a high rate of remarriage in societies which stress the importance of fertility.*

There is a close relationship between marital stability and remarriage. For example, *unions between previously married people are less stable than between those who are married for the first time. The divorce rate tends to increase with successive marriages.*

There are certain important characteristics of divorced women involved in remarriages. *The divorced woman in a social setting which is ambivalent about her status, and, to some extent, does not approve of her divorced status is likely to be pushed towards remarriage.* However, education seems to determine the fastness with which a divorcee remarries. For example, *college-educated divorcees move into a new marriage more slowly than do those divorcees with high-school or grammar-school education.*

Goode and his associates identified a few economic dimensions related to divorcees. *Remarried divorcees have higher income expectations than those not remarried. These are less likely to expect to work than are those who have not remarried.* Besides, *remarried divorcees claim that economic improvement follows their remarriage but their remarriage is often associated with less continuity of child-support payments by the ex-husband.*

The divorcee is least likely to feel unhappy at the idea of her ex-husband's remarriage if she has already remarried while he has not remarried, and most unhappy if he has remarried and she has not.

The position of children in reconstituted families has received some attention in sociological studies. The presence of children in many cases creates certain interpersonal problems between spouses in a remarriage and between step-children and step-parents and among the step-children. In some cases, children enhance the prospect of remarriage and in others they reduce it. For instance, *a divorced parent with children will remarry sooner than will a widowed parent with children.* Also *widowed or divorced women with children are more likely than those with no children to remarry quickly or not at all.*

The fact of divorce and remarriage itself leaves a serious impact on the child's emotional capacity to adjust. *The longer the child has been in an intact family the more difficult it is for him to adjust to a new marriage after the former has been dissolved. Children of broken homes are likely to show more anxiety if the parent remarries than if he/she does not.*

The preceding summation provides a glimpse of sociological understandings based on empirical findings. A careful review of the literature presents us with findings that are often contradictory. On the one hand, some studies reveal that the reconstituted families have unique problems including interpersonal conflicts between step-children and step-parents, competition between step-brothers and between step-sisters, and between parents and step-parents in relation to affection, concern, and so on. These problems are compounded by the fact that remarriages tend to be less stable than the first marriage (see Goode's aforementioned proposition). On the other, there is evidence on the tremendous adaptability, resourcefulness, resiliency, and accommodation on the part of remarried couples. Remarried couples, based on their previous experiences, tend to be cautious about situations which lead to marital discord and attempt to correct these before they assume unmanageable proportions.

CANADIAN DATA

As evident from Table 9:1, in 1973, 18.1 per cent of the total marriages were second marriages. From 1966 to 1973 this percentage has increased from 12.4 to 18.1 per cent. In 1973, 50,638 Canadians who had been married previously remarried. Table 9:2 summarizes these data.

The data indicate that more men than women were involved in second unions. Of these Canadians 71.3 per cent were divorced and 28.7 per

Table 9:1 Canada: Showing Remarriage Rates by Marital Status of Brides and Grooms, 1950–73

Marital Status Bridegroom	Bride	As Per Cent of Total Marriages									As Per Cent of Total Remarriages								
		1950–1964 Average	1966	1967	1968	1969	1970	1971	1972	1973	1950–1964 Average	1966	1967	1968	1969	1970	1971	1972	1973
Single	—Widowed	2.0	1.5	1.5	1.5	1.3	1.2	1.2	1.1	0.74	15.5	12.2	12.2	12.2	8.5	7.6	7.0	6.2	4.1
Single	—Divorced	2.3	2.4	2.4	2.4	3.2	3.5	3.7	3.8	4.87	18.1	19.1	19.2	19.3	21.2	21.7	22.3	22.5	26.7
Widowed	—Single	2.0	1.2	1.1	1.0	1.0	0.9	0.9	0.8	1.03	13.8	9.4	8.8	8.3	6.3	5.5	5.2	4.8	5.7
Widowed	—Widowed	2.4	2.3	2.2	2.2	2.1	2.1	2.0	2.0	1.9	19.1	18.4	18.2	18.3	14.2	13.0	12.2	11.7	10.5
Widowed	—Divorced	0.4	0.5	0.4	0.4	0.7	0.7	0.7	0.7	0.9	3.2	3.6	3.6	3.4	4.4	4.1	4.2	4.2	5.2
Divorced	—Single	2.3	2.6	2.5	2.6	3.4	3.9	4.1	4.3	4.2	18.4	20.8	20.7	20.8	22.8	24.3	24.5	25.8	23.0
Divorced	—Widowed	0.5	0.6	0.6	0.6	0.9	0.9	0.9	0.9	0.8	3.8	4.7	5.0	4.8	5.9	6.0	5.7	5.6	4.3
Divorced	—Divorced	1.0	1.4	1.5	1.6	2.5	2.8	3.1	3.2	3.7	8.0	11.5	12.2	12.7	16.7	17.7	18.8	19.1	20.4
Total		13.1	12.4	12.3	12.3	15.0	16.0	16.5	16.8	18.1									

Source: D.B.S., Nuptiality: 1950–1694; D.B.S., and S.C. *Vital Statistics*, 1966, 1967, 1968, 1969, 1970, 1971, 1972, 1973, various tables. Adapted from: S. P. Wakil, 1976.

Table 9:2 Previously Married Men and Women Who Remarried— Canada, 1973

	Widowed	Average Age	Divorced	Average Age	Total
Males	6,838	58.4 yrs.	18,871	38.7 yrs.	25,709
Females	7,715	52.7 yrs.	17,241	35.3 yrs.	24,929
Total	14,553		36,112		50,638

cent were widowed. The average ages of the divorced-remarried fall into the 35–39-year range while the average widowed ages fall in the 52–58-year range. More than two and a half times as many divorced Canadians marry for the second time than do the widowed.

Although there is little empirical evidence on the reasons for the continuing increase in the numbers of those who are remarrying, some tentative explanations can be offered.[2] For example, Wakil 1976: 42) suggests that, among other factors, a steady increase in the rate of divorce has resulted in a corresponding increase in remarriages. This could be due to the greater degree of societal tolerance and acceptability of both divorce and remarriage. This is evident from the data presented in Table 9:3, which indicate that about 50 per cent of the remarriages involved single persons (i.e., neither married or divorced before).

Patterns of Remarriages

An analysis of who marries whom in a remarriage context reveals certain patterns. In Table 9:3, four dominant patterns of remarriages in 1973 are presented.

Table 9:3 The Four Largest Combinations in Second Unions—Canada, 1973

Bridgegroom		Bride	Per Cent
1. Single	—	Divorced	26.7
2. Divorced	—	Single	23.0
3. Divorced	—	Divorced	20.4
4. Widowed	—	Widowed	10.5

Source: Statistics Canada, 1974.

The data indicate that in seventy per cent of these unions at least one of the spouses was divorced. Also obvious is that a divorced person appears to prefer a single spouse rather than a divorced partner. In fifty per cent of the unions a single person is involved with a previously married partner.

The divorced person is usually younger than the widowed and thus may be more eligible as a partner in a second union. There is also the possibility that a divorced person is more eager to resume family life either to prove to him/herself that he/she is not a failure, but also in some cases to marry the person with whom one fell in love while going through the divorce or prior to the divorce action. It is of interest to note that in the two most frequent combinations of second unions single partners are involved.

CHARACTERISTICS OF REMARRIAGES

In this section we will present a few major characteristics of remarriages in Canada and these stem primarily from the studies conducted by the author over several years.[3]

Demographic Aspects

Our discussion of the demographic aspects is based upon a recent study conducted by the author in the Toronto area.[4] However, to the extent that we can assess, the figures tend to be in line with our previous studies. The average age at time of remarriage for males was 37 years and for females 32 years; for divorced male was 36.5 years and the divorced female 33.5 years. Widowed males were on the average 45 years at time of remarriage and widowed females were 37 years. Single men who married a spouse who had been married before were 32 years and single females, 27 years. The widowed females are considerably older at time of remarriage than either divorced or single women. The average age at time of first marriage according to Statistics Canada figures is 25 years for males and 22 years for females. Thus, single people who married the widowed or divorced are generally older than those who choose a single spouse for their first marriage.

Of those who married for the second time (divorced or widowed), the average age at time of their first marriage was 24 years for both widowed and divorced males, 22 years for widowed females, and 21 for divorced females. In other words there was virtually no difference between widowed and divorced with regard to age at the time of their first marriage.

The average length of the first marriage for divorced males was 11 years and for divorced females 9 years. For the widowed male the average length of first marriage was 17 years and for the widowed female it was 19 years. As might be expected, first marriages of the widowed were of longer duration than those of the divorced.

The average time lapse between first and second marriage was 1.5 years for the divorced male and 2 years for the divorced female. For the widowed male it was 3 years and for the widowed female 7 years. It appears that the widowed respondents waited longer between marriages than the divorced, and that for both widowed and divorced the female reported a longer time lapse between marriages than did the male.

The most common cause for break-up for both males and females was emotional incompatibility (an inability to communicate and engage in a reciprocal relationship) which led to emotional and sexual distance. Other stated reasons for marriage breakdown included poor relations with parents and in-laws, primarily because of the inadequate separation of one or both partners from their family of origin, alcoholism, physical violence, and mental illness.

Courtship Process in Remarriage

The courtship process among the remarried does not seem to be as elaborate as the one in their first marriages. The length of acquaintance seems relatively short. The widowed male and female had the shortest period of acquaintance with the prospective spouse before remarriage; the males knew the propsective spouse for less than six months before marriage. In a majority of cases, spouses met through friends or at work. It was the divorced males and females and single females who met prospective spouses at work.

The reasons for breakup of the first marriage led them to seek different qualities in the second than in the first mate. Some of these qualities were stability, strength of personality, moral integrity, maturity, aggressiveness, and flexibility. A caring person who could be independent and "real", and someone with whom they could achieve sexual compatibility was preferred.

PROFILES OF MARITAL LIFE AMONG THE REMARRIED

A remarriage for a person offers a comparative perspective and this to some extent enables them to adjust to the everyday routine of marital life with relative ease. In our studies we identified several dimensions of marital life of the married in which such comparisons exercised an important influence on an effective reconstruction of life. In this section we will briefly outline some of these dimensions.

First and Second Marriages: Similarities and Differences

Among a great many of those who had remarried, particularly the divorced, there was a vast difference between their first and second marriages. Indications were that in the current marriage there was a much greater focus on family togetherness and home-centred activities. Both spouses were keenly involved with the children (in first marriages some husbands were not) and shared activities as a family. There was a closeness and warm emotional atmosphere. Because of increasing age and experience the second marrieds felt themselves and their family life to be more settled and stable than in the previous union, and stated that they had more realistic expectations of a marriage and a better understanding of what they themselves could contribute to it. In the second marriage there was an intimate and more open relationship in which there was freer communication and a greater ability to resolve any problems, also greater compatibility and more sharing of interests and activities.

Those who had children in the second marriage found that their life revolved more around the children than it did in their first marriage. But some also felt that they now managed to find more time for themselves as a couple, and that their life was not completely wrapped up in the children.

In discussing how the present family life seems similar to family life in the previous marriage, a great many of the divorced people felt that there was absolutely no similarity, or "the wedding ring is the only thing". Others said the only common features were "the role of mother and housewife" or "basic material similarities which aren't that important".

Adjustment in Second Marriages

In identifying the components of a successful remarriage, the second-married indicated that emotional compatibility, agreement on lifestyle and goals, and companionship were most important. Ultimately they spoke of maturity, which leads to an ability to respect one's partner. The remarried saw a successful relationship as an equal relationship, one in which you do not try to mould the other person, and in which you convey empathy, not sympathy. Maturity was variously described as knowing what is important to oneself, what one wants, needs, values, not expecting perfection, understanding, the importance of compromise, the capacity to trust each other, and the ability to make use of the first marriage experience to grow as a person, and develop tolerance and compassion in order to grow together in the relationship. A resolution of one's past was vital and led to an intimacy and openness in the relationship.

REMARRIED AND THEIR SIGNIFICANT OTHERS

Remarriages generally necessitate a careful restructing of social networks. An effective restructing involves redefinition of such "significant others" as former spouse, extended kin, friends, and neighbours. At present there is little sociological evidence on the process of reorganization of interpersonal networks. In our research, we were able to identify certain attitudinal and behavioural dispositions towards such significant others. What follows is a brief sketch of this aspect.

The Former Spouse

The most commonly mentioned attitude to the former spouse of the present mate was one of indifference, particularly when the form of marriage dissolution was divorce rather than death. Generally women indicated that they had feelings of resentment and anger towards the former spouse. Some of the reasons given were active interference by the ex-spouse in the current marriage, continued contact with the ex-spouse because of the children, and the financial demands created by the husband's paying alimony. Many second-marrieds said that they discuss former spouses in the present marriage.

The discussion of the former marriage appeared to have no effect on the present relationship. One of the explanations given was that it formed a small part of one's total life experience and should neither be forgotten nor unduly emphasized. Another was that any discussion of the former marriage was incidental and that the whole subject had been thoroughly discussed and worked out before the remarriage.

Extended Kin and Friends

The extent to which the remarried maintain effective contact with their extended kin depends on the degree of support and understanding offered by the latter during the dissolution process. In general, our observation suggests that only one out of five of the remarried feels that there was clear denial of support from their kin for the second marriage. The single and widowed female in a remarriage tended to maintain very close ties with their significant kin. The least contact was between the single and widowed male and their extended kin.

Regarding friends, they were either supportive or indifferent towards their remarriage. However, in comparison with extended kin most remarried tend not to be influenced by the opinions of their friends.

Children

Many parents recognized that there were difficulties in the adjustment that children had to make in areas of sharing a natural parent, trusting and accepting the new parent's personality and ways, and fitting into the new family system with siblings. However, a gradual adjustment period was indicated as being the usual pattern, with this period of "getting to know one another" starting very often during the courtship of the parents. Many step-parents realized that there were differences between the biological parent and the new parent that took time to adjust to, so that competition of the step-parent with this other parent was not deemed wise.

Previously divorced step-fathers cited the problem of adjusting to increased activity in the home, especially where teenagers were involved, and could not readily accept the children's habits. They were concerned about the amount of involvement with the children, exercising discipline and showing affection. Some found it difficult to accept the children emotionally, and they had to cope with their own jealousy, and occasionally with manipulation by female children. Winning their status was a gradual process. On a practical level, they worried about increased costs.

Among divorced women, negative community attitudes and interference from relatives, especially grandmothers, posed a problem. Mothers were concerned about privacy; they were afraid the children would get on their husband's nerves and wanted them to be more independent and less clinging. Some expressed difficulty with discipline and maintaining neutrality, and wanted to open communication channels between children, especially teenagers and spouse. There was a need to assuage the children's fear of a break-up, and to cope with their disturbance after visiting their natural father.

Single men expressed fear of stepping into a ready-made family, specifically citing acceptance by children, coping with the first husband's resentment and the children's visits with him as problematical. They were uncertain about the degree and type of discipline they should exercise, amount of affection, and gaining the children's trust.

Single women joining an existing family faced the problem of discipline especially of older boys, establishing new house rules, and promoting cooperation within the household. They had to accept that the children's habits and behaviour would not meet their expectations, and face their own feelings about wanting their husbands to themselves. Sometimes men and their children formed alliances against the new wife. Their own role was ill-defined, with comparisons made to the natural mother and grandmother, and feelings of resentment from the step-children.

CONCLUSIONS

What general patterns concerning remarriages in Canada may be discerned from the previous discussion? First, it is clear from the demographic evidence that the incidence of remarriages is steadily increasing. Second, in view of the increased acceptance of divorce as a solution to an unsatisfactory marriage, remarriage has emerged as a legitimate means for restructuring an orderly life. Third, the remarriages display certain structural characteristics that set them apart from first marriages. These include notably briefer, less ritualistic, less romantically oriented, and more pragmatic courtship. At the same time the proportion of divorces involving older couples including those with young children is increasing (see Chapter 8 on this point) and this, in turn, leads to remarriages which are more likely to involve families than in the past. Fourth, with regard to marital adjustment, although the remarried are likely to encounter problems common to all marriages, they may be at a slight advantage in coping because of a more rational approach to marriage. Finally, the strength of marriage, as an institution, is revealed not only because people choose to remarry when other options are available, but because of increasing social acceptance of remarriage.

Notes

1. The actual propositions from the Inventory compiled by Goode, Hopkins, McClure (1971: 593–95) are italicized for an easy identification. Students who wish to know more about Reconstituted Families are referred to Nye and Berardo (1973: 520–29), Bernard (1956), Duberman (1975), and Glen and Weaver (1977).

2. There is a scarcity of material available in Canada on reconstituted families. Kuzel and Krishnan (1973) examined the 1961–66 trends in remarriage, and Messinger (1976) discussed remarriage between divorced people and suggested an educational program for those who are planning or are in second unions. A bimonthly bulletin called *Stepparents' Forum* was started in Montreal in 1975. This bulletin discusses the situations faced by RF.

3. Due to the limitations of space, details of these studies have been omitted but these are available from the author upon request.

4. The author would be pleased to supply information on samplings and data-collection for the interested reader.

SELECTED BIBLIOGRAPHY

BERNARD, JESSIE. *Remarriage*, New York.
    1956
DUBERMAN, LUCILE. *The Reconstituted Family*, New York.
GLEN, NORVALL, D. and CHARLES H. WEAVER. "The Marital Happiness of Remarried Divorced Persons", *Journal of Marriage and the Family*, Vol. 39 (May), pp. 331–38.
GOODE, WILLIAM J., E. HOPKINS and HELEN M. MCCLURE. *Social Systems and Family*
    1971   *Patterns: A Propositional Inventory*, New York.

KUZEL, PAUL and P. DRISHNAN. "Changing Patterns of Remarriage in Canada: 1961–
 1973   66", *Journal of Comparative Family Studies*, Vol. 4 (Autumn), pp.
       215–24.
MESSINGER, LILLIAN. "Remarriage Between Divorced People with Children from
 1976   Previous Marriages", *Journal of Marriage and Family Counselling*, Vol.
       1 (April), pp. 193–200.
NYE, IVAN F. and FELIX M. BERARDO. *The Family: Its Structure and Functions*,
 1973   New York.
SCHLESINGER, BENJAMIN. "Remarriage as Family Reorganization for Divorced Per-
 1970   sons: A Canadian Study", *Journal of Comparative Family Studies*,
       Vol. 1 (Autumn), pp. 101–18.
———. *The One-Parent Family: Perspectives and Annotated Bibliography*, third ed.,
 1975   Toronto.
Stepparents Forum. Published bi-monthly, Westmount, Quebec.
WAKIL, S. PARVEZ. "Marriage and Family in Canada", *Journal of Comparative
 1976   Family Studies*, Calgary.

Non-Traditional Family and Marriage

10

ROBERT N. WHITEHURST

The preceding chapters in this book have dealt with the more traditional and expected concerns of people in marriages and families, but as the late 1960s and early 1970s have shown, a variety of alternative forms of living arrangement have also arisen, raising some questions about their relationship to the more common forms. This chapter will be a survey of some of these alternative forms, at least the most popular and visible of these, and will involve a sociological interpretation of their theoretical relevance to the future of families as well as an evaluation of their contemporary impact.

The importance of so-called alternative lifestyles has been relentlessly questioned by some authors, since their apparent decline and the advent of more difficult economic times in the early seventies, but there is little doubt of the increasing impact of the women's movement, sexual liberation, and the basic questioning of the sacredness of institutions as was begun in the sixties (Libby and Whitehurst, 1977). The problem of adequate research and the thorny problem of a lack of consensus regarding terminology describing these variants in family forms remain problematic. In this chapter, I will refer to the behaviour generally found under the rubric "alternatives" as variant marriage or family forms, simply implying that the participants may or may not have opted in any real sense for making the choice of the lifestyle they live (the term alternative implies choice—and all alternative lifestyles do not involve real choices) and that these forms simply vary—in some more or less regular way—statistically speaking, and not in a normative sense of being deviant—from more expected and conventional lifestyles.

The chapter is organized in terms of a perspective, explaining why alternative or variant lifestyles arose as they did at this time in the twentieth century, analysis of some of the dominant modes of sociological thought—and thinkers—as applied to variants today in Canada and more broadly in North America, and finally some speculative discussion as to what all this means for further changes in marriage and family forms—both in the near and the distant future.

PERSPECTIVES

Bennett Berger noted as early as 1967 that the older patterns related to Bohemianism were once more reasserting themselves in the "flower-child" movement of the late 1960s.[1] Earlier English socialists and free-thinkers had sold all the new ideas—from communes to free-sex—in an earlier era to any audiences they could find, but some contemporary sociologists thought that the media-assisted mass movement of the sixties might be different on several scores: the flower-children were a product of a televised society and were probably more susceptible to mass-society influences than any previous group. The decade of the sixties saw a re-surgence of the irreverence begun in the twenties—and that had faded with the depression in the thirties. This irreverence was in part a function of urbanization, the rapid mobility of families, which loosened the social-control possibilities of kin, and the general strengthening of secular values which accompanied the decline of organized religion as it formerly in-fluenced people's sense of moral rectitude, and gave strong direction to, and support for, existing institutions. Universal education and liberaliza-tion of job opportunities and careers for women were also factors which led to a changed social order. High divorce rates after the Second World War were associated with a trend toward greater personal freedom in mate-choice and appeared to have made divorce an easier option than before—simply by demonstrating that it could be done, and survived, more readily than had been supposed by many in previous times. Tech-nology also was implicated in a great number of ways providing increased leisure, less need for working on the part of the young, more automobiles that induced travel and ephemeral acquaintances, and of course such factors as improved conception-controls, especially the pill, would have to be included. In these alienating and anomic contexts variant family and lifestyles emerged (Conover, 1975: 457).

Despite their conspicuous nature, variant marriage and family forms have not attracted the attention of most mainstream theorists in sociology. Consequently, adequate theoretical explanation in this regard is scarce. In the following discussion we will attempt to place the non-traditional or variant forms of family in three major theoretical contexts: functional, conflict, and symbolic-interaction.

Functionalist Perspective

The functionalist theory holds that all societies tend to provide for the basic necessities—ordinarily through institutional organization—for the survival of the society. Although institutions are resistant to change, they do change, however, and as gaps in services or human needs are not met by institutions as they currently exist, new social forms will arise to fill the gaps and meet those unmet needs. The variant family and marriage forms can be seen as gap-fillers. In the case of the sixties and seventies, there was apparently a great need to express a sense of community, kin, and shared brotherhood, sometimes including sensuality and sexuality, that somehow went unmet by the more conventional ties of family. We know that a number of young people expressed real feelings of belonging—when they entered such movement activities as communes and other collective activities—and that they proclaimed they had not received these at home or in their families in a desired quantity. From this vantage point, these groups must be seen as functional, in terms of at least providing interim status to people who were dissatisfied with their existing family life, previous to seeking out some variant form or other. Most traditional functionalists, however, are likely to stress the disfunctionality of variant forms as disrupters of conventional family life, and would likely see short-term liaisons in quasi-families or other groupings as disfunctional as well. It is, as Merton has suggested, possible to use functionalist theory to support any ideological viewpoint.

Conflict Perspective

A variant of Marxist conflict theory might be used to analyse the appearance of variant families when they arose; the rise of those family forms can be said to have been caused by several types of inequality in the sixties, not all of which are purely economic, but most of which have some economic consequences associated with them: sex-role and sexual inequality, racial inequality, love-scarcity (although we have no good economic or exchange theory of love as yet), and the generally unsettled social conditions associated with a conflict-period in which many vested interests were at variance, related to larger issues such as war, racism, state secrecy, corporate power, and so on.

Symbolic-Interactionist Perspective

Symbolic-interactionist theory may be of some use in understanding the social changes that have fed the building of variant family and marriage forms. The changing nature of our symbol systems, including their transmission, (i.e., television, broad-based newspaper readership, radio, films, and so forth) may be seen as assisting in the reformulation of the meanings of family, marriage, and change in our society. Not the least of these communication items to be noted must be the fact of enhancing the range of available reference groups—some of which aid the development of variant forms of cohabitation. There have been some basic changes in our definitions of the appropriateness of sexuality in life during the post-Second World War period that appear to lend to the further widening of sexuality and sexual experimentation; broad-scale sex education, recognition of children's rights, more freedom for young people to spend time together, further selling of sexuality via media messages enhancing the attractiveness of sexuality, greater awareness of non-marital sexuality, more in-depth studies that lend an aura of normality to sexuality, and so forth. Sexual socialization in this culture is continuous and subtle in ways that affect our attitudes and behaviour and consequently change us as sexual beings. The basic trend is doubtless toward liberalization.

To summarize so far, it is useful to look at the advent of marriage and family variants as not necessarily new, but that there are some powerful, and probably new social forces, impinging on us as members of society today, that made their appearance probable when they came on the scene. Several styles of theory can be used to help explain their recent development, including functionalist theory, conflict theory, and symbolic-interactionism. Others would no doubt have relevance as well, but these are some of the major theoretical frameworks that seem appropriate.

CURRENT STATUS OF VARIANTS

A moderate polarizing effect appears to be operating currently in both Canada and the U.S. with respect to recent changes affecting variant lifestyles. On the one hand, the onset of tighter economic times, beginning about 1971 or 1972, heralded the cessation of the flow of youth on the road during the summer months as well as at other times. This could be interpreted as a response to a felt scarcity of jobs—and therefore money—which no doubt affected decisions to actively look for jobs, think about the future with respect to education, and other more sober responses that were unlike the earlier carefree times of the flower-child in the late sixties (Sussman, 1975). With a more serious attitude toward life, people often shunned the more flamboyant lifestyles, modes of dress, and other signals that marked out variants and non-traditional ways of expressing sexuality and attitudes toward life in general. Fear of economic reprisals from living too conspicuous and/or deviant a lifestyle seems to have predominated in the thinking of some erstwhile radicals of the early 1970s. Yet many of their radical actions (of the 1960s) have been diffused into the larger society. For example, one of the supposedly rare variants of living together unmarried in the 1960s has become widespread in the 1970s and has achieved a reluctant acceptance on the part of many adults as a normal phenomenon. It is in this changing economic and political context that we propose to examine the current state of some specific variant family forms.

Extramarital Sexuality

In terms of most frequent or most likely variant lifestyles, the old adaptation of conventional marriage—with some extramarital sexuality (EMS) on the side—must be considered as the continuing dominant variant. Although estimates vary and reliable data are lacking, it is likely that in North American cities, married people will approximate rates of EMS totalling about 60 to 70 per cent. Whether in fact EMS in a conventional marriage constitutes a variant is an open question, since it has always been a part of societal behaviour and more or less accepted—at least as a standard for men. The change now involves the move toward equality of participation by women; like other social movements, however, the female equality movement has not involved more than a small minority of women, but they have been often vocal and at times appear aberrant to their more conventional counterparts. What people may miss who see militant feminists simply as "bra burners" or lesbians is the fact that no social movement can get anywhere unless it can first capture the popular attenion. At any rate, standard or conventional EMS is the most likely adaptation—if we assume it is a variant on the normal family—of the normal family. The rationales for this ... em straightforward: having affairs is by now a conventionalized, if not fully accepted, means of expressing needs for variety, romance, or whatever it is that people look for outside their own marriage relationships. This means that there is an implied code that people who indulge EMS more or less come to understand and can communicate with each other. It is the most accepted, albeit not fully so, variant and at the same time least endangers one's social position, occupation, or other family status in the eyes of the community. Its popularity, in short, rests in the fact that it does not seriously upset the status quo; in fact it must be considered a real part of it.

Living Together

Very similar to the normalized practice of EMS in Canada is the habit of living together in the unmarried state. Reports from even small towns and northern regions suggest that it is rapidly becoming more or less acceptable for people with serious relationships to live together. There are apparently two problematic areas in understanding the current nature of cohabitation: first, does it replace marriage or simply replace older forms of engagement? Secondly, does it pose a problem for real changes in the institution of marriage? At this time, cohabitation seems more properly considered as more or less a replacement for older forms of engagement since a preponderance of cohabitants at some time or other tend to marry. In fact, resisting marriage in this society is still pretty difficult for all but the hard-core singles. Of course, this is a growing group, but most still marry and seem to be fairly conventional after one or two periods of cohabitation. This, in a sense, seems to answer the second question—that of the implications for changes in marriage wrought by cohabitation. Cohabitation may rationalize and liberalize mate-selection, but seems to have little total effect—at least at this time— on the marriages that ensue. There is little information available to suggest that those who have cohabited for some time do not eventually regress (in spite of their original intentions) to more conventional and normal sex-role styles of interaction as their lives proceed and children and other daily routines intrude. To this time, it seems that cohabitation tends to be overpowered by marriage much more frequently than is the institution of conventional marriage changed by cohabitation. Of course, there is interchange and effects both ways (in terms of what changes what and how much and what is cause and effect), but it is very difficult to make the case that cohabitation has seriously altered marriage today. Its most likely effects are to slightly retard age at first marriage, contribute to what Farber has called the "permanent availability" model of mate-selection (Farber, 1964) by adding to a more or less permanent pool of more or less available mates in ways that more conventional marriages do not do quite so easily. Finally cohabitation *may* in some instances create a greater awareness of the potential for androgyny or equality in the sex-roles allocation. This latter effect is far from clear except for select populations who cohabit, such as university students and professional people.

Modified Open Marriage

Other forms which are some kind of variants on the idea of marriage as a conjugal pair seem somewhat less important today in Canada and perhaps the U.S. as well. The most usual kind of adaptation to marriage which probably could not even be considered a variant—but rather a modification of marriage itself—is the tendency of men to become more involved with what were formerly described as feminine roles as women increasingly become enmeshed in the labour force. This modified open marriage most frequently includes some relatively minor changes in the role prescriptions as these are allotted within the marriage and family. The implication that arises from this change is already being seen; some husbands are singularly unwilling to yield to their wives' demands for more participation in household chores—the result being increased strains and tensions and more divorces.

A more radical variant of the conjugal pair involving open sexuality with awareness of the partners is a very uncommon adaptation in our society today. Five or so years ago there was much talk about open marriages, including sexually open ones, but those who tried it seem to have returned to a more basic monogamous lifestyle. There is no doubt that many partners were exchanged, both in terms of divorces and less formalized exchanges, but the habit of allowing a spouse open sexuality outside of the primary dyad is extremely uncommon. Our experimental orientation and the overall sense of failure at having heard about such experiments has contributed to changes in the common view of the practicability of such lifestyles. Open marriages never really got much of a fair hearing in this culture and were probably doomed to failure from the start; this failure as a built-in outcome is probably due to several factors in a monogamous society including structured jealousy, a sense of partner possession, and poor social support systems to make such a scheme workable for all but the most intrepid experimenters.

Singlehood

Probably one of the most profound changes in the social structures relating to marriage and the family this century is related to the singles phenomenon (Stein, 1975; Libby, 1977). Being single is not specifically a variant on the family, but if increasing numbers either shun marriage in the first place or opt for singlehood after trying marriage, it is obviously important to understand as a part of the larger scheme of male-female relations. Singlehood is thus seen as an alternative, but not necessarily a variant on marriage. The increasing numbers of singles today is probably the most spectacular change, creating impacts for current and future male/female relationships.

There appears to have been a bandwagon effect associated with singlehood. Although there is a dual image of singles, both involving extreme stereotypes, the actualities of singlehood are being increasingly seen by the public as at least a semi-desirable lifestyle in contrast to former views of singlehood. Formerly, our views of single women involved the notion of pitying the poor hapless female who could not snare a husband. Men who stayed single have always been subjected to match-makers who assumed automatically they must be entirely deprived of all life's goodies. Thus, our stereotypes lead us to see singles as either a seriously deprived, and probably a bit neurotic, minority to be pitied because they miss the goodness of wedded bliss, or to see them as swinging fun-loving people who are on an endless round of exciting parties and social events, coupled with complete freedom to do their own thing. Both of these stereotypes are obviously exaggerated and are seldom seen in reality. Single life is much like life in any other status—a mix of benefits and privileges, woes and problems. The essential point is that all lifestyles involve costs and rewards and more people are opting for the reward side of singlehood these days and avoiding the costs of marriage. As people view singlehood as a viable option for themselves and see living examples of people who seem to get along well as singles an increase in the bandwagon effect will occur. As a result of this, singles have for the first time begun to organize into coalitions and associations that provide for their needs as singles.

Although singles organizations are well developed in large cities, such changes have yet to occur on any scale in smaller cities or more rural places. Cities thus act as a magnet for those who occupy transitional status such as singlehood. The increasing level of organized activity will tend to solidify singles' statuses and create specialization in the ranks of singles. For example, clubs, bars, or other social places will tend to cater to specific kinds of singles' orientations, much as has happened with the gay scene in large cities; some will cater to simple sexual pleasure, some to more serious mate-hunting types, while others are likely to become places where sociability and more permanent friendships will be formed and made, perhaps along special interest lines, such as clubs formed on the basis of culture, sports, and travel. Already these are in evidence in large cities, even though the specialization is less evident now than it is likely to be in the future. The point is that singles will come to know that they can survive, and that they can get various needs met once they become wise to the ways of the singles' scene. This information is likely to spread the notion of attractiveness to potential singles, increasing its positive pull as a status.

Yet another factor adding to the pull toward singlehood is the tendency within marriage to expect ever-increasing increments of interpersonal satisfaction from spouses. Some experts feel that marriage adjustment or marriage relationships have not deteriorated over the years in general— but that ever increasing expectations of performance in marital roles creates a necessary disappointment with marriage that in turn creates higher divorce rates. If this is true, and there are many plausible reasons to believe it is, then we must expect the singles' model of lifestyle to become even more adapted to as a means to solve the problems implicit in living with one partner for a lifetime. There is no reason to believe at this time that becoming single in fact relieves or solves all these problems inherent in a limited relationship with one person in a monogamous marriage, but if people define single status as the place where it is possible to get *more* of what they want, then singlehood will be "where it's at". There is a two-sided set of obstacles that tend to inhibit the shift to singlehood as a major swing in our society: first, there is an ever-present and still highly valued pull into marriage, although this pull per se does not necessarily mean that people will not at some point in their lives turn to a period of singlehood.

Second, singlehood demands persons who can adapt to a more autonomous lifestyle in which needs are met on a more intermittent basis than marriage often gives. Of course, many are now viewing that security and stable need-meeting that occurs within marriage more as a burden and a kind of security that hobbles, while singlehood is more frequently viewed as a liberating experience that challenges the individual to grow and change, and to attack life with a sense of creative intelligence in order to solve problems on a more daily basis. Just how many people are apt to see life in these latter (single) terms is unknown, but the rapid changes in urban single populations is obvious. Whether marital failure creates the pool of singles in a much-enlarged form, or whether the failure of couples simply adds to the pool is an open question. What is obvious from talking about the meaning of life with singles is that they have (often) opted for this lifestyle as a conscious choice and choose to live with the daily uncertainties of relationships in terms that are much less stable than marriage. No doubt the rising set of expectations that are associated with long-term relationships makes for a very high probability of failure of many of these relationships. There is thus now a tension in North American values, between the one that propels us toward experimentation, taking up challenges, and growth-and-change norms and the ones that cause us to seek stability, even at the risk of boredom and over-predictability.

Other Variants

Other variants, which we will now discuss, seem at least for the moment statistically unimportant in terms of their effects on most of the population. This does not mean, however, that some kind of future shortages, changes in the political, economic, or social climate may not act as catalysts which could drastically change the above speculation. It merely means that it would be unsafe at this time to guess what impacts such eco-catastrophes or political changes might bring with them. Such an example might include fuel shortages which would force single-family dwellings to be used on a multi-family basis; continued inflation, which might have the same result; or extremely high unemployment might have the same effect. General poltical crises may continue as a threat to the stability of our way of life and be responded to by increasing numbers who seek subsistence farming collectively as a means to secure, at least, some semblance of coherence and control over their lives.

In the meantime, the potential for disaster and the increased consciousness of at least some in our society to act in ecologically responsible ways, the need to enact a social ethic which will minimize social isolation, and the tendency to undo the perceived evils of rampant individualism and competition are seen as rationales for working at cooperative lifestyles. This combined ethos will probably eventuate in the slow proliferation of urban collectives and communes. Insofar as current trends continue (high prices and inflation, shortages, decreased emphasis on the work ethic, etc.) there will probably be a continued and perhaps notable trend toward collectivization in cities as well as the less apparent trend toward survival farming in rural areas. Some training places are now available to teach survival farming as a successful potential whereas the tendency in the late sixties and early seventies was for people without skills, land, or tools to go forth into poor farming places. Obviously nearly all of these failed. Now, since it is less a fad-like thing to do and people are being better prepared, the few who adapt will likely be more successful. They will still constitute an unimportant minority for the foreseeable future.[2]

One variation on the theme of ecological soundness and economic sharing has been attempted by various groups, including churches in Canada. This involves what may loosely be called forming quasi-kin units, in which the predominating themes involve sharing social and recreational time with others, baby-sitting, and possibly some of the expensive hard-goods of the household, such as washing equipment. These adaptations have been reasonably successful and may well proliferate as the aforementioned scarcities and consciousness of waste increase in our society.

No mention has, as yet, been made of the gay adaptation to life in marriage or the family as it may affect the future of these institutions. At this time, it seems that the backlash reactions to the gay movement are in full swing and that gains are likely to be damaged by recent events. Even if there were no serious reactionary efforts to repress the gay movement and their freedoms, it is highly unlikely that in a society such as the current Canadian setting, gay freedoms (to marry for example) would likely be forthcoming. The idea of something like legitimate marriage between gays is simply stretching the mores too far for the average citizen of this land as a legitimate probability. If political and economic pressures remain no more repressive than they now are, gays will probably move forward extremely slowly in terms of gaining their basic rights as human beings. If the repressive and reactionary forces persist in their persecution of gays, this forward momentum may be slowed considerably. It is obvious, however, at this time that gays do not receive full and equal treatment in society—simply because they are gay. No other minority is so subjected to scrutiny and inordinately harsh judgment because of sexual orientation, a double standard in effect which someday will be minimized if not eradicated. That day is not yet at hand.

Probably of least significance (at least statistically speaking) in its impacts on Canadian society would have to be considered the phenomenon of group marriages, including triads in which three-way sexuality is experienced. Research on such groups is extremely difficult to find and seems to be non-existent in Canada. It is probably safe to conclude that either people who engage in such relationships are very secretive about them and maintain only underground connections with respect to their knowledge and information, or they are so ephemeral and short-lived that they dissipate before most people become aware of them as the kinds of multiple living units they may be. In any case, even the folklore and exaggerated stories about such phenomena have all but ceased to be part of the language of even the most sophisticated cocktail set. Other priorities seem to have surfaced and it is likely that the utopian vision of the earlier period has vanished in favour of a more hard-core search for immediate gratification at less cost than the extreme complexity that group marriages and the like entail.

Although there may be a number of hidden triads in various places in Canada, they are probably not of numerical significance. Three people living together can fairly easily disguise the odd person as a friend of the same-sex person of the dyad living in the house, thus it is fairly simple to hide a *ménage à trois* and have few but the most intimates be aware of the sexual habits of the three people sharing housing and a more or less complete lifestyle.

CONCLUSIONS

Certain trends can be perceived from the foregoing discussion. First, the traditional family is definitely in change, the stability and once-felt sacredness of nuclear or extended families is no longer as viable or as stable as we once felt these forms to be. The individual seems more often to be replacing the family as a unit of living, treatment, and societal organization. As a result, life is less predictable, less planned and much more *ad hoc* in terms of the kinds and styles of relationships we have. The sets of expectations we once held for permanence and stability are less often found even though still desired by most people. Further, this set of conditions seems to result in people living in what might be called "expectation-free" relationships more often than many would like, simply because they are unable to negotiate from a solid, long-term base of equality and similar expectations about relationships.

Second, as a result of the women's movement and the increased divorce rates, people, women especially, are seeking more of a sense of independence and autonomy in their lives. The happy balance between belonging and independence is seldom found as compared with former times when people had fewer choices in their lives.

Third, there is greater toleration of breakups and thus more of an expectation that they will happen frequently. The self-fulfilling prophecies thus set into motion by this temporary kind of definition of relationships add to the potential for more breakups, more toleration of breakups, and so forth.

Fourth, it seems improper to define changes in Canadian lifestyles as containing major changes for most people; this does not deny however that serious changes have been made in the society that affect us, but that these changes have not been felt by the majority and that social and political conditions are not now ripe for further changes that will make for an increased visibility of variant family forms. Recent political, social, and economic forces, may, however, serve to bring about changes in unpredictable ways that will change this rapidly.

Variants in marriage and family forms thus face an uncertain future, but from the past have left a lingering impact on the lives of many Canadians.

Notes

1. Bennett Berger noted the similarity to the 1920s in his address to the American Sociological Association by calling attention to Malcom Crowley's book, *Exile's Return*.

2. Conover claims that the youth of the sixties and seventies, having never experienced poverty, aimed their energies at saving resources not creating them (Conover, 1975).

SELECTED BIBLIOGRAPHY

CONOVER, PATRICK W. "An Analysis of Communes and Intentional Communities
1975   with Particular Attention to Sexual and General Relations", *The Family Coordinator*, Vol. 24, No. 4 (October), pp. 453–64.

ERIKSON, KAI T. "The Sociology of Deviance", in E. C. McDonagh and J. E. Simpson, eds., *Social Problems: Persistent Challenges*, New York.
1965

FARBER, BERNARD. *Family: Organization and Interaction*, San Francisco, California.
1964

LIBBY, ROGER W. and ROBERT T. WHITEHURST. *Marriage and Alternatives: Exploring*
1977   *Intimate Relationships*, Glenview, Illinois.

MERTON, ROBERT K. *On Theoretical Sociology*, New York.
1967

SKOLNICK, ARLENE. *The Intimate Environment*, Boston.
1973

STEIN, PETER J. "Singlehood: An Alternative to Marriage", *The Family Coordinator*,
1975   Vol. 24, No. 4 (October), pp. 489–504.

SUSSMAN, MARVIN B. "The Four F's of Variant Family Forms and Marriage Styles",
1975   *The Family Coordinator*, Vol. 24 (October), pp. 553–76.

Courtship, Marriage, and the Family in Canada:

An Overview

G. N. RAMU

11

In the preceding chapters, eight scholars have outlined what we know to date about certain aspects of marriage and the family in Canada. In this concluding chapter we propose to bring together the essentials of their analyses and place these in a conceptual context in order to give the reader a composite picture. To this end the following perspective is intended as a means for summarizing the main findings and not as an exercise in theory-construction.

A PERSPECTIVE

Three general themes are implicit in the empirical materials on courtship, marriage, and family life reviewed in this book: *stability*, *change*, and *convergence*. The organization of marriage and family life centres around the ideal of stability. In Canadian society, for example, there are uniform sets of beliefs about the type of family that one should form, the nature of marital life that one should lead, and the manner in which children should be reared. Such normative codes prevail not only across ethnic, religious, or class lines but appear to be relatively strong, and, hence relatively impervious. Basic to the notion of stability is a set of values, norms, and roles that people hold important and these are hard to change.

The emphasis on stability is evident in most major analyses of marriage and family behaviour and stated in functional terms—asks how it affects society and the individual? In the context of the family, stability is equated with continuity of certain social practices and the maintenance of social order. This point is underscored in Chapter 5 on sex roles and especially in Chapter 9 on divorce where Peters outlines the legal impediments of marital dissolution. Social arrangements are geared to promoting a sense of order and stability through many institutions and the family is crucial in this respect. In fact, a careful reader of this volume would infer that in Canada the family, perhaps, is the most conservative institution with regard to resistance to change, along with other aspects of the society such as the economy and polity.

Although important in its own right as an ideal and a reality, stability alone cannot provide the key for understanding Canadian families. Part of the dual-reality of marital and family life stems from recent changes in both attitudes and behaviour. For example, there has been a sharp decline in the birth rate, resulting in smaller families as well as an increase in premarital sexual permissiveness and marital dissolution. Although pockets of traditionalism and conservatism remain, it is clear that the attitudes (if not behaviour) of the majority of Canadians are changing with regard to numerous issues surrounding the family. Thus the complex relationship between the family and the maintenance of ethnicity (insofar as the former influences the persistence of the latter) has become increasingly tenuous and problematic. There continues to be concerted pressure to liberalize divorce laws which had already been substantially modified a decade ago, as there continue to be attempts on the part of some who are frustrated with the current marriage and family relationships to engage in "alternate or experimental" lifestyles. The net effect of such changes and experiments has been a partial erosion of the stability previously characteristic of Canadian marriage and family patterns.

Although no major empirical study has clearly mapped the direction of such changes, there are numerous allusions throughout this book that such changes are indicative of more general convergent tendencies toward uniformity in family patterns. For example, in Chapter 3 Hobart concludes that in terms of sexual attitudes and behaviours there is a convergence between the French and the English on the one hand, and males and females on the other. Similarly, in Chapter 7, Tavuchis suggests a convergence of family patterns cutting across ethnic lines. Therefore, although the rates of change may differ among various groups, available evidence suggests increased consonance. Lacking more rigorous and reliable data, we can only speculate that the forces of urbanization, industrialization, and secularization have in fact not only influenced the direction of change but have also promoted homogeneity rather than diversity.

In short, we recognize that both continuity and change characterize marital and family behaviour in Canada and assume that the concepts of stability, change, and convergence are useful in providing a perspective for understanding concrete events.

COURTSHIP PROCESS

In reviewing courtship in Canada we shall focus on three elements: (1) principles of mate-selection, (2) dating behaviour, and (3) premarital sexual attitudes and behaviour.

Principles of Mate-Selection

In contemporary Canada, one can identify at least two conflicting ideologies and practices with regard to mate-selection. At the societal level there exists a generalized but unstated expectation that marriage is an important factor in the orderly continuity of culture and population. Although not all those who marry form families, data show that a majority do and there is clear societal pressure encouraging endogamy. At the individual level, however, the commitment to the freedom of choice with few or no barriers or constraints prevails. Individuals hold that it is a matter of personal right to marry whomever they wish. But as Moon points out in Chapter 3, such a belief is practised only in approximately two out of three cases. Race, religion, and ethnicity continue to exercise a dominant influence in mate-choice and take precedence over other considerations. In fact, change in the area of endogamy has been remarkably slow compared to the magnitude of changes that are taking place in other aspects of social life.

The empirical evidence presented in this volume suggests that religion and ethnicity continue to play an important role in mate-selection, e.g., in 1972, nearly 80 per cent of Canadians married within their own faith. Of these, Jews are most likely to marry within their group followed by Catholics and Protestants. While it is true that religion and ethnicity are crucial, there are other equally critical criteria such as race and class. At present we have no data on how and to what extent these restrict marital choice.

In the last five decades almost all religious and ethnic groups have demonstrated some flexibility in relation to endogamy. Such flexibility stems from at least two sources. First, the size and distribution of certain ethnic groups relative to others. In general, studies indicate that the smaller the ethnic group or the larger the demographic imbalance, the greater the tendency for exogamy or out-marriage. Secondly, the combined forces of industrialization, urbanization, and secularization seem to minimize the importance of religion and ethnicity, if not race, with respect to intermarriage. In a study of the relationship between Jewish outmarriage and social cohesion, Cohn (1976: 104) suggests that, "Outmarriages by Jews may be considered either as a sign of breakdown of Jewish communal solidarity or as a sign of the integration of Jews into the social solidarity of their surroundings or both."

Undoubtedly, a host of other variables also shapes and determines mate-selection procedures, e.g., the romantic love complex, personal attributes, marital aspirations, the mass media, social class, etc. At present, it is impossible to assess their relative weights or to provide the reader with any illuminating generalizations because of the lack of empirical studies that go beyond small selective samples.

Dating Behaviour

Despite all its recognized shortcomings, dating remains the primary means by which individuals are inducted into the courtship process which eventually leads to binding commitments such as marriage. Statements concerning its demise and outmoded nature notwithstanding there are few institutionalized alternatives to dating as the initial phase in bringing marriageable individuals together. In general, most young Canadians start dating in their early teens (approximately fourteen for girls, fifteen for boys) and continue for about eight years. Urban dwellers tend to start slightly earlier than rural residents and there are only a few sex differences in dating behaviour. For example, females tend to have more dates and date more frequently with different partners than boys. Males tend to view dating in a recreational context and appear to be more sexually-oriented than females. Females, on the other hand, view dating as part of the courtship and marriage process, and more likely to confine their sexual activities to one partner with an emphasis on emotional commitment. However, Whitehurst's study discussed in Chapter 2 casts doubt on the strictly matrimonial function of dating. Although it is true that dating as we know it today is mainly recreational, there is no evidence that other methods of mate-choice have replaced dating. Whether among cosmopolitan Torontonians or among the traditional Hutterites, some variant of dating remains as the primary means for selection of a partner.

It is difficult to gauge the extent to which the norms of endogamy are expressed in dating behaviour. In a study of Saskatoon university students, Wakil found that considerations such as religion, ethnicity, and class did not play a significant part in the choice of dating partners. However, generalizations in this regard cannot be made owing to the nature of the samples studied. For instance, in almost all studies, the respondents are drawn from college or university campuses. Given that approximately 15 per cent of those eligible to attend universities do so, and that two-thirds of these individuals have middle- and upper-class backgrounds of the dominant ethnic groups, it is clear that most samples are unrepresentative.

Premarital Sexual Attitudes and Behaviour

Of the three elements of courtship process discussed here, certain notable changes have occurred in premarital sexual attitudes and behaviour. Studies cited in Chapter 3 by Hobart indicate that in general the changes are in the direction of increasing permissive attitudes and behaviour. For example, studies by Packard and Perlman show that the majority of the respondents state that sexual intercourse is permissible after engagement.

In two of his own studies about ten years apart (1968 and 1977) Hobart explored further the issue of increasing permissiveness. He found that English-speaking respondents showed a marked increase in permissive attitudes. Those who felt that sexual intercourse is acceptable for those who are in love or engaged increased from 59 per cent in 1968 to 82 per cent in 1977. The greatest increase was shown by females who felt intercourse is acceptable when engaged. At the attitudinal level, however, males tended to conform to the "double standard", i.e., sexual intercourse should be permissible for men but not women. In addition, Hobart found that in 1968 French-Canadian males and females were more conservative than English but by 1977, the differences had decreased.

Evidence on premarital sexual behaviour in 1960s and 1970s also indicates that permissiveness is on the increase. Packard's research during the 1960s showed that of five national samples (the United States, Canada, England, Germany, and Norway), Canadians were the most conservative. These findings are complemented by Hobart's studies which reported an increase in the incidence of intercourse by about 20 and 15 per cent respectively for English females and males. French females, on the other hand, seem to have registered the highest percentage increase (more than double, see Table 3:6) and as a consequence, more French women than men reported having had sexual intercourse.

Chapter 3 also notes the association between permissiveness and other social characteristics. For example, Catholics and Jews tend to be less permissive than Protestants. Those who attend church infrequently, live in settings such as campus residence halls, and in urban areas, report dissatisfaction with the kind of sex instruction provided by parents, and those who come from lower-income and upper-middle-class backgrounds tend to be more permissive than others.

Finally, Hobart notes that significant changes in premarital sexual permissiveness also reveal certain converging trends. Canadian attitudes towards and experiences in premarital sex closely correspond to the American in this respect. The discrepancy between the males and the females in liberality is vanishing mainly because women are "catching up" with men. Finally, the differences between the Canadian French- and English-speaking person which were sharp a decade ago, have practically disappeared. The 1977 data demonstrate that French Canadians (and especially women) now express more permissive attitudes than do English Canadians.

ASPECTS OF MARRIAGE AND THE FAMILY

The discussion of demographic materials in the introductory chapter has underscored the pervasiveness of marriage and the family as primary social institutions. In chapters 4 through 7, our contributors have assessed in detail some of the conditions which facilitate continuity of marriage and the family in Canada and also attempted to delineate changes occurring in these institutions. In what follows, our main purpose is to stress the highlights and major points in these chapters.

Profiles of Marriage

The demographic data on marriage in Chapter 1 make a convincing argument that marriage is more than holding its own—at least at the aggregate statistical level. In fact, one could even say it has never been more popular, especially when we hear of many individuals and couples who are experimenting with alternatives to marriage. Moreover, Canadians are marrying at a younger age than they did a generation ago and the age differences between spouses continue to decrease.

To what extent changes in the demographic characteristics of marriage have affected interpersonal relationships is difficult to fathom at this time. But if the studies Nett discusses in Chapter 4 in any way reflect the sentiments of Canadians, marriage continues to be an ambivalent and challenging enterprise. For example, many studies suggest that "marriage results in a loss of individuality" and "a decline in conjugality". That such attitudes reflect reality may be inferred from increasing divorce rates and single-person households. From some of the studies one may get an impression that all is not well with marriage. If one looks at the demographic data, however, one is hard-pressed to understand not only the increasing marriage rate, but also the desire to marry early and/or to marry shortly after divorce.

The image of marriage as the locus of both continuity and change becomes clear when we examine Nett's analysis of literature on the division of labour within marriage and family contexts. Public opinion, in general, strongly adheres to the idea that the married woman's major role is to care for young children at home. A majority of Canadians also believe that women's participation in the labour force has a harmful effect on the family life. Consequently, the division of labour continues to be determined along sex lines. When women work outside the home they usually end up having two careers, one at home and the other outside. As Chapter 4 indicates, whether it is in the Toronto suburb of Crestwood Heights or on a farm in the Prairies, the rigidity of a sex-based division of labour and the dual obligations of females persist. As Nett notes, there seems to be a strong commitment (at least by men) to a division of labour in which most of the household labour is performed by wives whether or not they are in the labour force part- or full-time.

Yet data on participation of women in the labour force in the last seven decades show a significant increase. For example, in 1901 only 14 per cent of the labour force consisted of women and this figure rose to 36.7 per cent in 1975. Furthermore, there has been a steady increase in the proportion of married women in the labour force to the point where they outnumber other females. In 1962, 21.6 per cent of all married women were in the labour force, and in 1975 this percentage rose to 41.6 per cent. What such an increase points to is that either more women are choosing (or being forced) to work outside the home even if it means bearing the burdens of two jobs or that there have been structural changes in the domestic division of labour. Existing evidence fails to support the latter assumption. But studies of married employed women elsewhere do suggest that the role of the husband has increasingly become flexible especially when he perceives that the wife's earnings are important for the family economy.

As Nett observes in Chapter 4, we know very little about marital interaction in the areas of decision-making, conflict, adjustment, and satisfaction since we are restricted to isolated studies some of which deal with aforementioned issues only tangentially. For example, conflict among working-class couples revolves around the employment of both spouses and the tension it creates in their social and sexual lives.

Profiles of the Family

Demographically the size of the Canadian family has fluctuated between 3.7 and 3.9 in the last four decades. This, as we noted in the introductory chapter, is a consequence of the continuing decline in birth rate. The latest available data show that the average Canadian family includes the husband, the wife, and one or two children. Even in regions traditionally known for their high fertility the birth rate is falling sharply and beginning to reflect national patterns of family size.

There are few sociological studies that provide conclusive explanations for the complex phenomenon of falling birth rates. Nevertheless, a plausible hypothesis as any (and partially substantiated by the demographic experience of other nations) is that most Canadians pressed by increasing economic, social, and psychological costs of child-rearing, coupled with rising material expectations are committed to having one or two children at the most. What is important to recognize here is the persistence of parenthood in the face of various competing and alternative lifestyles and ideologies. From this point of view, the Canadian family reflects an orderly continuity.

But one cannot draw such inferences regarding the prevailing notions about socialization. In Chapter 5, Nett outlines how familial and societal structures encourage the continuity of sex-typed socialization and subtly, but effectively, continue to resist the transformation of the traditional inflexible role models. For example, most children in Canada continue to be socialized along strict sex lines and parents tend to inculcate the traditional values and beliefs about male and female roles and responsibilities. Ironically, as some studies reveal, the younger generation tends to be more traditional in terms of role specialization based on sex identity than the older. However, as Nett notes, the findings are not entirely consistent on this point. Males tend to be less enthusiastic, if not reluctant, to change their beliefs and practices related to sex roles and as a result experience greater stress than females. Females, on the other hand, project ambivalence in that they value their femininity, the security, protection, and prestige conferred on them by males, and their domestic roles but at the same time also reject their image as a satisfied homemaker. In essence, the Canadian female tends to be much more flexible and, therefore, more prone to change with respect to sex-role ideology and behaviour than the Canadian male.

Undoubtedly the increasing participation of married women in the labour force necessitates changes in the stereotypical perceptions of women as happy homemakers which can be transmitted to the next generation. The changes occur in relation to decision-making processes, re-allocation of domestic chores, and other aspects of conjugal interaction. The restructuring of domestic duties entails not so much the conception of work based on male-female competence as the bargains struck before marriage at the time of employment, and other crucial phases of the family cycle. Such structural changes are bound to leave an impression on children's perceptions of parental roles which they emulate, at least partially. The image of father, for example, as a patriarch who is the sole bread-winner will increasingly have little cultural or empirical relevance for children if present trends continue. Sociological investigations in Canada have not yet addressed these issues. Although such dual-career or employed families are still statistically small, they cannot be ignored because they increasingly serve as reference points and models for other married couples.

An analysis of literature on kinship reveals that in Canada most families are nuclear in structure and autonomous. Although there appears to be a general preference to be close to relatives, especially parents and siblings, geographic mobility is common and there is contradictory evidence on how this has affected the functioning of kin networks. Available data suggest that the relevance and importance attached to kin varies from one ethnic group to the other, e.g., as opposed to the English, French and Italian Canadians maintain a cohesive kin structure which is reinforced by frequent visits, mutual aid, ritual occasions, etc.

The overview presented in Chapter 6 suggests that in urban Canada, kinship networks are maintained not so much on the basis of binding obligation or as an element of social organization but rather on voluntary and selective criteria. People choose certain kin from a large kin universe for sociability and sentimental purposes as well as pragmatic concerns involving mutual aid. The number of relatives so chosen, the frequency of visits, and the nature of interaction are to a large extent determined by residential proximity, class differences, mutual interests, and genealogical distance. What is evident in the literature is that there is a persistence of values supportive of extended kin contacts and that the nuclear family continues to be the primary medium through which kin solidarity is expressed.

The relationship between the family and other social institutions and processes is an important area of concern and analysis. Unfortunately our present knowledge is inadequate and superficial. The influence of religion, government, the economy, and the mass media on contemporary Canadian families and vice versa is far from clear and although there have been many theoretical allusions we have few empirical insights into such matters. In Chapter 7 Tavuchis attempts to identify the intricate relationship between ethnicity and family. As he notes, in a society which emphasizes ethnic pluralism the family has a strategic significance, in that it has the prime responsibility of socializing the next generation to its beliefs and practices which, in turn, are derived from ethnic culture.

Consequently, the family becomes the first line of defence against assimilative influences.

According to Tavuchis, the family as an institution is ultimately and inextricably linked to the vitality and persistence of ethnicity insofar as it is able and willing to foster allegiance and conformity to traditions. First-generation immigrants and certain persecuted minority groups such as the Anabaptist and Jewish groups tend to resist acculturation into the larger Canadian society. Until the 1950s the French Canadians also resisted the influence of modern secular forces including cultural assimilation by the dominant English.

The Canadian family as a rampart of ethnicity is fast losing ground in recent decades and the author's discussion suggests three reasons for this. First the unavoidable and irresistible forces of industrialization which exert pressures toward convergence in all aspects of social life including the family. Such uniformity is reflected in the birth rate, the nature of family life, kinship orientations, and adherence to standardized legal codes pertaining to marriage and divorce. Second, the English language and culture are pervasive and dominating vehicles which press toward homogeneity with ethnicity increasingly confined to certain residual elements rather than the total cultural complex. The French-Canadian and the Polish-Canadian families illustrate this point. Third, courtship practices, such as dating and premarital sex, neutralize the continuity of particularistic ethnic differences. (As Hobart notes in Chapter 3, the French and English respondents demonstrate similar attitudes and behaviour with regard to premarital sex.) Further, ethnic intermarriages over time reduce the prospects of the survival of ethnic differences.

In sum, Tavuchis's review argues that despite the pockets of resistance, ethnic family patterns are losing their distinctiveness and converging toward a general Canadian pattern that mirrors urban-industrial societies throughout the world.

DIVORCE AND REMARRIAGE

The rising incidence of divorce and remarriage in Canada not only highlights the transitions occurring in Canadian marital and family life but also the growing tension between traditional and modern values. Despite the liberalizing of Canadian divorce laws in 1968, they continue to reflect a conservative turn of mind. On the other hand, prompted by the increasing number of divorces, the complex and often insensitive legal procedures have been increasingly subjected to reformist pressures (from both liberals and conservatives) aimed at making the legal system more responsive and humane in the light of contemporary mores and conditions. At present, various interest groups are pressing for "no fault" divorce, and a reduction of the separation period to one year, from the present three, before the final decree is granted. As we noted in chapters 8 and 9, divorce and remarriage are no longer the stigmatized social situations they once were in Canadian society.

Divorce

In Chapter 8, Peters traces the evolution of divorce laws in Canada and concludes that recent changes in divorce laws which took place in 1968 partially reflect the response to changes in family life. However, as even a cursory review of the reformed law would suggest, the major grounds on which legal dissolution of a marriage can be sought remain unchanged. The only element of progress one can note in the reformed divorce law is the introduction of the "marital breakdown" clause. In recent years, over one-third of marriages terminated were done so on the grounds of "marital breakdown" (for details, see Chapter 9). While certain interest groups have kept up their pressure for further liberalization of divorce laws, the State, indirectly supported by the Church, has not yet yielded to such pressures.

An examination of demographic and sociological evidence by Peters sheds light on some of the social patterning of divorce. For example, there is an inverse relationship between age and income, and the incidence of divorce. Those who marry early (earlier than the median age at marriage in Canada, especially teenage marriages), and those who come from low income families tend to have a high degree of divorce-proneness. In this connection, Peters notes that in 1975, of those divorced, 43 per cent of women, and 13 per cent of men were married when they were 20 years old or younger. Whether a couple live in rural or urban areas also appears to contribute to marital stability or instability, with individuals in cities showing a higher divorce rate than those in rural areas. Contrary to popular belief, children do not have a stabilizing influence on a marriage, and increasingly are participants in the divorce experience. (Almost two-thirds of divorces decreed in 1975 involved children.)

Despite rigid legal codes, the divorce rate in Canada has registered consistent increases during the past decade. The most frequently cited grounds for divorce are marital breadown and adultery. In general, there appears to be a greater degree of social acceptance and tolerance of divorce and the divorced.

Remarriage

It is not clear as to what proportion of those whose marriages are dissolved by death or divorce remarry, but there has been an increase in the proportion of second marriages in the total population of the married. From 1966 to 1973 this has increased from 12.4 to 18.1 per cent. This datum indicates that divorce does not necessarily represent disillusionment with marriage but with one's spouse and, in fact, those who remarry do so within two years after their divorce.

Schlesinger's investigations of remarried couples show that such marriages are less romantically inclined and based on more realistic expectations. The mate-selection process involves a careful scrutiny of competence in handling interpersonal relationships. Most couples studied by Schlesinger noted that there was a change in the quality of their relationship although remarriages were not free from problems. Essentially, problems were related to initial adjustment between spouses, adjustment between step-children and step-parent, and the occasional intrusion of the former spouse into the new marriage because of his or her relationship to the children.

The discussion of divorce and remarriage in chapters 8 and 9 again emphasizes continuity and change. On the one hand, it is clear that marriage as a social institution continues to thrive in Canada. On the other hand, the increasing divorce rate clearly reflects both the relative ease of legal divorce, the high expectations of marriage, and the reluctance to tolerate situations that do not fulfill expectations and perceived needs. For an increasing number of individuals, marriage is defined as a voluntary association in which the couple seek to meet each other's needs and their mutual commitment is contingent upon their ability to meet each other's expectations. In effect, what determines the stability of marriage is not religious bonds or social pressures from kith and kin but the nature and quality of interpersonal relationships. In this sense, divorce and remarriage patterns signify the changing definition of marriage among some Canadians.

ALTERNATIVES

In Chapter 10, Whitehurst assesses the significance of the so-called alternate lifestyles and their impact on marriage and family relations. He attributes the emergence of variant family movement to the influence of mass media, the demand for human rights and choices of various kinds, the decline of kin control and organized religion, flexible divorce laws, the feminist movements, and two negative concomitants of rapid industrialization and urbanization—anomie and alienation. In addition, the well-publicized alternate lifestyles in the United States (e.g., communes, swinging) have inspired many innovative or disillusioned Canadians to adapt these in a bid for a better life.

As Whitehurst correctly stresses, however, variant forms have barely left their mark on conventional patterns either statistically or as enduring and viable variants. There is little evidence of the success of communes on the west coast. Swinging does not appear to have gained popularity nor has the practice of "open-marriage" become widespread or accepted by most couples. Nevertheless, as Whitehurst observes, the pattern of unmarried people living together is gaining a certain degree of social acceptance. "At this time cohabitation seems more properly considered as more or less a replacement for older forms of engagement since the preponderance of cohabitants at some time or other tend to marry. . . . Cohabitation may rationalize and liberalize mate-selection, but seems to have little total effect . . . on the marriages that ensue" (Chapter 10, p. 171).

The interplay of and the resultant tensions between conservative and liberal forces in Canada are apparent in the area of sexuality both within and outside marriage, and with respect to homosexual marriages. Although conjugal fidelity as a marital norm is still strongly supported, there has not only been a weakening increase in extramarital sexuality, but also a weakening of the traditional double standard. Whitehurst summarizes such trends as follows: "the old adaptation of conventional marriage—with some extramarital sexuality on the side—must be considered as the continuing dominant variant" (p. 170). In effect, phenomena such as "swinging" or "open marriage" do not seem to have left an enduring mark on conventional patterns of conjugal fidelity or infidelity and are limited to a small proportion of the population.

By religious decree and majority preference, heterosexual unions have always been accorded the highest prestige and protection in Canada as in most societies. But now homosexual groups are exerting pressures for social recognition of their sexual preference and legitimation of marriages between persons of the same sex. Their cause has been sympathetically received by certain liberal-minded people. These developments have prompted many conservatives to align themselves in a crusade to block any further progress of homosexuals in either legal or social contexts. What we are witnessing here are conflicting conceptions of marriage by the dominant and minority groups. The dominant groups are resisting any changes that may result in marriage and sexual practices in Canada because of the pressures applied by homophile groups. For the foreseeable future, however, "the idea of something like legitimate marriage between gays is simply stretching the mores too far for the average citizen of this land as a legitimate probability" (Chapter 10, p. 177).

RESEARCH ON MARRIAGE AND THE FAMILY IN CANADA: SOME IMPRESSIONS

Our primary task in this volume has been to provide an overview of the significant research in the area of courtship, marriage, and the family in Canada. This has been an unenviable if not ambitious task for several reasons. First, the most obvious fact is that research in the sociology of marriage and the family is extremely sparse compared to other substantive specialties. There are numerous gaps in our knowledge and these are underscored by the virtually unanimous complaints about the paucity of data made by the contributors to this volume. A cursory review of most chapters reveals that the authors have based their analyses on only a handful of research articles and monographs. Second, given the lack of pertinent materials, many of our contributors have extensively reviewed materials of marginal relevance to their topics (e.g., Nett and Tavuchis). Third, because of the aforementioned problems, many contributors have had to dwell upon theoretical aspects instead of concrete evidence (e.g., Moon's discussion of mate-selection theories), while some topics have been treated rather descriptively (e.g., remarriage). Perhaps such problems are endemic to an area which has not attracted empirical research. However, such a rationalization should not preclude an analysis of the reasons for the lethargic pace of research in the areas discussed in previous chapters.

As noted elsewhere (Ramu and Tavuchis, 1977) approximately fifteen years ago Elkin (1964) alerted us to the empirical lacunae in family sociology in Canada. Based on our understanding of the discussions in previous chapters, we would conclude that many of the problems cited by Elkin have been neither addressed nor resolved. It appears that research on marriage and family patterns in Canada continues to be fragmented, lacks direction, and fails to meet the standards found in other developed nations regardless of size. With very few exceptions, our over-all research efforts do not seem to be related to larger trends or theoretical foci. To be sure, gains have been made by some solo researchers who have directed their sustained attention to certain specific problems (e.g., Hobart on premarital sexuality). But it would take the efforts of a large contingent of researchers to bridge the gaps in our knowledge which Elkin documented in 1964. We hope that our overview of the field in this volume will serve as a bench-mark for what we have accomplished so far, and what needs to be done in the future.

SELECTED BIBLIOGRAPHY

COHN, WERNER. "Jewish Outmarriages and Anomie", *Canadian Review of Sociology*
1976   *and Anthropology*, Vol. 3, No. 1 (February).
RAMU, G. N. and N. TAVUCHIS. Reviews of books on Canadian marriage and the
1977   family, *Journal of Marriage and the Family*, Vol. 39, No. 3 (August).

Bibliography

ABELL, HELEN C. "Adaptation of the Rural Family to Change", in S. Parvez-Wakil,
1975   ed., *Marriage, Family, and Society: Canadian Perspectives*. Toronto:
     Butterworth.

ABERNATHY, THOMAS J. and MARGARET ARCUS. "The Law and Divorce in Canada",
1977   *The Family Coordinator*, Vol 26, No. 4 (October), pp. 409–13.

ADAMS, BERT N. *Kinship in an Urban Setting*. Chicago: Markham.
1968

———. *The Family: A Sociological Interpretation*. Chicago: Rand McNally.
1975

Advisory Council on the Status of Women. *Annual Report*, 1974–75. Ottawa:
1975   Queen's Printer.

AMBERT, ANNE-MARIE. *Sex Structure*. Second ed. Don Mills: Longman Canada.
1976

AMES, MICHAEL M. and JOY INGLIS. "Tradition and Change in British Columbia Sikh
1976   Family Life", in K. Ishwaran, ed., *The Canadian Family*. Revised ed.
     Toronto: Holt, Rinehart and Winston.

BANDURA, A. "The Role of the Modeling Processes in Personality Development", in
1969   Donna M. Gelfand, ed., *Social Learning in Childhood*. Belmont, Cali-
     fornia: Brooks Cole.

BARCLAY, HAROLD D. "The Lebanese Muslim Family", in K. Ishwaran, ed., *The Cana-*
1971   *dian Family*. Toronto: Holt, Rinehart and Winston.

BAUMAN, KARL E. "Volunteer Bias in a Study of Sexual Knowledge, Attitudes and
1973   Behaviour", *Journal of Marriage and the Family*, Vol. 35 (February),
     pp. 27–31.

——— and ROBERT R. WILSON. "Sexual Behaviour of Unmarried University Students
1974   in 1968 and 1972", *The Journal of Sex Research*, Vol. 10, pp. 327–33.

BAXTER, E. H. "Children's and Adolescents' Perception of Occupational Prestige",
1976   *Canadian Review of Sociology and Anthropology*, Vol. 13, No. 2, pp.
     229–38.

BAYER, ALAN E. "Sexual Permissiveness and Correlates as Determined Through
1977   Interaction Analyses", *Journal of Marriage and the Family*, Vol. 39,
     pp. 29–40.

B.C. Divorce Guide. Third ed. Vancouver: Self-Counsel Press.
1973

BEATTIE, JOHN. *Other Cultures: Aims, Methods and Achievements in Social Anthro-*
1964   *pology*. New York: The Free Press.

BECKER, GARY. "A Theory of the Allocation of Time", *Economic Journal*, Vol. 75
1965   (September).

BELL, ROBERT R. *Premarital Sex in a Changing Society*. Englewood Cliffs, New
1966   Jersey: Prentice-Hall.

——— and JAY B. CHASKES. "Premarital Sexual Experience Among Coeds, 1958–
1970   1968", *Journal of Marriage and the Family*, Vol. 32 (February), pp.
     81–84.

——— and SYLVIA CLAVAN. "Settings and Techniques in Marital Sexuality", unpub-
1973   lished manuscript, Temple University.

———. *Marriage and Family Interaction*. Homewood, Ill.: Dorsey Press.
1975

BEM, SANDRA L. and DARYL J. BEM. "Case Study of Nonconscious Ideology: Train-
1970   ing the Woman to Know Her Place", in D. J. Bem, ed., *Beliefs, Atti-*
     tudes and Human Affairs. Monterey, California: Brooks Cole.

BENNETT, JOHN W. "A Comparison: Hutterite Women and Their Families", a sup-
1976   plementary essay in Seena Kohl. *Working Together*. Toronto: Holt,
Rinehart and Winston.
BERGER, PETER and HANSFRIED KELLNER. "Marriage and the Construction of Re-
1971   ality", in Hans Peter Drietzel, ed., *Recent Sociology No. 2: Patterns of
Communicative Behaviour*. New York: Macmillan.
BERNARD, JESSIE. *Remarriage*. New York: Dryden Press.
BEYER, MARY ALICE and ROBERT N. WHITEHURST. "Value Change with Length of
1976   Marriage: Some Correlates of Consonance and Dissonance", *Inter-
national Journal of Sociology of the Family*, Vol. 6 (Spring), pp. 109–20.
BIENVENUE, RITA M. "Intergroup Relations: Ethnicity in Canada", in G. N. Ramu
1976   and S. D. Johnson, eds., *Introduction to Canadian Society: Sociological
Analysis*. Toronto: Macmillan.
BIRDSALL, NANCY. "Women and Population Studies", *Signs: Journal of Women in
1976   Culture and Society*, Vol. 1, No. 3 (Spring), pp. 699–712.
BLAU, PETER. *Exchange and Power in Social Life*. New York: John Wiley.
1964
BOHANNAN, PAUL, ed. *Divorce and After*. New York: Doubleday.
1970
——. "The Six Stations of Divorce", in Marcia E. and Thomas E. Lasswell, eds.,
1973   *Love, Marriage, Family*. Glenview, Ill.: Scott, Foresman.
BOISSEVAIN, JEREMY. "Family and Kinship Among Italians in Montreal", in K.
1976   Ishwaran, ed., *The Canadian Family*. Revised ed. Toronto: Holt, Rinehart and Winston.
BOLTON, CHARLES D. "Mate Selection as the Development of a Relationship", *Mar-
1961   riage and Family Living*, Vol. 23, pp. 225–36.
BOSSARD, JAMES H. S. "Residential Propinquity as a Factor of Mate Selection",
1932   *American Journal of Sociology*, Vol. 38, pp. 219–24.
BOTT, ELIZABETH. *Family and Social Network*. London: Tavistock Publications.
1957
BOWERMAN, CHARLES E. and BARBARA R. DAY. "Test of the Theory of Complementary
1956   Needs, *American Sociological Review*, Vol. 21, pp. 602–05.
BOYD, MONICA. "Equality Between the Sexes: The Results of Canadian Gallup Polls,
1974   1953–1973", paper presented at the Annual Meeting of the Canadian
Sociology and Anthropology Association.
——, MARGRIT EICHLER, and JOHN R. HOFLEY. "Family: Functions, Formation and
1976   Fertility", in Gail C. A. Cook, ed., *Opportunity for Choice: A Goal
for Women in Canada*. Ottawa: Statistics Canada.
BRETON, RAYMOND and JOHN C. MCDONALD. "Occupational Preferences of Canadian
1971   High School Students", in B. Blishen *et al.*, eds., *Canadian Society*. Third
ed.(abr.) Toronto: Macmillan.
BROGAN, DONNA and NANCY G. KUTNER. "Measuring Sex-Role Orientation: A Norma-
1976   tive Approach", *Journal of Marriage and the Family*, Vol. 38, No. 1,
pp. 31–41.
BUCHLER, IRA R. and HENRY A. SELBY. *Kinship and Social Organization: An Intro-
1968   duction to Theory and Method*. New York: Macmillan.
BURGESS, ERNEST and PAUL WALLIN. *Engagement and Marriage*. Philadelphia: J. B.
1953   Lippincott.
BURKE, RONALD J. and TAMARA WEIR. "Husband-Wife Helping Relationships: The
1974   'Mental Hygiene' Function in Marriage", paper presented at the American Psychological Association Convention, New Orleans.
—— and ——. "Relationships of Wives' Employment Status to Husband, Wife

1976a   and Pair Satisfaction and Performance", *Journal of Marriage and the Family*, Vol. 38, No. 2 (May), pp. 279–87.

——, ——, and DENISE HARRISON. "Disclosure of Problems and Tensions Experi-
1976b   enced by Marital Partners", *Psychological Reports*, Vol. 38, pp. 531–42.

BURR, W. R. "Satisfaction with Various Aspects of Marriage over the Life Cycle",
1970   *Journal of Marriage and the Family*, Vol. 32, pp. 26–37.

——. *Theory Construction and the Sociology of the Family*. New York: John Wiley.

BUTLER, PETER M. "Single and Dual Earning and Family Involvement in the Work
1976   World", in K. Ishwaran, ed., *The Canadian Family*. Revised ed. Toronto: Holt, Rinehart and Winston.

CAMPBELL, A. "The American Way of Mating: Marriage si, Children only Maybe",
1975   *Psychology Today*, May, pp. 37–43.

Canadian Ethnic Studies. Bulletin of the Research Centre for Canadian Ethnic
Studies, University of Calgary.

Canadian Mother and Child, The. Third ed. Ottawa: Information Canada.
1967

CANNON, KENNETH L. and RICHARD LONG. "Premarital Sexual Behaviour in the Six-
1971   ties", in Carlfred B. Broderick, ed., *A Decade of Family Research and
Action*. Minneapolis: National Council on Family Relations.

CARISSE, COLLETTE. *Planification des Naissances en Milieu Canadien-Francais*. Mont-
1964   real: Presses de l'Université de Montreal.

——. "Cultural Orientations in Marriages Between French and English Canadians",
1975a   in S. Parvez-Wakil, ed., *Marriage, Family, and Society: Canadian Perspectives*. Scarborough, Ontario: Butterworth.

——. "The Family: The Issue of Change", in Dennis Forcese and Stephen Richer,
1975b   eds., *Issues in Canadian Society: An Introduction to Sociology*. Scarborough, Ontario: Prentice-Hall.

——. "Life Plans of Innovative Women: A Strategy for Living the Feminine Role",
1976a   in Lyle E. Larson, *The Canadian Family in Comparative Perspective*.
Scarborough, Ontario: Prentice-Hall.

——. "Cultural Orientations in Marriages Between French and English Canadians",
1976b   in Lyle E. Larson, *The Canadian Family in Comparative Perspective*.
Scarborough, Ontario: Prentice-Hall.

CATTELL, RAYMOND B. and JOHN R. NESSELROADE. "'Likeness' and 'Completeness'
1967   Theories Examined by 16 Personality Factors Measured on Stably and
Unstably Married Couples", advanced publication No. 7, University of
Illinois, Urbana.

CHIMBOS, PETER D. "Marital Violence: A Study of Husband-Wife Homicide", in
1976   K. Ishwaran, ed., *The Canadian Family*. Revised ed. Toronto: Holt,
Rinehart and Winston.

CHODOROW, NANCY. "Family Structure and Feminine Personality", in Michelle Zim-
1974   balist Rosaldo and Louise Lamphere, eds., *Women, Culture, and Society*. Stanford, California: Stanford Press.

CHRISTENSEN, HAROLD T. and CHRISTINA F. GREGG. "Changing Sex Norms in America
1970   and Scandinavia", *Journal of Marriage and the Family*, No. 32, pp.
616–27.

CLAYTON, RICHARD R. "Religious Orthodoxy and Premarital Sex", *Social Forces*, Vol.
1969   47 (June), pp. 469–74.

——. "Premarital Sexual Intercourse: A Substantive Test of the Contingent Con-
1972   sistency Model", *Journal of Marriage and the Family*, Vol. 34 (May),
pp. 273–81.

COLE, WILLIAM G. *Sex in Christianity and Psychoanalysis*. New York: Oxford
1955   University Press.

CONOVER, PATRICK W. "An Analysis of Communes and Intentional Communities
1975   with Particular Attention to Sexual and General Relations", *The Family Coordinator*, Vol. 24, No. 4 (October), pp. 453–64.

COOK, GAIL C. A. *Opportunity for Choice: A Goal for Women in Canada*. Ottawa:
1976   Information Canada.

COOMBS, ROBERT H. "Value Consensus and Partner Satisfaction Among Dating
1966   Couples", *Journal of Marriage and the Family*, Vol. 28, pp. 166–73.

CORELLI, R. "One Year's Separation Proposed as Only Ground for Divorce",
1973   *Toronto Star*, 29 August.

COSER, ROSE and GERALD ROKOFF. "Women in the Occupational World: Social Dis-
1974   ruption and Conflict", in Rose Laub Coser, ed., *The Family: Its Structure and Functions*. Second ed. New York: St. Martin's Press.

CRUIKSHANK, JULIA. "Matrifocal Families in the Canadian North", in K. Ishwaran,
1975   ed., *The Canadian Family*. Toronto: Holt, Rinehart and Winston.

CRYSDALE, S. "Family and Kinship in Riverdale", in W. E. Mann, ed., *Canada: A*
1968   *Sociological Profile*. Toronto: Copp Clark.

DANZIGER, KURT. *The Socialization of Immigrant Children*. Toronto: Institute of
1971   Behavioural Research, York University.

——. "Differences in Acculturation and Patterns of Socialization Among Italian
1975   Immigrant Families", in Robert M. Pike and Elia Zureik, eds., *Socialization and Values in Canadian Society*, Vol. II. Toronto: The Carleton Library, Macmillan.

——. "The Acculturation of Italian Immigrant Girls", in K. Ishwaran, ed., *The*
1976   *Canadian Family*. Revised ed. Toronto: Holt, Rinehart and Winston.

DAVIDSON, J. KENNETH, SR. and GERALD R. LESLIE. "Premarital Sexual Intercourse:
1977   An Application of Axiomatic Theory Construction", *Journal of Marriage and the Family*, Vol. 39, pp. 15–25.

DAVIS, K. E. "Sex on Campus: Is There a Revolution?", *Medical Aspects of Human*
1970   *Sexuality*.

DECKERT, PAMELA and LANGELIER RAGIS. "A Comparative, Crosscultural Study of
1977   Divorced Canadians", paper presented at the National Council on Family Relations Conference, San Diego, October.

DOUVAN, ELIZABETH. "Employment and the Adolescent", in Ivan Nye and Lois
1963   Hoffman, eds., *The Employed Mother in America*. Chicago: Rand McNally.

DUBERMAN, LUCILE. *The Reconstituted Family*. New York: Nelson-Hall.
1976

——. *Marriage and Other Alternatives*. New York: Praeger.
1977

EASTMAN, WILLIAM F. "First Intercourse", *Sexual Behaviour*, Vol. 2 (January), pp.
1972   22–27.

ECKLAND, BRUCE. "Theories of Mate Selection", *Eugenics Quarterly*, Vol. 15, pp.
1968   71–84.

Edmonton Journal. "Unmarried Couples Rise", 2 August, p. 15.
1977

EDWARDS, JOHN. "Familial Behaviour as Social Exchange", *Journal of Marriage*
1969   *and the Family*, Vol. 31, pp. 518–26.

—— and ALAN BOOTH. "Sexual Behaviour In and Out of Marriage: An Assessment
1976   of Correlates", *Journal of Marriage and the Family*, Vol. 38 (February), pp. 73–82.

EHRMANN, WINSTON W. "Influence of Comparative Social Class of Companion upon
1955   Premarital Heterosexual Behavior", *Marriage and Family Living*, Vol. 17, No. 1, pp. 48–53.

———. *Premarital Dating Behavior.* New York: Bantam Books.
1959

EICHLER, MARGRIT. "Sociological Researh on Women in Canada", *Canadian Re-*
1975a   *view of Sociology and Anthropology,* Vol. 12, No. 4 (November),
pp. 414–81.

———. "The Egalitarian Family in Canada", in S. Parvez-Wakil, ed., *Marriage, Fam-*
1975b   *ily, and Society: Canadian Perspectives.* Scarborough, Ontario: Butterworth.

———. "The Prestige of the Occupational Housewife", paper delivered at symposium,
1976   The Working Sexes, The Institute of Industrial Relations, University
of British Columbia.

———. *Grow Paper #6: Towards a Sociology of Feminist Research in Canada.* First
1977   draft, mimeographed (February).

ELKIN, FREDERICK. *The Family in Canada.* Ottawa: Vanier Institute of the Family.
1964

———and GERALD HANDEL. *The Child and Society: The Process of Socialization.* Sec-
1972   ond ed. New York: Random House.

ERIKSON, KAI T. "The Sociology of Deviance", in E. C. McDonagh and J. E. Simp-
1965   son, eds., *Persistent Challenges.* New York: Holt, Rinehart and Winston.

EVANS, RICHARD I. *Conversations with Carl Jung.* Princeton: Van Nostrand.
1964

Family Law. Law Reform Commission, Information Canada.
1976

Family Law Reform. Ministry of the Attorney General, 18 King Street East, Toronto, Ontario.

The Family Planning Federation of Canada. *Resource Catalogue.* Second ed.
1975   Ontario.

FARBER, BERNARD. *Family: Organization and Interaction.* San Francisco, California:
1964   Chandler Publications.

FERRELL, MARY A., WILLIAM L. TOLONE, and ROBERT H. WALSH. "Maturational and
1977   Societal Changes in the Sexual Double-Standard: A Palen Analysis",
Journal of Marriage and the Family, Vol. 39, pp. 255–71.

FIRTH, RAYMOND. *Two Studies of Kinship in London.* London: Athlone Press.
1956

FORCESE, DENNIS. *The Canadian Class Structure.* Toronto: McGraw-Hill Ryerson.
1975

FOX, ROBIN. *Kinship and Marriage.* Baltimore: Penguin.
1967

FRANCIS, E. K. *In Search of Utopia: The Mennonites in Manitoba.* Altona, Manitoba:
1955   D. W. Friesen.

FREEMAN, LINTON C. "Marriage Without Love: Mate-Selection in Non-Western
1974   Societies", in Robert F. Winch and Graham B. Spanier, eds., *Selected
Readings in Marriage and the Family.* New York: Holt, Rinehart and
Winston.

GARIGUE, PHILIPPE. "French-Canadian Kinship and Urban Life", *American Anthro-*
1956   *pologist,* Vol. 58. Reprinted in *Marriage, Family, and Society: Canadian
Perspectives,* ed., S. Parvez-Wakil. Scarborough, Ontario: Butterworth.

———. *La Vie Familiale des Canadiens Francais.* Montreal: Presses de l'Université
1962   de Montréal.

———. "The French Canadian Family", in Bernard R. Blishen *et al.* eds., *Canadian
1968   Society.* Toronto: Macmillan.

———. "The French Canadian Family", in Bernard R. Blishen *et al.* eds., *Canadian
1971   Society.* Third ed. Toronto: Macmillan.

———. "French Canadian Kinship and Urban Life", in K. Ishwaran, ed., *The Cana-*
1976   *dian Family.* Revised ed. Toronto: Holt, Rinehart and Winston. (First
       published in *American Anthropologist,* Vol. 58, December 1956, pp.
       1090–1100.)

GARRISON, ROBERT, V. E. ANDERSON, and SHELDON REED. "Assortative Marriage",
1968   *Eugenics Quarterly,* Vol. 15, pp. 113–27.

GEORGE, P. M. and H. Y. KIM. "Social Factors and Educational Aspirations of Cana-
1971   dian High School Students", in James E. Gallagher and Ronald D.
       Lambert, eds., *Social Process and Institution.* Toronto: Holt, Rinehart
       and Winston.

GIBRAN, KAHIL. *The Prophet,* various editions.
1929

GIBSON, J. "Kin Family Network: Overheralded Structure in Past Conceptualiza-
1972   tion of Family Functioning", *Journal of Marriage and the Family,* Vol.
       3, No. 2.

GLAZER-MALBIN, NONA. "Housework: A Review Essay", *Signs: Journal of Women in*
1976   *Culture and Society* (Summer), pp. 905–34.

GLEN, NORVALL D. and CHARLES H. WEAVER. "The Marital Happiness of Remarrried
1977   Divorced Persons", *Journal of Marriage and the Family,* Vol. 39 (May),
       pp. 331–38.

GLICK, PAUL. "A Demographer Looks at American Families", *Journal of Marriage*
1975   *and the Family,* Vol. 37, No. 1 (February), pp. 15–26.

GOLD, DOLORES. "Relations between Maternal Employment and Development of
1976   Nursery School Children", paper presented at the CPA Convention, To-
       ronto.

———. "Full-Time Employment of Mothers in Relation to Their Ten-Year-Old
1977   Children", *Atlantis,* Vol. 2, No. 2, pp. 98–105.

GOODE, WILLIAM J. "The Theoretical Importance of Love", *American Sociological*
1959   *Review,* Vol. 24, pp. 38–47.

———. *World Revolution and Family Patterns.* Glencoe, Illinois: The Free Press.
1963

———.*The Family.* Englewood Cliffs, New Jersey: Prentice-Hall.
1964

———. "Family and Mobility", in R. Bendix and S. M. Lipsett, eds., *Status and*
1966   *Power: Social Stratification in Comparative Perspective.* New York:
       Free Press.

———. "A Sociological Perspective on Marital Dissolution", in M. Anderson, ed.,
1971   *Sociology of the Family.* London: Penguin Modern Sociology.

———, E. HOPKINS and HELEN M. MCCLURE. *Social Systems and Family Patterns:*
1971   *A Propositional Inventory.* New York: Bobbs Merrill.

———. "Family Disorganization", in R. K. Merton and R. Nisbet, eds., *Contempor-*
1976   *ary Social Problems.* New York: Harcourt Brace Jovanovich.

GORDON, MILTON M. *Assimilation in American Life.* New York: Oxford University
1964   Press.

GREENFIELD, S. M. "Love and Marriage in Modern America: A Functional Analysis",
1965   *The Sociological Quarterly,* Vol. 4.

GREGOROVICH, ANDREW, ed. *Canadian Ethnic Groups Bibliography.* Toronto: On-
1972   tario Department of the Provincial Secretary and Citizenship.

GRINDSTAFF, CARL F. and G. EDWARD EBANKS. "Male Sterilization in Canada", in
1971   James F. Gallagher and Ronald D. Lambert, eds., *Social Process and*
       Institution: The Canadian Case. Toronto: Holt, Rinehart and Winston.

HARDY, KENNETH R. "An Appetitional Theory of Sexual Motivation", *Psychological*
1964   *Review,* Vol. 71, pp. 1–18.

HARTLEY, RUTH E. "A Developmental View of Female Sex-Role Identification", in

1966   B. J. Biddle and E. J. Thomas, eds., *Role Theory*. New York: John Wiley.

HEER, DAVID M. and CHARLES A. HUBAY, JR. "The Trend of Interfaith Marriages in
1975   Canada: 1922 to 1972", in S. Parvez-Wakil, ed., *Marriage, Family, and Society: Canadian Perspectives*. Scarborough, Ontario: Butterworth.

HENSHEL, ANNE-MARIE. "Swinging: The Sociology of Decision-Making", in S. Parvez-
1975   Wakil, ed., *Marriage, Family, and Society: Canadian Perspectives*. Scarborough, Ontario: Butterworth.

HELTSLEY, MARY E. and CARLFRED B. BRODERICK. "Religiosity and Premarital Sexual
1969   Permissiveness, A Re-examination of the Reiss Traditionalism Proposition", *Journal of Marriage and the Family*, Vol. 31, pp. 441–43.

HILL, CHARLES T., ZICK RUBIN and LETITIA ANNE PEPLAU. "Breakups Before Marriage:
1976   The End of 103 Affairs", *Journal of Social Issues*, Vol. 32, pp. 14–168.

HOBART, CHARLES W. *Italian Immigrants in Edmonton: Adjustment and Integration*.
1966   Ottawa: Information Canada.

——. "Orientations to Marriage Among Young Canadians", *Journal of Compara-
1972a   tive Family Studies*, Vol. 3 (Autumn), pp. 171–93.

——. "Sexual Permissiveness in Young English and French Canadians", *Journal
1972b   of Marriage and the Family*, Vol. 34, No. 2, pp. 292–303.

——. "Attitudes Toward Parenthood Among Canadian Young People", *Journal of
1973   Marriage and the Family*, Vol. 35, No. 1, pp. 71–81.

——."The Social Context of Morality Standards Among Anglophone Canadian
1974   Students", *Journal of Comparative Family Studies*, Vol. 5, No. 1, pp. 26–40.

——. "Ownership of Matrimonial Property", *The Canadian Review of Sociology
1975   and Anthropology*, Vol. 12, No. 4 (November), pp. 440–52.

——. "The Changing Family Patterns Among Ukrainian-Canadians in Alberta",
1976   in Lyle E. Larson, *The Canadian Family in Comparative Perspective*. Scarborough, Ontario: Prentice-Hall.

HOLLINGSHEAD, AUGUST B. "Cultural Factors in the Selection of Marriage Mates",
1950   *American Sociological Review*, Vol. 15, pp. 619–27.

HOMANS, GEORGE C. *Social Behaviour*. New York: Harcourt, Brace and World.
1961

HOSTETLER, JOHN A. and GERTRUDE E. HUNTINGTON. *The Hutterites in North Amer-
1967   ica*. New York: Holt, Rinehart and Winston.

——. *The Hutterites*. Baltimore: Johns Hopkins University Press.
1974

IRVING, HOWARD. *The Family Myth: A Study of Relationships between Married
1972   Couples and Their Parents*. Toronto: Copp Clark.

ISHWARAN, K. "Family, Church and School in a Dutch-Canadian Community", in
1971   K. Ishwaran, ed., *The Canadian Family*. Toronto: Holt, Rinehart and Winston.

——, ed. *The Canadian Family*. Revised ed. Toronto: Holt, Rinehart and Winston.
1976

——. *Family, Kinship, and Community: A Study of Dutch-Canadians*. Toronto:
1977a   McGraw-Hill Ryerson.

——. *Family, Kinship and Community*. Toronto: Holt, Rinehart and Winston.
1977b

JANSEN, CLIFFORD J. "The Italian Community in Toronto", in John L. Elliott, ed.,
1971   *Immigrant Groups*. Vol. II. Scarborough, Ontario: Prentice-Hall.

Journal of Social Issues. Divorce and Separation edition, Vol. 32, No. 1.
1976

KAATS, GILBERT and KEITH E. DAVIS. "The Dynamics of Sexual Behavior of College

1970   Students", *Journal of Marriage and the Family*, Vol. 32, No. 3, pp. 390–99.

KAGAN, JEROME. "Acquisition and Significance of Sex Typing and Sex Role Iden-
1964   tity", in M. L. Hoffman and L. W. Hoffman, eds., *Review of Child Development Research*, Vol. I. New York: Russell Sage Foundation.

KALBACH, WARREN E. *The Impact of Immigration on Canada's Population.* Ottawa:
1970   Dominion Bureau of Statistics.

—— and WAYNE W. MC VEY. *The Demographic Bases of Canadian Society.* Toronto:
1971   Macmillan.

——. "Propensities for Intermarriage in Canada as Reflected in the Ethnic Origins
1974   of Native-Born Husbands and Their Wives: 1961 and 1971", paper presented at the Annual Meeting of the Canadian Sociology and Anthropology Association, Toronto, August.

——. "The Demography of Marriage", in S. Parvez-Wakil, ed., *Marriage, Family,*
1975   *and Society: Canadian Perspectives.* Scarborough, Ontario: Butterworth.

——. "Canada: A Demographic Analysis", in G. N. Ramu and S. D. Johnson,
1976a   eds., *Introduction to Canadian Society: Sociological Analysis.* Toronto: Macmillan.

—— and WAYNE W. MC VEY. "The Canadian Family: A Demographic Profile", in
1976b   Lyle E. Larson, ed., *The Canadian Family in Comparative Perspective.* Scarborough, Ontario: Prentice-Hall.

KALLEN, EVELYN. "Family Life Styles and Jewish Culture", in K. Ishwaran, ed.,
1976   *The Canadian Family.* Revised ed. Toronto: Holt, Rinehart and Winston.

KELLY, JEFFREY A. and LEONARD WORELL. "Parent Behaviours Related to Mascu-
1976   line, Feminine, and Androgynous Sex Role Orientations", *Journal of Consulting and Clinical Psychology*, Vol. 44, No. 5, pp. 843–51.

KEPHART, WILLIAM M. "Occupational and Marital Disruption", *American Socio-*
1955   *logical Review*, Vol. 20, pp. 456–65.

——. *The Family, Society and the Individual.* Boston: Houghton Mifflin.
1961, 1972

KERCHOFF, ALAN and KEITH E. DAVIS. "Value Consensus and Need Complementarity
1962   in Mate Selection", *American Sociological Review*, Vol. 27, pp. 295–303.

KIMBALL, MEREDITH M. "Socialization of Women: A Study in Conflict", in S.
1975   Parvez-Wakil, ed., *Marriage, Family, and Society: Canadian Perspectives.* Scarborough, Ontario: Butterworth.

KINSEY, ALFRED C., WARDELL POMEROY and CLYDE E. MARTIN. *Sexual Behavior in the*
1948   *Human Male.* Philadelphia: W. B. Saunders.

—— and PAUL GEBHARD. *Sexual Behavior in the Human Female.* Philadlephia:
1953   W. B. Saunders.

KIRKENDALL, LESTER A. *Premarital Intercourse and Interpersonal Relationships.* New
1961   York: The Julian Press.

—— and ROGER W. LIBBY. "Interpersonal Relationships: Crux of the Sexual Renais-
1966   sance", *Journal of Social Issues*, Vol. 22, pp. 45–59.

KIRKPATRICK, CLIFFORD. "A Statistical Investigation of the Psychoanalytic Theory of
1973   Mate Selection", *Journal of Abnormal and Social Psychology*, Vol. 32, pp. 427–30.

KOHL, SEENA B. *Working Together: Women and Family in Southwestern Saskatch-*
1976   *ewan.* Toronto: Holt, Rinehart and Winston.

KRALT, JOHN. *Ethnic Origins of Canadians.* Ottawa: Census of Canada, Profile
1977   Studies, Demographic Characteristics. Bulletin 5. Catalogue 99–790, pp. 1–9.

KRISHNAN, P. "War and Depression Effects on Canadian Marriage Rates: A Macro-
1977   analysis", paper presented at the Canadian Anthropology and Siocology
meetings, Fredericton, New Brunswick.

KUBAT, DANIEL and DAVID THORNTON. *A Statistical Profile of Canadian Society*.
1974   Toronto: McGraw-Hill Ryerson.

KUROKAWA, MINAKO. "Mennonite Children in Waterloo County", in John L. Elliott,
1971   ed., *Immigrant Groups*, Vol. II. Scarborough, Ontario: Prentice-Hall.

KUZEL, PAUL and P. KRISHNAN. "Changing Patterns of Remarriage in Canada: 1961–
1973   66", *Journal of Comparative Family Studies*, Vol. 4 (Autumn), pp.
215–24.

LACASSE, FRANCOIS D. "Women at Home: The Cost to the Canadian Economy of the
1971   Withdrawal from the Labour Force of a Major Proportion of the
Female Population", studies of the Royal Commission on the Status of
Women. Ottawa: Information Canada.

LAING, LORY and R. KRISHNAN. "First-Marriage Decrement Tables for Males and
1976   Females in Canada, 1961–1966", *Canadian Review of Sociology and
Anthropology*, Vol. 13, pp. 217–28.

LAMBERT, R. D. "Sex Role Imagery in Children: Social Origins of the Mind", studies
1971   of the Royal Commission on the Status of Women in Canada, No. 6.
Ottawa: Information Canada,

LAMBERT, W. E., A. YACKLEY, and R. N. HEIN. "Child Training Values of English
1971   Canadian and French Canadian Parents", *Canadian Journal of Behav-
ioral Sciences*, Vol. 3, pp. 217–36.

LAROQUE, P. "The Evolution of the Canadian Divorce Law", MA thesis, Queen's
1969   University.

LARSON, LYLE E. "Multilevel Family Interpersonal Perception of Ideal Marital Roles:
1975   An Exploratory Study", *Journal of Comparative Family Studies*, Vol.
6, No. 2, pp. 223–37.

——. *The Canadian Family in Comparative Perspective*. Scarborough, Ontario:
1976a   Prentice-Hall.

——. "Courtship and Mate Choice", in Lyle E. Larson, ed., *The Canadian Family
1976b   in Comparative Perspective*. Scarborough, Ontario: Prentice-Hall.

LATOWSKY, EVELYN. "Family Life Styles and Jewish Culture", in K. Ishwaran, ed.,
1971   *The Canadian Family*. Toronto: Holt, Rinehart and Winston.

Law Reform Commission of Canada. *Divorce*. Working paper 13. Ottawa: Informa-
1975a   tion Canada.

——. *Family Property*. Working paper 8. Ottawa: Information Canada.
1975b

LESLIE, GERALD R. *The Family in Social Context*. New York: Oxford University
1976   Press.

LEVINGER, GEORGE, DAVID SENN, and BRUCE JOGENSEN. "Progress Toward Perma-
1970   nence in Courtship: A Test of the Kerckhoff-Davis Hypotheses",
Sociometry, Vol. 33, pp. 427–33.

——. "A Social Psychological Perspective on Marital Dissolution", *Journal of
1967   Social Issues*, Vol. 32, No. 1, pp. 21–47.

LIBBY, ROGER W. "Creative Singlehood as a Sexual Lifestyle: Beyond Marriage as
1977a   a Rite of Passage", in Roger W. Libby and Robert N. Whitehurst, eds.,
Marriage and Alternatives. Glenview, Ill.: Scott, Foresman.

—— and ROBERT N. WHITEHURST. *Marriage and Alternatives: Exploring Intimate
1977b   Relationships*. Glenview, Ill.: Scott, Foresman.

LITWAK, E. "Geographic Mobility and Extended Family Cohesion", *American Socio-
1960a   logical Review*, Vol. 30.

————. "Occupational Mobility and Extended Family Cohesion", *American Socio-*
1960b   *logical Review,* Vol. 29.

————. "Use of Extended Family Group in Achievement of Social Goals: Some
1960c   Policy Implications", *Social Problems,* Vol. 7.

LOO, ROBERT and PAMELA LOGAN. "Investigations of the Attitudes Toward Women
1977   Scale in Western Canada", *Canadian Journal of Behavioural Sciences,*
Vol. 2, No. 2, pp. 201–04.

LOPATA, HELEN ZNANIECKI. "Review Essay: Sociology", *Signs: Journal of Women*
1976   *in Culture and Society,* Vol. 2, No. 1, pp. 165–76.

LYNN, DAVID. "Sex Role and Parental Identification", *Child Development,* Vol. 33,
1962   pp. 555–64.

MCDOUGALL, JOYCE. "Homosexuality in Women", in Signe Hammer, ed., *Women,*
1975   *Body and Culture.* New York: Harper & Row.

MACCOBY, E. E. and C. N. JACKLIN. *The Psychology of Sex Differences.* Stanford,
1974   California: Stanford University Press.

MANN, W. E. "Canadian Trends in Premarital Behavior", *Bulletin,* The Council for
1967   Social Service, No. 198.

————. "Sex Behavior on the Campus", in W. E. Mann, ed., *Canada: A Sociological*
1968a   *Profile.* Toronto: Copp Clark.

————. "Non-Conformist Sexual Behavior on the Canadian Campus", in W. E. Mann,
1968b   ed., *Deviant Behavior in Canada.* Toronto: Social Science Publishers.

————. "Sex at York University", in W. E. Mann, ed., *The Underside of Toronto.*
1970   Toronto: McClelland and Stewart.

MARANELL, GARY M., RICHARD A. DODDER, and DAVID F. MITCHELL. "Social Class and
1970   Premarital Permissiveness: A Subsequent Test", *Journal of Marriage*
and the Family, Vol. 32 (February), pp. 85–88.

MARGOLIN, G. and G. R. PATTERSON. "Differential Consequences Provided by Mothers
1975   and Fathers for Their Sons and Daughters", *Developmental Psychology,*
Vol. 2, pp. 537–38.

MARSH, ROBERT M. and ALBERT R. O'HARA. "Attitudes Toward Marriage and the
1961   Family in Taiwan", *American Journal of Sociology,* Vol. 67, pp. 1–8.

MASTERS, WILLIAM H. and VIRGINIA E. JOHNSON. *Human Sexual Response.* Boston:
1966   Little, Brown.

———— and ————. *Human Sexual Inadequacy.* Boston: Little, Brown.
1970

MAYKOVICH, MINAKO KUROKAWA. "The Japanese Family in Tradition and Change",
1971   in K. Ishwaran, ed., *The Canadian Family.* Toronto: Holt, Rinehart
and Winston.

————. "Ethnic Variation in Success Value", in Robert M. Pike and Elizabeth
1975   Zureik, eds., *Socialization and Values in Canadian Society,* Vol. II.
Toronto: The Carleton Library, Macmillan.

————. "Alienation and Mental Health of Mennonites in Waterloo County", in K.
1976   Ishwaran, ed., *The Canadian Family.* Revised ed. Toronto: Holt, Rinehart and Winston.

MEISSNER, MARTIN, ELIZABETH W. HUMPHREYS, SCOTT M. R. MEIS, and WILLIAM J.
1975   SHEU. "No Exit for Wives: Sexual Division of Labour", *The Canadian*
Review of Sociology and Anthropology, Vol. 12 (November), pp.
424–39.

————. "Sexual Division of Labour and Inequality: Labour and Leisure", in Marylee
1977   Stephenson, ed., *Women in Canada.* Don Mills, Ontario: General
Publishing.

MERTON, ROBERT K. *On Theoretical Sociology.* New York: Free Press.
1967

MESSINGER, LILLIAN. "Remarriage between Divorced People with Children from
1976   Previous Marriages", *Journal of Marriage and Family Counselling*,
Vol. 1 (April), pp. 193–200.

MIDDENDORP, C. P., W. BRINKMAN, and W. KOOMEN. "Determinants of Premarital
1970   Sexual Permissiveness: A Secondary Analysis", *Journal of Marriage and
the Family*, Vol. 32 (August), pp. 369–79.

MINDEL, CHARLES H. and ROBERT W. HABENSTEIN, *Ethnic Families in America: Pat-
1976   terns and Variations*. New York: Elsevier.

MIRANDE, ALFRED M. "Reference Group Theory and Adolescent Sexual Behavior",
1968   *Journal of Marriage and the Family*, Vol. 30 (November), pp. 572–77.

MONEY, JOHN. "Psychosexual Differentiation", in Signe Hammer, ed., *Women,
1975   Body and Culture*. New York: Harper & Row.

MOREUX, COLETTE. "The French Canadian Family", in M. Stephenson, ed., *Women
1973   in Canada*. Toronto: General Publishing.

MORGAN, L. H. *Systems of Consanguinity and Affinity in the Human Family*. Wash-
1966   ington: Humanities Press Incorporated.

MORGAN, D. H. *Social Theory and the Family*. London: Routledge and Kegan Paul.
1975

MURDOCK, G. P. *Social Structure*. New York: Free Press.
1949

——. "Family Stability in Non-European Cultures", *Annuls of the American Acad-
1950   emy of Political and Social Science*, Vol. 270.

MURSTEIN, BERNARD. "Stimulus-Value-Role: A Theory of Marital Choice", *Journal
1970   of Marriage and the Family*, Vol. 32, pp. 465–82.

NETT, E. M. "The Changing Forms and Functions of the Canadian Family: A
1976a   Demographic View", in K. Ishwaran, ed., *The Canadian Family*. Second
ed. Toronto: Holt, Rinehart and Winston.

——. "The Social Psychological Effects on the Family of the Women's Movement",
1976b   *Canadian Home Economics Journal*, Vol. 26, No. 1, pp. 12–19.

——. "Wife-Husband Interaction: A Review of the Canadian Literature", paper
1977   presented at the Canadian Anthropology and Sociology meetings,
Fredericton, New Brunswick.

NYE, IVAN F. and FELIX M. BERARDO. *The Family: Its Structure and Functions*. New
1973a   York: Macmillan.

—— and ——. *The Family: Its Structure and Interactions*. New York. Macmillan.
1973b

OAKLEY, ANN. *Sex, Gender and Society*. San Francisco: Harper & Row.
1972

O'BRYAN, K. G., J. G. REITZ, and O. M. KUPLOWSKA. *Non-Official Languages: A Study
1976   of Canadian Multiculturalism*. Ottawa: Supply and Services Canada.

OSTERREICH, HELGI. "Geographical Mobility and Kinship: A Canadian Example",
1965   *International Journal of Comparative Sociology*, Vol. 6 (March), pp.
131–45.

——. "Geographic Mobility and Kinship: A Canadian Example", in K. Ishwaran,
1976   ed., *The Canadian Family*. First published in *International Journal of
Comparative Sociology*, Vol. 6, 1965.

OTTO, HERBERT A. "Marriage and Family Enrichment Programs in North America—
1975   Report and Analysis", *The Family Coordinator*, Vol. 24 (April), pp.
137–42.

PACKARD, VANCE. *The Sexual Wilderness*. Toronto: Musson Book.
1968

PALMER, SALLY E. "Economic Conflict in Marriage", *The Social Worker–Le Travail-
1972   leur Social*, Vol. 40, No. 3 (September), pp. 145–52.

————. "Divorcing Families: A Case Study in Southwestern Ontario", in K. Ish-
1976   waran, ed., *The Canadian Family*. Revised ed. Toronto: Holt, Rinehart
and Winston.
PARK, ROBERT E. "Human Migration and Marginal Man", *American Journal of*
1928   *Sociology*, Vol. 33, No. 7.
PARSONS, TALCOTT. "The Kinship System of the Contemporary United States",
1943   *American Anthropologist*, Vol. 45.
————. "Family, Structure and the Socialization of the Child", in T. Parsons and
1955   R. F. Bales, eds., *Family Socialization and Interaction Process*. New
York: Basic Books.
PERLMAN, D. "The Sexual Standards of Canadian University Students", in D.
1973   Koulack and D. Perlman, eds., *Readings in Social Psychology, Focus
on Canada*. Toronto: John Wiley.
Perspectives Canada. Ottawa: Information Canada.
1975
PETER, KARL. "The Hutterite Family", in K. Ishwaran, ed.,*The Canadian Family*.
1971   Toronto: Holt, Rinehart and Winston.
————. "The Hutterite Family", in K. Ishwaran, ed., *The Canadian Family*. Revised
1976   ed. Toronto: Holt, Rinehart and Winston.
PETERS, JOHN F. "Divorce in Canada: A Demographic Profile", *Journal of Com-*
1976a   *parative Family Studies*, Vol. VII, No. 2, pp. 335–49.
————. "A Comparison of Mate Selection and Marriage in the First and Second
1976b   Marriages", *Journal of Comparative Family Studies*, Vol. VII, No. 3,
pp. 483–90.
———— and LAIRD CHRISTIE. "Mate Selection Among the Chirishana Yanomama",
1978   forthcoming.
PIDDINGTON, RALPH. "A Study of French Canadian Kinship", *International Journal*
1961   *Of Comparative Sociology*, Vol. 2 (March), pp, 3–22.
————. "A Study of French Canadian Kinship", in K. Ishwaran, ed., *The Canadian*
1971   *Family*. Toronto: Holt, Rinehart and Winston.
————. "The Kinship Network Among French Canadians", in G. L. Gold and Marc-
1973   Adelard Trembley, eds., *Communities and Culture in French Canada*.
Toronto: Holt, Rinehart and Winston.
————. "A Study of French Canadian Kinship", in K. Ishwaran, ed., *The Canadian*
1976   *Family*. Toronto: Holt, Rinehart and Winston.
PIKE, ROBERT. "Legal Access and the Incidence of Divorce in Canada", in *The*
1975   *Canadian Review of Sociology and Anthropology*, Vol. 12, No. 2
(May), pp. 115–33.
PINEO, PETER C. "The Extended Family in a Working-Class Area of Hamilton",
1968   in B. R. Blishen *et al.* eds., *Canadian Society*. Toronto: Macmillan.
————. "The Extended Family in a Working-Class Area of Hamilton", in B. R.
1971   Blishen *et al.* eds., *Canadian Society*. Third ed. Toronto: Macmillan.
————. "The Extended Family in a Working Class Area of Hamilton", in K. Ish-
1976   waran, ed., *The Canadian Family*. Toronto: Holt, Rinehart and Winston.
PITCHER, EVELYN GOODENOUGH. "Fathers, Mothers, and Sex Typing", in Signe Ham-
1975   mer, ed., *Women, Body, and Culture*. New York: Harper & Row.
PORTER, JOHN. *The Vertical Mosaic: An Analysis of Social Class and Power in*
1965   *Canada*. Toronto: University of Toronto Press.
PROPPER, ALICE MARCELLA. "The Relationship of Maternal Employment to Adoles-
1972   cent Roles, Activities, and Parental Relationships", *Journal of Marriage
and the Family*, Vol. 34, No. 3, pp. 417–21.
PYKE, S. W. "Childrens Literature: Conceptions of Sex Roles," in Elia Zureik and

1975   Robert M. Pike, eds., *Socialization and Social Values in Canada*. Toronto: New Press.

RADECKI, HENRY. *Polish-Canadian, Canadian-Polish, or Canadian?* Toronto: York
1970   University, Mimeograph.

—— with BENEDYKT HEYDENKORN. *A Member of a Distinguished Family: The*
1976   *Polish Group in Canada*. Toronto: McClelland and Stewart.

RAMU, G. N. "The Family and Marriage in Canada", in G. N. Ramu and Stuart D.
1976   Johnson, eds., *Introduction to Canadian Society: Sociological Analysis*.
         Toronto: Macmillan.

—— and NICHOLAS TAVUCHIS. "Sociology of Marriage and the Family in Canada:
1977   A Review", *Journal of Marriage and the Family*. Forthcoming.

REED, PAUL. "A Preliminary Analysis of Divorce Actions in Canada 1969–72",
1975   paper presented at the Canadian Learned Society meetings, Edmonton,
         May 28–31.

REISS, IRA L. *The Premarital Sexual Standards in America*. New York: Free Press.
1960

——. "The Sexual Renaissance in America: A Summary and Analysis", *Journal*
1966   *of Social Issues*. No. 22, pp. 123–37.

——. *The Social Context of Premarital Sexual Experience*. New York: Holt, Rinehart and Winston.
1967   hart and Winston.

—— and BRENT C. MILLER. "A Theoretical Analysis of Heterosexual Permissiveness", *Technical Report* II. Minneapolis, Minnesota. The Minnesota
1974   ness", *Technical Report* II. Minneapolis, Minnesota. The Minnesota
         Family Study Center.

——. *Family Systems in America*. Second ed. Hinsdale, Ill.: Dryden.
1976

REISS, P. J. "Extended Kinship System: Correlates and Attitudes on Frequency
         Interaction", *Marriage and Family Living*, Vol. 24.

Report of the Royal Commission on the Status of Women. Ottawa: Statistics
1970   Canada.

Revised Statutes of Canada. Vol. III. Ottawa: Queen's Printer.
1970

ROBINS, L. and M. TOMANEC. "Closeness to Blood Relatives Outside the Immediate
1962   Family", *Marriage and Family Living*, Vol. 24.

ROBINSON, IRA E., KARL KING, CHARLES J. DUDLEY, and FRANCIS J. CLUNE. "Change
1968   in Sexual Behavior and Attitudes of College Students", *The Family
         Coordinator*, Vol. 17 (April), pp. 119–23.

——, ——, and JACK O. BALSWICK. "The Premarital Sexual Revolution Among
1972   College Females", *The Family Coordinator*, Vol. 21 (April), pp. 189–
         94.

Royal Bank of Canada. "The Family: Cradle of Culture, Strength of the Nation,
1972   Stronghold of Civilization", a collection of Monthly letters. Head Office
         of the Royal Bank of Canada (February), Montreal.

RUBIN, ZICK. *Liking and Loving: An Invitation to Social Psychology*. New York:
1973   Holt, Rinehart and Winston.

—— and GEORGE LEVINGER. "Theory and Date Badly Mated: A Critique of Murstein's SVR and Lewis's PDF Models of Mate Selection", *Journal of
1974   stein's SVR and Lewis's PDF Models of Mate Selection", *Journal of
         Marriage and the Family*, Vol. 36, pp. 226–31.

SAFILIOS-ROTHSCHILD, CONSTANTINA. "Dual Linkages Between the Occupational and
1977   Family Systems: A Macrosocial Analysis", *Journal of Marriage and
         the Family*, Vol. 1, No. 3, pt. 2, pp. 51–60.

SAWHILL, ISABEL V. "Economic Perspectives on the Family", *Daedalus* (Spring),
1977   pp. 115–25.

SCANZONI, JOHN. *Sexual Bargaining: Power Politics in the American Marriage*.

1972   Englewood Cliffs, New Jersey: Prentice-Hall.
——and LETHA SCANZONI. *Men and Women and Change: A Sociology of Marriage*
1976   *and Family.* New York: McGraw-Hill.
SCHELHENBERG, JAMES A. and LAWRENCE S. BEE. "A Re-examination of the Theory
1960   of Complementary Needs in Mate Selection", *Marriage and Family
        Living*, Vol. 22, pp. 277–332.
SCHLESINGER, BENJAMIN. *Families: A Canadian Perspective.* Toronto: McGraw-Hill
1970a   Ryerson.
——. "Remarriage as Family Reorganization for Divorced Persons: A Canadian
1970b   Study", *Journal of Comparative Family Studies*, Vol. 1 (Autumn), pp.
        101–18.
——, ed., *The Chatelaine Guide to Marriage.* Toronto: Macmillan.
1975a
——. *The One-Parent Family: Perspectives and Annotated Bibliography.* Toronto:
1975b   University of Toronto Press.
SCHLUDERMANN, SHIRIN and EDUARD SCHLUDERMANN. "Adolescent Perceptions of
1973   Themselves and Others in Hutterite Communal Societies", paper pre-
        sented at the 1974 meeting of the American Anthropological Associa-
        tion.
SCHNEIDER, D. M. *American Kinship: A Cultural Account.* Englewood Cliffs, New
1968   Jersey: Prentice-Hall.
—— and GEORGE C. HOMANS. "Kinship Terminology and American Kinship System",
1955   *American Anthropologist*, Vol. 57.
SCHULZ, DAVID A. and STANLEY F. RODGERS. *Marriage, the Family, and Personal Ful-
1975   fillment.* Englewood Cliffs, New Jersey: Prentice-Hall.
SEELEY, JOHN, R. A. SIM, and E. W. LOOSLEY. *Crestwood Heights: A Study of the
1956   Culture of Suburban Life.* New York: John Wiley.
——, ——, and ——. *Crestwood Heights: A Study of the Culture of Suburban Life.*
1967   New York: John Wiley.
SHANAS, E. and G. STREIB. *Social Structure and the Family.* Englewood Cliffs, New
1965   Jersey: Prentice-Hall.
SHIBUTANI, TAMOTSU and KIAN M. KWAN. *Ethnic Stratification: A Comparative Ap-
1965   proach.* New York: Macmillan.
SIMMONS, ALAND B. and JEAN. E. TURNER. "The Socialization of Sex Roles and
1976   Fertility Ideals: A Study of Two Generations in Toronto", *Journal of
        Comparative Family Study*, Vol. 7, No. 2, pp. 2–5–272.
SKOLNICK, ARLENE. *The Intimate Environment.* Boston: Little, Brown.
1973
SLABY, R. G. and K. S. FREY. "Development of Gender Constancy and Selective At-
1975   tention to Same-Sex Models", *Child Development*, Vol. 46 (December),
        pp. 849–56.
SMIGEL, E. O. and R. SEIDON. "Decline and Fall of the Double Standard", *Annals
1968   of the American Academy of Political and Social Science*, pp. 6–17.
SNYDER, ELOISE. "Attitudes: A Study of Homogamy and Marital Selectivity",
1964   *Journal of Marriage and the Family*, Vol. 26, pp. 332–36.
——. "Marital Selectivity in Self-Adjustment Social Activity and I.Q.", *Journal
1966   of Marriage and the Family*, Vol. 28, pp. 188–89.
SPENCER, JOHN, ed. *An Inventory of Family Research and Studies in Canada:
1967   1963–1967.* Ottawa: Vanier Institute of the Family.
SPIRO, M. E. *Kibbutz: A Venture in Utopia.* New York: Shocken Books.
1956
SPUHLER, J. N. "Assortive Mating with Respect to Physical Characteristics",
1968   *Eugenics Quarterly*, Vol. 15, pp. 129–34.

STEIN, PETER J. "Singlehood: An Alternative to Marriage", *The Family Coordinator*,
1975   Vol. 24, No. 4 (October), pp. 489–504.

STEPHENS, WILLIAM N. *The Family in Cross Cultural Perspective*. New York: Holt,
1963   Rinehart and Winston.

Stepparents Forum. Published bi-monthly, Box 4002, Westmount, Quebec. H3Z 2X3.

STOLL, CLARICE STASZ. *Female and Male: Socialization, Social Roles and Social*
1974   *Structure*. Debuque, Iowa: Wm. C. Brown.

SUSSMAN, MARVIN B. "The Help Pattern in the Middle Class Family", *American*
1953   *Sociological Review*, Vol. 18.

——. "Isolated Nuclear Family: Fact or Fiction", *Social Problems*, Vol. 6.
1959

—— and LEE BURCHINAL. "Parental Aid to Married Children: Implications for
1962   Family Functions", *Marriage and Family Living*, Vol. 24.

——. "Relationships of Adult Children with Their Parents in the United States",
1965   in E. Shanas and G. Streib, eds., *Social Structure and the Family*.
        Englewood Cliffs, New Jersey: Prentice-Hall.

——. "The Four F's of Variant Family Forms and Marriage Styles", *The Family*
1975   *Coordinator*, Vol. 24, No. 4 (October), pp. 563–76.

TAVUCHIS, N. *Family and Mobility Among Greek Americans*. Athens: National
1972   Centre of Research.

——and WILLIAM J. GOODE, eds. *The Family Through Literature*. New York:
1975   McGraw-Hill.

——. "Mobility and Family: Problems and Prospects", *Cornell Journal of Social*
1976   *Relations*, Vol 11, No. 2.

TAYLOR, K. W. and NOEL SCHACTER. "Divorce Petition Study", unpublished paper.
1977

TEEVAN, JAMES J., JR. "Reference Groups and Premarital Sexual Behavior", *Journal*
1972   *of Marriage and the Family*, Vol. 34 (May), pp. 283–91.

THIBAUT, JOHN W. and HAROLD H. KELLEY. *The Social Psychology of Groups*. New
1959   York: John Wiley.

THOMPSON, S. K. "Gender Labels and Early Sex-Role Development", *Child Develop-*
1975   *.ment*, Vol. 36 (June), pp. 339–47.

TREMBLAY, MARC-ADELARD and MARC LAPLANTE. *Famille et Parente en Acadie*.
1971   Ottawa: Musee National du Canada.

——. "Authority Models in the French-Canadian Family", in Gerald L. Gold and
1973   Marc-Adelard Tremblay, eds., *Communities and Culture in French*
        Canada. Toronto: Holt, Rinehart and Winston.

TURK, JAMES L. and NORMAN BELL. "Measuring Power in Families", *Journal of*
1972   *Marriage and the Family*, Vol. 34 (May), pp. 215–22.

UDRY, J. RICHARD, KARL E. BAUMANN, and NAOMI M. MORRIS. "Changes in Premarital
1975   Coital Experience of Recent Decade-of-Birth Cohorts of Urban Amer-
        ican Women", *Journal of Marriage and the Family*, Vol. 37, pp. 783–87.

United Nations. *Demographic Year Book 1975*. Department of Economic and
1969   Social Affairs. New York: United Nations.

Vanier Institute of the Family. *An Inventory of Family Research and Studies in*
1967   *Canada, 1963–67*. Ottawa: Vanier Institute of the Family.

——. *Canadian Resources on the Family Catalogue*. Ottawa: The Vanier Institute
1974   of the Family.

VAUGHTER, REESA M. "Psychology: Review Essay", *Signs: Journal of Women in*
1976   *Culture and Society*, Vol. 2, No. 1, pp. 120–46.

VERNER, ARTHUR M. and CYRUS S. STEWARD. "Adolescent Sexual Behavior in Middle
1974   America Revisited: 1970–1973", *Journal of Marriage and the Family*,
        Vol. 36 (November), pp. 728–35.

VERNON, PHILIP E. "Sex Differences in Personality Structure at Age 14", *Canadian*
1972   *Journal of Behavioural Sciences*, Vol. 4, pp. 283–97.
Vital Statistics. Volume II. Marriages and Divorces, pp. 84–205. Ottawa: Statistics
1975   Canada.
———. *Marriage, Family, and Society: Canadian Perspectives*. Scarborough, Ontario:
1975   Butterworth.
———. "Marriage and Family in Canada", *Calgary Journal of Comparative Family*
1976   *Studies*. Monograph.
WAKIL, S. P. and F. A. WAKIL. "Campus Dating: An Exploratory Study of Cross-
1973a   National Relevance", *Journal of Comparative Family Studies*, Vol. 4,
pp. 286–94.
——— and ———. "Campus Mate Selection Preferences: A Cross-National Compari-
1973b   son", *Social Forces*, Vol. 51, No. 4 (June), pp. 471–77.
——— and ———. "Marriage and Family in Canada: A Demographic Cultural Pro-
1976   file", in K. Ishwaran, ed. The Canadian Family. Revised ed. Toronto:
Holt, Rinehart and Winston.
WALKER, TIMOTHY B. "Beyond Fault: An Examination of Patterns of Behaviour in
1971   Response to Present Divorce Laws", *Journal of Family Law*, Vol. 10,
No. 3, pp. 267–99.
WALLER, WILLARD. *The Family: A Dynamic Interpretation*. New York: Dryden.
1938
———. "The Rating and Dating Complex", *American Sociological Review*, Vol. 2,
1973   pp. 727–34.
WALSH, ROBERT H., MARY Z. FERRELL, and WILLIAM L. TOLONE. "Selection of Refer-
1976   ence Group, Perceived Reference Group Permissiveness, and Personal
Permissiveness Attitudes and Behaviour: A Study of Two Consecutive
Panels (1967–71; 1970–74)", *Journal of Marriage and the Family*, Vol.
38, pp. 495–507.
WARGON, S. "Fertility and Some Selected Demographic Aspects of the Family in
1976   Canada", in S. P. Wakil, ed., *Marriage, Family, and Society: Canadian
Perspectives*. Toronto: Butterworths.
WEISSLEDES, W. "No-Illusion Marriage and No-Fault Divorce", *Canadian Review
of Sociology and Anthropology*, Vol. 11, No. 3, pp. 214–29.
WESTLEY, W. A. and N. B. EPSTEIN. *Silent Majority*. San Francisco: Jossey-Bass.
1969
WILLIAMS, J. E., S. M. BENNET, and D. L. BEST. "Awareness and Expression of Sex
1975   Stereotypes in Young Children", *Developmental Psychology*, Vol 11,
pp. 635–42.
WILSON, SUSANNAH J. "The Changing Image of Women in Canadian Mass Circulat-
1977   ing Magazines, 1930–1970", *Atlantis*, Vol. 2, No. 2 (Spring), pp. 33–42.
WINCH, ROBERT F. *Mate Selection*. New York: Harper & Row.
1958
———. *Identification and Its Familial Determinants*. Indianapolis: Bobbs Merrill.
1962
———. *The Modern Family*. Third ed. New York: Holt, Rinehart and Winston.
1971
WIRTH, LOUIS. "Urbanism as a Way of Life", *American Journal of Sociology*, Vol.
1938   44.
WHITEHURST, ROBERT N. and BARBARA PLANT. "A Comparison of Canadian and
1971   American University Students' Reference Groups, Alienation and Atti-
tudes Toward Marriage", *International Journal of Sociology of the
Family*, Vol. 50, pp. 75–82.
———. "Youth Views Marriage: Some Comparisons of Two Generation Attitudes

1973   of University Students", in Roger W. Libby and Robert N. Whitehurst, eds., *Renovating Marriage: Toward New Sexual Life Styles.* Danvill, California: Consensus.

—— and G. R. FRISCH. "Sex Differences in Dating Orientations: Some Comparisons
1974   and Recent Observations", *International Journal of Sociology of the Family*, Vol. 4, pp. 213–19.

——. "Youth and the Future of Marriage", unpublished paper.
1975

WOLFE, M. *Women and the Family in Rural Taiwan.* Stanford: Stanford University
1972   Press.

Woman's Bureau. *Facts and Figures* (1973 ed.) Vol. 1, Ottawa: Information
1974   Canada.

Women in Canada. Second ed. Toronto: Decision Marketing Research Ltd.
1976

WUESTER, T. S. "Canadian Law and Divorce", in S. Parvez-Wakil, ed., *Marriage,*
1975   *Family, and Society: Canadian Perspectives.* Scarborough, Ontario: Butterworth.

YOUNG, M. and P. WILLMOTT. *Family and Kinship in East London.* Baltimore:
1957   Penguin.

ZARETSKY, ELI. "Capitalism, the Family and Personal Life", in Nona Glazer and
1977   Helen Youngelson Waehrer, eds., *Women in a Man-Made World.* Chicago: Rand McNally.

ZIMMERMAN, CARLE C. *Family and Civilization.* New York: Harper & Row.
1947

Notes on Contributors

CHARLES W. HOBART is in the Department of Sociology, University of Alberta.

SUENG G. MOON is in the Department of Sociology, University of Manitoba.

EMILY M. NETT is in the Department of Sociology, University of Manitoba.

JOHN F. PETERS is in the Department of Sociology and Anthropology, Wilfrid Laurier University.

BENJAMIN SCHLESINGER is in the Faculty of Social Work, University of Toronto.

NICHOLAS TAVUCHIS is in the Department of Sociology, University of Manitoba.

ROBERT N. WHITEHURST is in the Department of Sociology, University of Windsor.

G. N. RAMU is in the Department of Sociology, University of Manitoba.

Author Index

Subject Index